TRAINING HUNT JUMPERS AND HACKS

By HARRY D. CHAMBERLIN
LIEUTENANT-COLONEL OF CAVALRY, UNITED STATES ARMY

AUTHOR OF

RIDING AND SCHOOLING HORSES

NEW YORK :: THE DERRYDALE PRESS

TWELVE HUNDRED AND FIFTY COPIES OF
TRAINING HUNTERS, JUMPERS AND HACKS
HAVE BEEN PRINTED BY EUGENE V. CONNETT
AT THE DERRYDALE PRESS

COPYRIGHT, 1937, THE DERRYDALE PRESS, INC.

The Author on "High Hat"
A good hunting seat. The horse is jumping boldly and freely in his stride.

TO

HELEN BRADMAN CHAMBERLIN

PREFACE

EQUITATION breaks itself naturally into two educational problems: that of the horse and that of the rider. To teach an utter novice how to ride on an untrained horse is an almost hopeless task; conversely, for the novice to undertake the training of a green colt is futile. Such procedure evokes the traditional two-horned dilemma upon which an Army captain once found himself. During the early days of a war crisis, having unexpectedly been supplied with one hundred unbroken remounts and as many raw recruits, he was directed to form a troop of cavalry. Devoid of assistance though not of dismay, he hastily telegraphed the War Department, "Have received one hundred men who have never seen a horse and one hundred horses which have never seen a man. Help!"

Properly breaking and training a colt so as to develop an agreeable mount presupposes an experienced rider with a good seat, sound theoretical knowledge of equitation, and skill in the use of his hands and legs as aids. In a former book, "Riding and Schooling

PREFACE

Horses," an effort was made by the present writer to describe a correct forward seat, to give the psychological principles on which training is based, and to indicate the proper use of the aids. In other words, it contained instructions and information necessary in the education of a good rider. One chapter briefly pointed out the qualities desirable in a well trained horse and gave a general outline of a rational method of training for the attainment of those qualities; for though two problems exist in educating horse and rider, they tend to merge at many points.

Under the assumption that the rider can sit his horse well and has the requisite coördination and knowledge to employ his hands and legs with moderate skill, the prime objective of this work is to set forth for his use precise descriptions of normal methods for breaking and training the horse from the time of purchase until his debut in the field or ring.

There is no doubt that many experienced horsemen with mediocre or even poor seats quite successfully "get along" with their horses. This is due to their good hands, common sense, general ability, and years of experience. However, "getting along" is far less thrilling than riding in perfect form. Also, were they to ride in form, these same riders would make life far more pleasant not only for themselves but for their horses, as a correct seat permits the latter greater free-

PREFACE

dom in the mechanics of movement, and the former far more ease and finesse in the use of the aids. All are therefore urged to study and practice a correct forward seat. Let it be pointed out, however, that rounding the back into a hump does not constitute a forward seat, nor does it facilitate or add grace to riding. While the subject of this work is training, a summarized description of the forward seat advocated by the author will be found at the end of Chapter III.

Chapter I, on selection, conformation and gaits, is a simple presentation of the relationship between beauty and mechanical ability. This knowledge is indispensable in selecting a hunter, jumper or hack. Chapter II continues in detail the examination into the beauties and defects of conformation. It is believed that experienced horsemen may find some items of information, hitherto unknown to them, therein.

Chapter III deals with the marks of an educated horse; in other words, the characteristics which must be present if he is to be considered well trained. By the same token, these characteristics are the objectives of training. The close relationship existing between the horse's head carriage and ultimate success in producing the characteristics just mentioned will be carefully brought out. The contents of this chapter are of tremendous importance as a theoretical basis for all equitation.

PREFACE

In the later chapters breaking and training will be thoroughly discussed and insofar as possible instructions as to length of time necessary for the various phases will be given. These cannot be definite rules since so many variable factors enter the individual equations of man and horse. The tact, skill, experience, patience and knowledge of the former, and the age, condition, disposition, conformation and adaptability of the latter, all modify the amount of time needed to teach any particular horse a specified lesson.

Credit for the system of training enunciated herein is due the French Cavalry School at Saumur. Evolved by many generations of skilled and highly intelligent horsemen, there is no system more scientifically founded or practically efficacious. Guerinière, Baucher, L'Hotte, d'Aure, Saint Phalle, Beauchesne, Champsavin are the names of but a few among the distinguished Frenchmen whose composite teachings and writings have aided in formulating the principles, doctrines and methods used at Saumur. This system of training, borrowed from the French School, has long dominated instruction at the United States Cavalry School at Fort Riley, Kansas.

Nothing in equitation is new. Disputes concerning the amount of flexion desirable in the horse's neck were current in the 16th century. In reading the opinions of Frederic Grison, Pluvinel, the Marquis de

PREFACE

Newcastle, Guerinière, d'Abzac, Baucher, Fillis and other masters, we find, as Comte d'Aure has written, that the differences are largely superficial and that their methods were in fact directed toward the same ends. The value of longeing and suppling exercises has been appreciated for centuries. Differences in methods have been caused, as time passed, by the variations in type of horse and in the work or sport for which he has been employed. The truth is, that in the days before the French Revolution the art of equitation was more flourishing and profoundly studied generally than at any time since. Only in the last two decades have the horsemen of the United States begun to be interested in understanding the principles and refinements of equitation and training. It is, in effect, a renaissance.

The last half-century has produced vast interest and activity in mounted sports, while modern warfare has brought a demand for extreme mobility in a cavalry now deemed by all the great World War leaders as more valuable on the field of battle than ever before. In view of these facts, all cavalry schools have forsaken the slow paces and the extreme collection of the manege and concentrated on extension, speed and freedom for the horse. Because of the demands for speed in jumping and cross-country work, some horsemen have turned to the extreme of abandoning all ef-

PREFACE

fort to supple, balance and collect their horses. This hardly answers the purpose of riders who want easily-handled and nicely-balanced hunters, jumpers, polo ponies and hacks. Proper gymnastic exercises during training to produce obedience, balance and suppleness are just as essential for the equine as for the human athlete. Such exercises as a means to an end are the basis of the methods set forth hereafter. Unfortunately some equestrians erroneously consider the exercises as the ends to be attained, rather than as a means of making the horse obedient and clever at his normal work.

Although it would be foolish not to admit that a great part of equitation remains an art, it must be realized that the continuity of purpose, study and instruction in the French Cavalry School has reduced much of equitation, through the written word, to a science. If the French precepts are correctly understood and applied, they will develop calmness, boldness, suppleness, brilliance and all other requisites of a well-trained horse.

Any normal person to some extent can learn to ride just as he can learn to play the piano. The difference between the average individual and the master, whether at the piano or on a horse, represents the difference between science and art. Hastily it must be added that much of success in any art results from

PREFACE

many hours of hard work, and as has been most truly said, "Genius is the capacity for infinite detail." From the above it seems permissible to deduce that the average man, through practice, perseverance and sound theoretical knowledge, eventually may become an expert horseman.

To give to the inexperienced amateur who desires to train his own horses the essential theoretical background of training, along with definite instructions as to its practical application, and to provide helpful additions to the knowledge possessed by more experienced owners are the purposes of this work. Nothing aside from the dearest human relationships can give the pleasure found in working and playing with a horse. That magnificent, powerful, yet dependent creature so willingly gives so much that surely it behooves his master to study thoroughly all things which may help in understanding his mute and faithful servant. An American cavalry general once remarked, "Association with the horse is ennobling." It is hoped that what follows may assist in making more pleasant that noble association between the reader and his horse.

H.D.C.

CONTENTS

Preface ix

Chapter I. Generalities Concerning Selection, Conformation and Gaits . . . 1

Chapter II. Details of Conformation . . 27

Chapter III. Head Carriage and Objectives of Training 95

Chapter IV. Breaking 129

Chapter V. Training 209

Chapter VI. Training the Horse to Jump 285

Conclusion 325

LIST OF ILLUSTRATIONS

THE AUTHOR ON "HIGH HAT"	*Frontispiece*
"HIGH LINE"—EXCELLENT TYPE OF SIRE	*Facing page* 1
ANATOMY OF THE HORSE	*Page* 10
"EQUIPOISE"	*Facing page* 12
"IMP. ROYAL MINSTREL"	*Facing page* 12
SKELETON OF THE HORSE	*Page* 15
A LONG STRIDING AND CADENCED CANTER	*Facing page* 22
HEAD WELL PLACED AT CANTER	*Facing page* 22

	Page
NORMAL SLOW GALLOP WITH THE RIGHT LEAD	24
BOTTOM OF FORE FOOT	28
CONTRACTED HEEL IN A FORE FOOT	28
BOTTOM OF HIND FOOT	28
DIAGRAMMATIC CROSS SECTION OF FOOT AND PASTERN	29
THE FORE LEG	31
PASTERNS	35
THE FORE LEG FROM KNEE DOWN	38
GOOD CONFORMATION OF LEGS	43
CROOKED LEGS	43
FORE LEGS	46

LIST OF ILLUSTRATIONS

	Page
THE GALLOPING TYPE	53
THE TROTTING TYPE	53
"JOE ALESHIRE"—A GREAT JUMPER	Facing page 54
"JOE ALESHIRE" IN ACTION	Facing page 54

	Page
HOCKS	58
THE HOCK JOINT	59
HIND LEG	60
SLOPING CROUP	69
WELL SHAPED CROUP	69
THE HEAD AND NECK	74
PROPORTIONS OF THE BODY	78
SWAY-BACKED	79
LONG, FLAT CROUP	79
HERRING-GUTTED	79
SHORT-DROOPED CROUP	79
CORRECTLY ADJUSTED CAVESSON	Facing page 140
A MILD SNAFFLE BRIDLE	Facing page 140

	Page
THE CAVESSON	140
LONGEING	142
RIGHT OPENING OR LEADING REIN	168

LIST OF ILLUSTRATIONS

	Page
BEARING OR NECK REIN	170
REIN OF DIRECT OPPOSITION	224
REIN OF INDIRECT OPPOSITION IN FRONT OF THE WITHERS	226
REIN OF INDIRECT OPPOSITION IN REAR OF THE WITHERS	228
CONTROLLED, LIGHT AND BALANCED MOVEMENT	Facing page 230
A TRAINED HORSE AT EXTENDED TROT	Facing page 230
BACKING WITH LOW HEAD CARRIAGE	Facing page 235
CORRECT HEAD CARRIAGE WHILE BACKING	Facing page 235

	Page
HALF-TURNS	237
TURNS	244
THE TURN ON THE HAUNCHES	247
SHOULDER-IN AT TROT	Facing page 253
"APPUYER" OR SHOULDER-IN AT TROT	Facing page 253
TWO TRACKING AT TROT	Facing page 283
TWO TRACKING ON RIGHT OBLIQUE AT TROT	Facing page 283
OBSTACLES OF THE PRIX DES NATIONS COURSE	Facing page 285

	Page
JUMPING ON THE LONGE	287

LIST OF ILLUSTRATIONS

	Facing page
GOOD BALANCE OF HORSE AND RIDER	293
DISPLAY OF EXCELLENT FORM	293

	Page
ELLIPTICAL PEN	296

	Facing page
EXCELLENT SHOW JUMPING SEAT	305
CORRECT FORM DURING DESCENT	305
CORRECT FORM IN LANDING	305
ILLUSTRATING FORM AND CALMNESS	319
LIGHT HANDS AND RELAXATION OF HORSE AND RIDER	319

	Page
OBSTACLES FOR JUMPING	321

TRAINING HUNTERS, JUMPERS AND HACKS

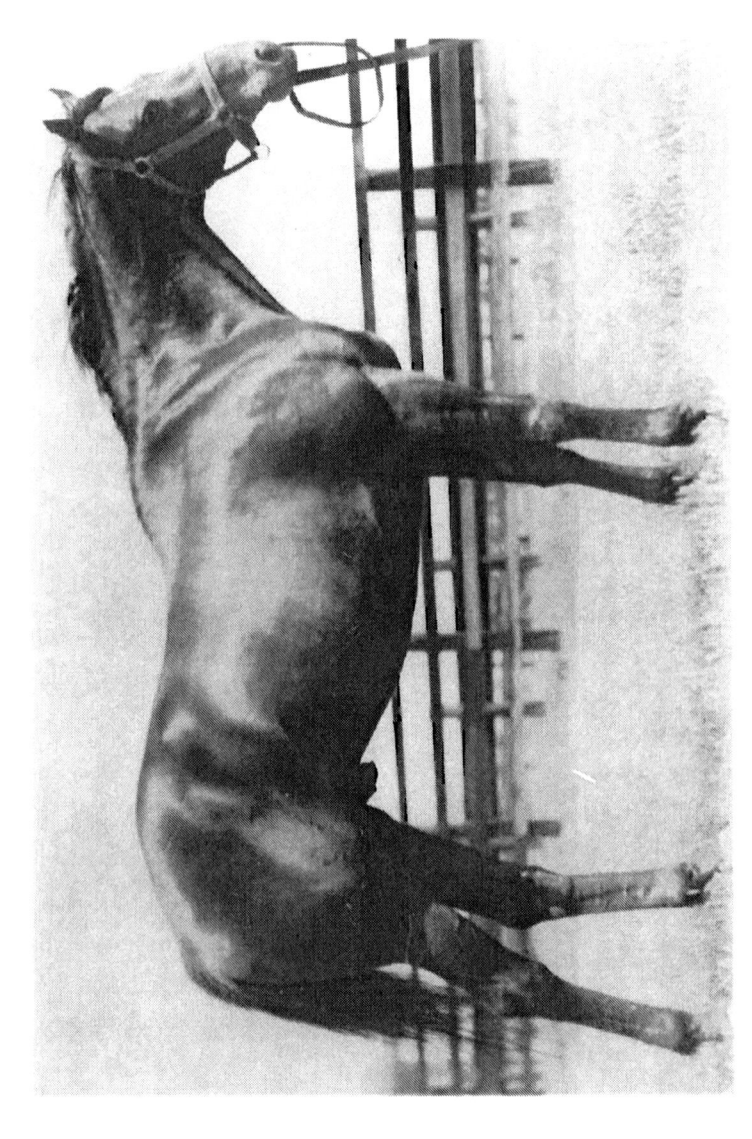

"High Line"—Excellent type of sire for hunters and jumpers.

CHAPTER I

GENERALITIES CONCERNING SELECTION, CONFORMATION AND GAITS

What Is Beauty in Conformation?

THE old adage concerning the chain's being only as strong as its weakest link, often and most aptly is applied to horses. It is true especially of hunters since their work requires great speed, strength and stamina. A French author sententiously has stated that "the beauty of man is ideal; that of the horse, mathematical." The statement was evoked because that particular appearance and form of any feature of the horse which make it most capable of withstanding wear and tear, and hence best adapted to perform the work required, gradually have come to be recognized as beautiful. A horse as a whole is considered beautiful when all his parts individually are so, and when they are so proportioned one to the other that he is perfectly adapted to his work. The type determines what is beautiful. Thus, a certain form of feature beautiful in a draft horse might be ugly in a thoroughbred. However, there are certain beauties common to all types which therefore are called absolute.

Scientific study of the horse's gaits and movements, since the advent of the motion picture camera, has discovered and analyzed quite exactly the mechanical advantages resulting from beautiful conformation. The study of the pictures merely has confirmed the observations of experienced horsemen.

When submitted to the strains of strenuous hunting and jumping, no horse with poorly conformed fore legs can remain sound and useful for any great period of time. The machine is faultily constructed and not mechanically balanced. Moreover, when galloping across hunting country, weaknesses in certain parts of the equine machine are apt to cause grave accidents through the horse's falling. Consequently, it behooves every person who rides to acquire knowledge of conformation, and more particularly so if he expects to own horses.

Learning to Judge Conformation

Contrary to common belief, it is not at all difficult to learn appreciation of the more important points of conformation. A little study and the mental deter-

SELECTION, CONFORMATION AND GAITS

mination to exercise one's power of observation are all that are necessary. It also should be understood by those who train young horses that the particular conformation of each colt ought to influence greatly the schedule and methods employed in his breaking and training. The variations necessary, depending on conformation, will be mentioned later.

In judging conformation, a certain fixed routine of inspection should be adopted and rigorously followed in each case. Routine makes thoroughness a habit, and the probability of overlooking grievous defects is eliminated.

Value of the First Impression of a Horse

First and foremost, when purchasing a horse, it is vitally important that his appearance as a whole please the buyer. Otherwise the latter is never completely happy with his possession, nor will he cease to regret having bought a horse that failed to meet the requirements he had in mind. Unfortunately any one of the many oversights which a purchaser easily may make never can be excused by his pride of possession. Even to apologize tacitly for his horse is the essence of bitterness to a horseman. From these facts an axiom is born: *never buy a horse which offends the eye at first glance.*

Best Age for Purchase

After weighing the various factors involved, the matter of age is one which each buyer must decide for himself. Buying an older horse, either wholly or partly trained, from a reliable person whose methods are known to be good, has many advantages. The usual disadvantage attending this course is a very high price. If the decision is made to purchase a young, untrained one, the most suitable age is four. With knowledge and time available, training provides a joyous satisfaction for the owner and at four years of age a colt is old enough so that serious work may be undertaken immediately and proceed continuously. This normally will produce a well trained horse at six. However, even through his sixth year, his work should be considered carefully, for the average horse is not fully matured until seven years of age. From seven until fifteen or older, a good hunter or jumper is in his prime.

If bought at the age of two or three, a colt may be gentled, broken and trained to some small extent, but when so young the liability to injury, the additional expense of upkeep, and the fact that very little work can be demanded, are distinct disadvantages. Staying off his back during his second and third years is the best way to safeguard his health, feet and legs. Hence it is more economical from all points of view not to own the colt until he is four. To begin mounted training at four is a recognized principle in the armies of all great nations, and the horse world generally acknowledges that the cavalry schools of these nations have evolved the soundest known principles of scientific equitation and training.

Before his fourth year, a colt simply is not strong enough to do hard work without great possibility of severe injury. When for any reason one is broken during his second or third year, he should not be given long rides or required to jump obstacles over three feet in height. It is far better at that tender age to require no jumping at all, and certainly *none while mounted*. Except for teaching him to bear the rider's weight for short periods at very slow paces, it is wisest to stay off his back. It is admitted that certain remarkable horses, despite their being required to do severe work during their second and third years under riders, manage to remain sound. Nevertheless, most intelligent horsemen, not professionally engaged in the horse business, follow the rule of commencing systematic mounted work at four.

The fact that our race tracks abound with two- and three-year-olds being exploited for money should in no way influence any genuine sportsman to start a colt destined to become a hunter or jumper at serious mounted work prior to his fourth year. Naturally, many breeders and dealers desire to sell or race their colts as early as possible; it is a matter of money, since the period of profitless upkeep is shortened. These mere babies are over-fed, over-trained, over-taxed, and a vast number become poor crippled things before they even approach maturity. And this, alas, is glorified under the name of sport! Fortunately, some of the true sportsmen who own racing stables are beginning to disparage the racing of two-year-olds. It is hoped that the number of these gentlemen increases and that they make loud their protests. Surely the gallant thoroughbred should be given every chance to improve; such a generous comrade and friend should not be commercialized, without a fair chance, by the avarice of those he serves. Sadly enough, the racing of two-year-olds and the short sprints now in vogue, which have replaced the long races of former days, have done much to harm the conformation of the thoroughbred. These lamentable conditions have caused, among other undesirable characteristics, straighter shoulders and pasterns, longer legs, drooped croups and more sloping arms.

Leaving this digression, which needs much publicity, and returning to the subject, it appears most logical to buy a four-year-old when the purchaser intends to break and train his own horse. It is, of course, advantageous if the colt selected has been gentled and

SELECTION, CONFORMATION AND GAITS

halter-broken. Then, under the mild work to be advocated for his fourth year, he will develop quickly, and at five, consider himself quite grown up, although at times his behavior may be unexpectedly childish. In any event, at five he will be just out of the baby category and his bones and muscles will have been partly hardened and prepared to resist without injury the violent and often accidental strains that come with galloping and jumping.

Inspecting the Colt in His Stall

Having decided upon the age and found the horse which from the first glance proved pleasing to the eye, the prospective purchaser, if possible, should see him in his stall. There it can be determined whether he is a cribber (chews the wood of his stall), windsucker (sucks in air after seizing hold with his teeth of a protruding piece of wood or other material), a weaver (sways back and forth, alternately shifting his weight from one fore leg to the other) or has other stable vices. The stall itself may show scars from habitual kicking. Excessive nervousness or irritability usually will be manifested when a stranger approaches. If possible, the visit to the stall should be unexpected both to the horse and the dealer.

The most beautiful conformation is of little value if the horse has a bad disposition, and a most reliable index to disposition is his eye. Its expression should be observed often and carefully. A beautiful eye is alert, brilliant, frank, limpid, large, mildly curious and friendly. To the true horseman his horses' eyes tell many things. Through their expressions he reads the moods and state of health of each individual in the stables. Only by such sympathetic interest can an owner understand and enjoy his horses to the fullest.

While in the stall if visibility is good, in addition to studying the expression of the eyes, a minute examination should be made to be sure that no cloudiness impairs the vision. Also, while standing a little to the rear of the horse's head, move a hand quickly upward, close to and past the eye, carefully noticing whether it blinks as it should. The glands just back of and under the lower jawbone may be felt to see that they are similar and not abnormal in size. The disease called "strangles" often leaves these glands so enlarged that they interfere with flexion of the jaw and poll. The poll (region of the neck just back of the ears) should be inspected for traces of "poll evil," an injury which often is very grave. In these examinations it will be discovered whether, as a result of bad treatment, poll evil, nervousness or viciousness, the horse is "head shy." His pulse and teeth should be examined. The pulse is felt just inside and under the lower jawbone. It should be full and strong, at normal temperatures varying between thirty-four and thirty-eight beats per minute. The count is higher, as a rule, in young horses than in older ones. A good pulse is an indication of excellent health, while a weak or irregular one signifies poor health and an irritable disposition. Naturally a young horse is less liable than an older one to have serious injuries and incurable vices.

If the legs are bandaged the cause should be determined. Frequently bandages are used for bracing and resting legs which are perfectly sound. On the other hand the legs may be weak or injured and, as a result, stock (swell) after exercise, in which case the bandages are used to prevent or reduce the swelling. Such habitual swelling indicates circulatory or lymphatic disorders.

Next the horse should be led outside the stable. Closely study the eyes again just as he comes into the bright daylight. An eye may be totally blind from a paralyzed retina and yet appear clear and normal. Many a horseman has failed to find this defect until weeks after a purchase. Only by noting the contraction which the light causes in the pupil of a good eye, and the blinking which occurs when a hand is passed close to it, can one be certain that this type of blindness does not exist.

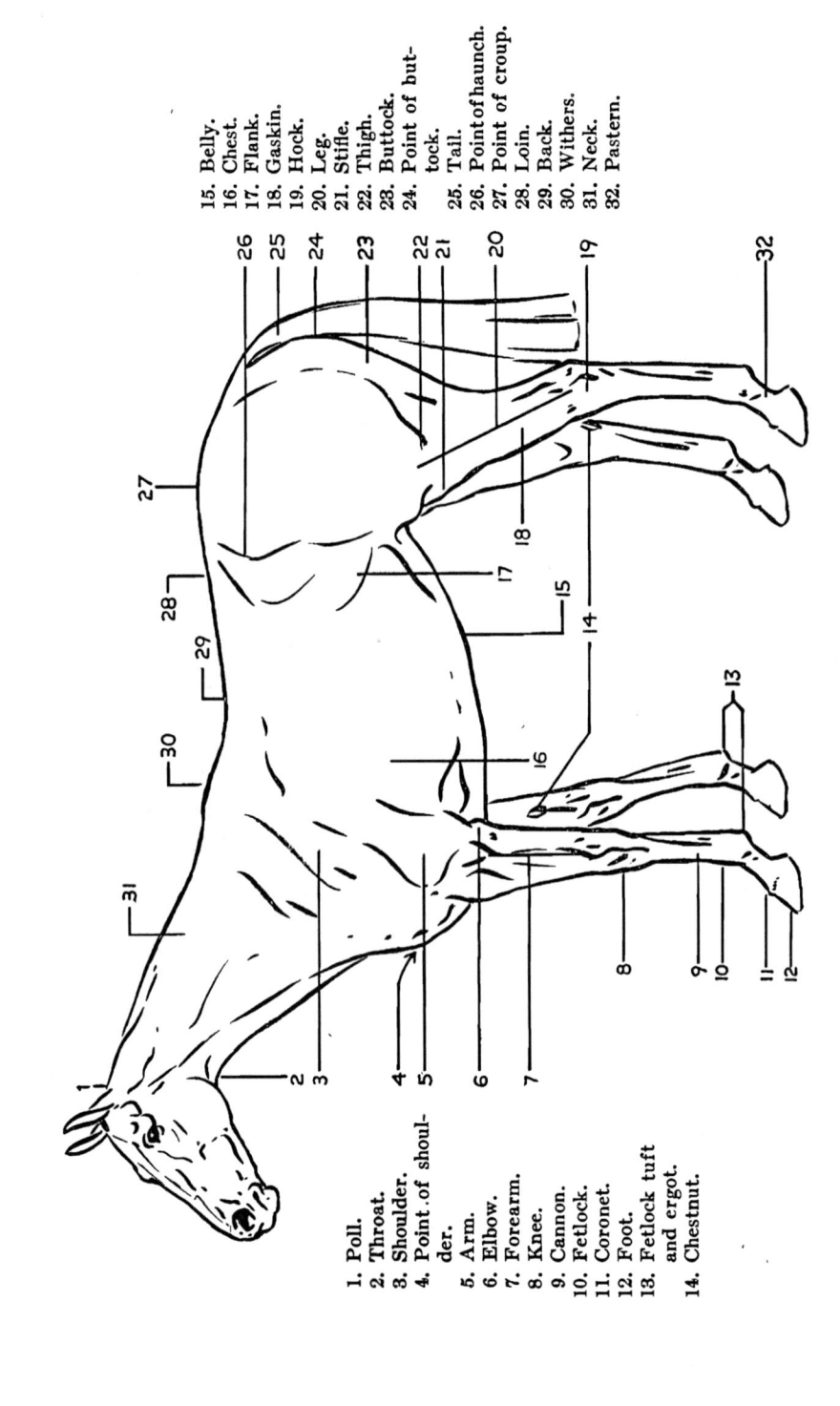

1. Poll.
2. Throat.
3. Shoulder.
4. Point of shoulder.
5. Arm.
6. Elbow.
7. Forearm.
8. Knee.
9. Cannon.
10. Fetlock.
11. Coronet.
12. Foot.
13. Fetlock tuft and ergot.
14. Chestnut.
15. Belly.
16. Chest.
17. Flank.
18. Gaskin.
19. Hock.
20. Leg.
21. Stifle.
22. Thigh.
23. Buttock.
24. Point of buttock.
25. Tail.
26. Point of haunch.
27. Point of croup.
28. Loin.
29. Back.
30. Withers.
31. Neck.
32. Pastern.

SELECTION, CONFORMATION AND GAITS

Study of the Horse's General Symmetry

In judging his general appearance the symmetry and harmony of the horse's height and length are important. Also, the length of his legs in relation to the size and height of his body, as well as the relative proportions of his head, neck and body must be studied. In a well made horse the height of his chest (often miscalled "depth") measured perpendicularly from the top of his withers to the bottom of his chest, or point where the cinch passes underneath the body, should equal approximately the distance from his chest to the ground. In the "ideal" horse the first measurement is a trifle greater. If not approximately equal he will appear "leggy" and "have too much daylight under him." "Legginess" indicates a small chest and lung capacity, as well as unstableness. After a little practice these relative proportions are readily judged, and an appreciation of balanced symmetry is developed by the eye.

If the horse has a long neck the head should be small, otherwise the weight of a big head on the long lever, formed by the neck, makes him heavy in front. His "balancer" (the head and neck) is unwieldy. If the neck is very short, a rather large head which adds the necessary weight to the balancer is desirable. The croup should be almost as long from hip to point of buttock (or end of ischium) as is the head. The shoulder, from its point to the top of the withers in a well-made horse, is as long as his head, as is also the distance from the point of the hock to the ground. In discussing conformation in detail, more information will be given concerning relative proportions which assist in determining the degree of symmetry and probable mechanical ability a horse possesses.

The Coat

The coat should be carefully noted. It is a distinctive indication of quality and good breeding if it is silky, fine-haired and glossy. A fine coat generally covers a skin which, when pinched between the thumb and forefinger, also feels fine and delicate. After exercise the veins on the legs, neck and body of a horse with a coat and skin as described stand out very prominently. These conditions are fairly reliable proof that the tissues beneath are of high quality and not laden with gross, superfluous fat. Just after a horse has been carefully groomed a poor coat often looks well. The buyer therefore must be able to recognize a good coat when the horse is in pasture, ungroomed, or "in the rough." This is accomplished by examining the texture of the individual hairs. A horse possessing a coat that shines like satin is spoken of as having "bloom." After great and long-continued exertion, a fine coat, a thin skin, and veins near the surface permit prompt

Photo copyrighted by L. S. Sutcliffe, Lexington, Ky.
"EQUIPOISE"
Mr. C. V. Whitney's great race horse and sire, the epitome of long muscled speed and proven quality. Note the beautiful scapula-humeral angle.

"IMP. ROYAL MINSTREL"
Mr. C. V. Whitney's thoroughbred. A magnificent type of sire for hunters.

recuperation through rapid cooling of the blood and underlying tissues. In horses required to hunt, race, play polo or jump difficult courses, such an efficient cooling system is vitally important.

Muscular Development

In an untrained colt, more than in an older horse, potential muscular development must be carefully estimated. The muscles of course will not be highly developed but the indications of quality, or lack thereof, are readily recognizable to the trained eye. Always it must be borne in mind that thick, heavy, bunchy muscles are not desirable in riding horses. On the contrary being capable of exerting very intense, but not necessarily swift, effort, they are considered beautiful in draft animals.

Veterinarians have determined scientifically that the intensity of muscular force increases as the square of the diameter of the muscle. A riding horse, however, should have long, low gaits. These do not require tremendous strength and are produced only by long, wiry muscles, capable of great amplitude in extension and contraction. Blocky, muscular horses, while stronger in slow draft, are completely outclassed by the long-muscled types in agility and fleetness under the saddle. While the intensity of muscular strength is a function of the square of the muscle's diameter, the weight to be moved is a function of the cube of the muscle's diameter. This explains why *beyond a certain height,* a horse carrying a load which is in fixed proportion to his own weight (say one-sixth, for example) must be a *better* horse mechanically than the similar, smaller horse just equaling that certain height. In other words, the increase in the taller horse's mass (a function of the cube of the muscles' diameters) exceeds the increase in the intensity of his muscular strength (function of the square) relative to the mass and strength of the smaller horse. Hence the smaller horse carries his load more easily than the bigger one which is worn out sooner by his greater weight.

Standing about fifteen hands three inches on legs short relative to the body's height is believed by eminent authorities to be the most efficient height for a thoroughbred destined to carry far and fast a weight of approximately one hundred eighty pounds. In general, endurance rides and the Equestrian Championships of the Olympic games tend to prove the moderate-sized horse's superiority. The weight-carrying ability of small horses and mules is well known. In the mountains, burros are seen carrying burdens all day long which almost equal their own weights. Below a certain height the disqualifying disadvantages of short and small horses are lack of speed and amplitude of stride.

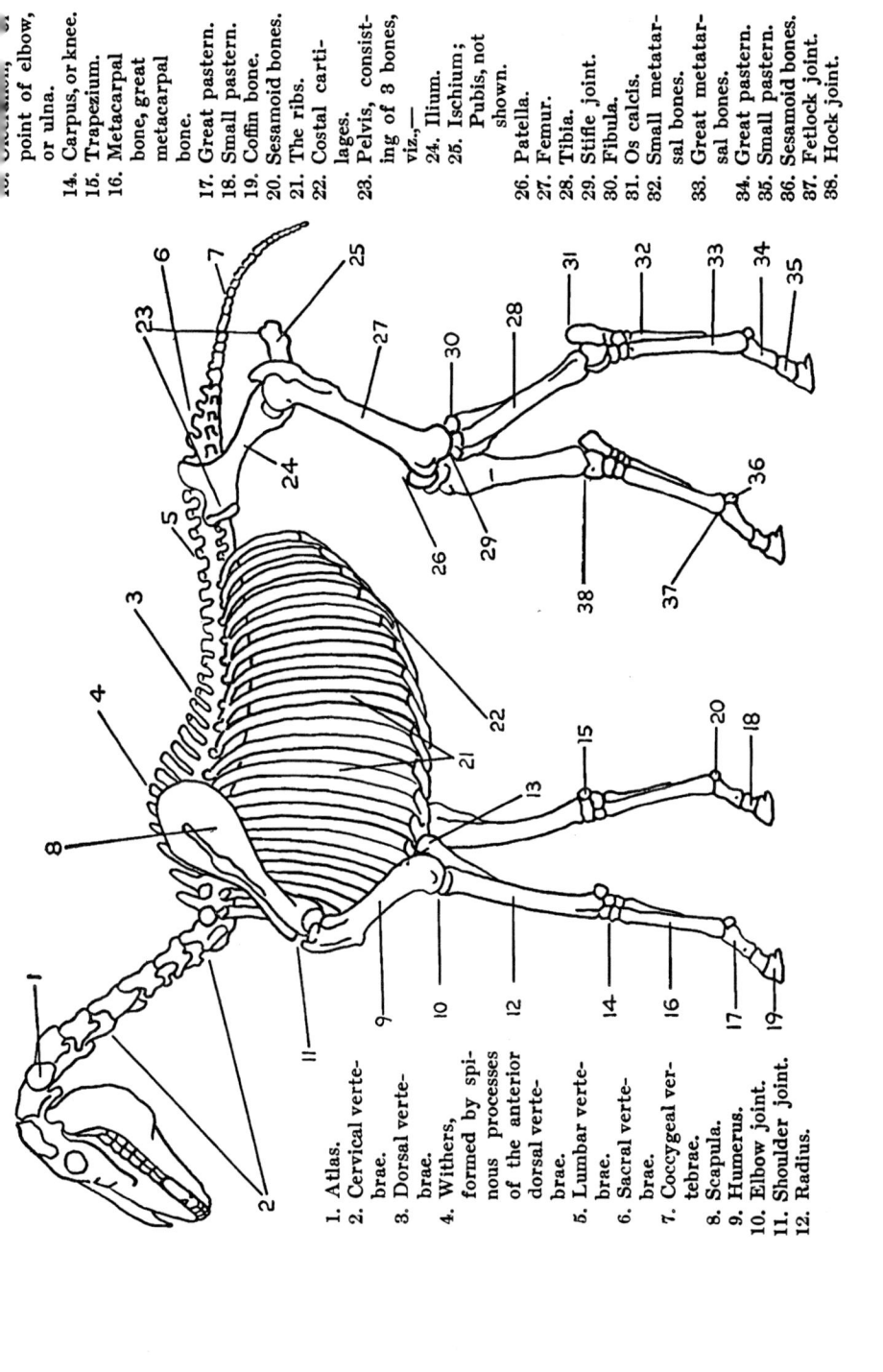

1. Atlas.
2. Cervical vertebrae.
3. Dorsal vertebrae.
4. Withers, formed by spinous processes of the anterior dorsal vertebrae.
5. Lumbar vertebrae.
6. Sacral vertebrae.
7. Coccygeal vertebrae.
8. Scapula.
9. Humerus.
10. Elbow joint.
11. Shoulder joint.
12. Radius.
13. Olecranon, point of elbow, or ulna.
14. Carpus, or knee.
15. Trapezium.
16. Metacarpal bone, great metacarpal bone.
17. Great pastern.
18. Small pastern.
19. Coffin bone.
20. Sesamoid bones.
21. The ribs.
22. Costal cartilages.
23. Pelvis, consisting of 3 bones, viz.,—
24. Ilium.
25. Ischium; Pubis, not shown.
26. Patella.
27. Femur.
28. Tibia.
29. Stifle joint.
30. Os calcis.
31. Fibula.
32. Small metatarsal bones.
33. Great metatarsal bones.
34. Great pastern.
35. Small pastern.
36. Sesamoid bones.
37. Fetlock joint.
38. Hock joint.

The Bony Framework

The direction and development of the muscles are closely allied to and dependent upon the shape and direction of the bones to which they are attached. *Therefore, the skeleton which forms the base of the structure is the determining factor in judging conformation.* The eye must learn to picture the framework even when hidden by layers of muscle and fat. It is far easier to judge conformation, and therefrom the probable adaptability and capability of a horse, when thin than when fat. Fat hides a multitude of sins and deceives many a man who flatteringly considers himself "a fine judge of horseflesh." Therein lies the error; he mistakes horseflesh for the bone and muscle that permit fine performance. That very soft roundness, which is an abomination in a fine cross-country horse, often is praised and sought for by superficial horsemen. In many show rings judges are timid about giving a prize to a big-boned, capable hunter unless he is rolling in fat. This fact appears too absurd for comment, but unfortunately many an owner who has hunted his horse and has him in fine, hard condition dares not enter him in a fall show. Disregarding the above absurdity, it is the horse which, when in hard condition, is clean cut, distinctly angular and almost rough-appearing due to his big, bony framework that makes the great hunter, galloper and jumper. The

SELECTION, CONFORMATION AND GAITS

horse broad across the hips; with big, clean, prominent joints; flat, hard-appearing bone; muscles not thick and heavy, but long and lean; a chiseled-out horse, not molded smoothly into round curves, is the type that will be blessed with speed, endurance and the mechanism necessary to stand hard galloping over rough country without breaking down.

If the manner in which muscles work is analyzed, the necessity and beauty of prominent joints, broad, angular hips, and a generally accentuated bony framework, are obvious. Those muscles used in locomotion lie for the most part parallel to, and along, the bones which, when the horse moves, partially rotate about an adjacent joint. The prominences at the ends of the bones and near the joints form levers, or give points of attachment for the muscles, and therefore should be large. In moving the bones which form the joints, since the muscles are parallel to them, the initial muscular effort is very great. Later, when the joint is partly flexed, the muscles act more perpendicularly to the bones which allows a decrease in the muscular effort necessary to continue the flexion. Thus it is seen that the accentuation of every bony prominence serves a beneficial purpose mechanically in facilitating some movement.

The above facts are of great importance in studying the conformation of the shoulders, croup and legs—

the agents of locomotion. Chapter II will cover these points in more detail.

Cause of Fatigue

In contracting, a muscle's work generates heat and poisonous acid. Upon relaxing for a fleeting instant after contraction it rests, and the poisonous acid is partly neutralized by the oxygen brought to the muscle by the blood. In the short and quick striding galloper the periods of relaxation are briefer and the consequent decrease in the time for rest and supply of oxygen hastens fatigue. This is the basic reason for the superiority as a "stayer" of the long-muscled, long-striding horse with great amplitude of movement to his joints. It also is the foundation for the old saying, "A horse gallops with his wind."

In résumé the examination of the horse thus far, both in and out of the stable, has helped to determine: the presence or absence of stable vices; type of disposition; obvious defects and injuries; character and condition of the eyes; general appearance as to symmetry; muscular development; and the quality of the coat.

If the prospective purchase passes satisfactorily the above cursory examination, and before going more minutely into the questions of soundness and conformation, the purchaser should see him in action.

SELECTION, CONFORMATION AND GAITS

Study of the Gaits

To see the horse move on a halter, longe, or at liberty is absolutely essential, for no matter how handsome he may be, without low, true, elastic and free gaits he will be of little value.

To have him led on a halter is perhaps the most satisfactory way of studying the walk and trot. The halter shank should be allowed to hang loosely so that it may interfere in no way with natural gestures made by the head and neck. A level, hard road is the best place to observe the gaits, for the horse, if sound, will travel uniformly and naturally on such footing. All three gaits should be studied from the side when the horse is moving past; from the front when moving toward; and from the rear when moving away from the observer.

The Walk

At the walk—called the "mother of the gaits"—the strides, when studied from the side, should be long, free, and close to the ground. In a good walk, each hind foot strikes the ground from four to ten inches or more in advance of the print made by the fore foot on the corresponding side. As the fore foot is carried to the front the shoulder moves easily and freely, the point appearing to slip forward smoothly and elastically, while the upper end of the blade moves similarly to the rear. The angle between the shoulder blade and arm displays great amplitude in opening and closing, the arm reaching well out to the front as the foot is grounded. No cramped or tight appearance is apparent if the horse is well conformed, sound, and walks well. Each fore leg snaps unhesitatingly to its full extension and the heel appears to strike the ground first. As western horsemen say, "He picks 'em up and lays 'em down." The knees are not raised high with good cannons which are short relative to the forearms. The fetlock joints are supple and softly springy. No stiffness is present in any part of the stride.

The hind leg moves freely with little perceptible flexion at the hock because the motion appears to be caused by the free, long gesture of the thigh (from the hip joint to the stifle) which swings the leg and cannon almost as one piece and engages the foot far forward under the horse's body. The fetlocks also should be very flexible and springy without, as a result of excessively long pasterns, breaking back too far when the feet are planted.

Viewed from the front, the fore legs should move in vertical planes with no throwing of the feet outward (paddling) or inward. Ample, but not excessive, room between the fore feet as they pass should exist. If too close together there will be interference and unstableness, especially when the horse is fatigued; if too far apart he will be stable but will lack agility, speed and suppleness at faster gaits. The front feet, when moving properly, remain square and true during the whole stride.

In watching the horse from directly in rear, his hind legs should exhibit no rotation of the foot or hock as the foot strikes the ground; the feet should travel squarely to the front without swinging outward or inward. Faulty twisting, grinding or swinging action means loss of efficiency and additional strain on articulations and tendons, with consequent likelihood of injuries.

The hind feet should follow accurately the same lines made by the fore; however, the hind leg does not always move in a vertical plane since, from the stifle down, it often slopes inward slightly toward the foot, particularly on broad-hipped horses.

With a good walk, the horse appears to glide along in a snakelike manner.

The Trot

At the trot, when observing the horse from the front and rear, similar conditions to those desired at the walk should exist relative to true, low action and the tracking of the feet. Contrary to what is often heard about a thoroughbred's not being able to trot well, since he is bred to gallop, it is noteworthy that a long-striding, springy trot is a reliable indication of an excellent galloper. The trot, though springy, should be low, with feet moving close to the ground as a result of a minimum flexion of knees and hocks. This gait quickly reveals the presence of natural "impulsion" when, although little effort is evident, great driving power is displayed by the hind legs and the strides are long. The horse with such a trot appears to glide along with little up and down motion apparent in any part of his body. A generally well made horse with a trot as described, if also graced by high withers, a somewhat sloping but long and well made croup and good hocks, usually will prove to be a long-striding galloper and good jumper.

At the trot, there should be no sidewise rocking of the hindquarters, which comes from legs set too far apart, or hips too broad, faults found where a strong cross of draft horse blood exists.

The Gallop

The gallop is the natural gait of the thoroughbred type when moving at speed. It is far less fatiguing to such horses than is a very fast trot. Incidentally a slow trot is less fatiguing than the walk when the latter gait is pushed to extreme speed for long periods of time. However, brief periods of the extended walk and trot are excellent gymnastics for training purposes.

A long striding and cadenced canter. Note impulsion shown by extension of right fore and engagement of right hind. Second beat of gallop with right lead.

Head well placed at canter. Correct length of stirrups for training and hacking.

SELECTION, CONFORMATION AND GAITS

The horse, when "galloping with the right lead," places the right lateral biped (the right fore and right hind) at each stride on the ground in advance of the left lateral biped (left fore and left hind). If galloping slowly (cantering) with the right lead, the gait has three beats; 1st—left hind; 2d—right hind and left fore; there is now an instant when three feet are in support, until the left hind is lifted leaving the right hind and left fore only in support; 3d—right fore. As the right fore grounds, the right hind and both front feet give again a tripedal support until the right hind lifts. This is followed by the lifting of the left fore, leaving only the right fore in support. The right fore leg, now used as a pole vaulter uses his pole, receives the impulsion from the hind legs which projects the whole mass of the horse into the air over this right fore into the period of suspension which occurs in each galloping stride.

As the gallop becomes fast, a four-beat gait results because the right hind comes to ground an instant ahead of the left fore. At a racing gallop the tripedal phases of support disappear, and all four feet are planted on approximately a single straight line.

The horse carries his croup slightly to the right, if leading right, which favorably disposes his two right legs to come to ground in advance of the left ones. It also places the bipedal supporting diagonal (left fore

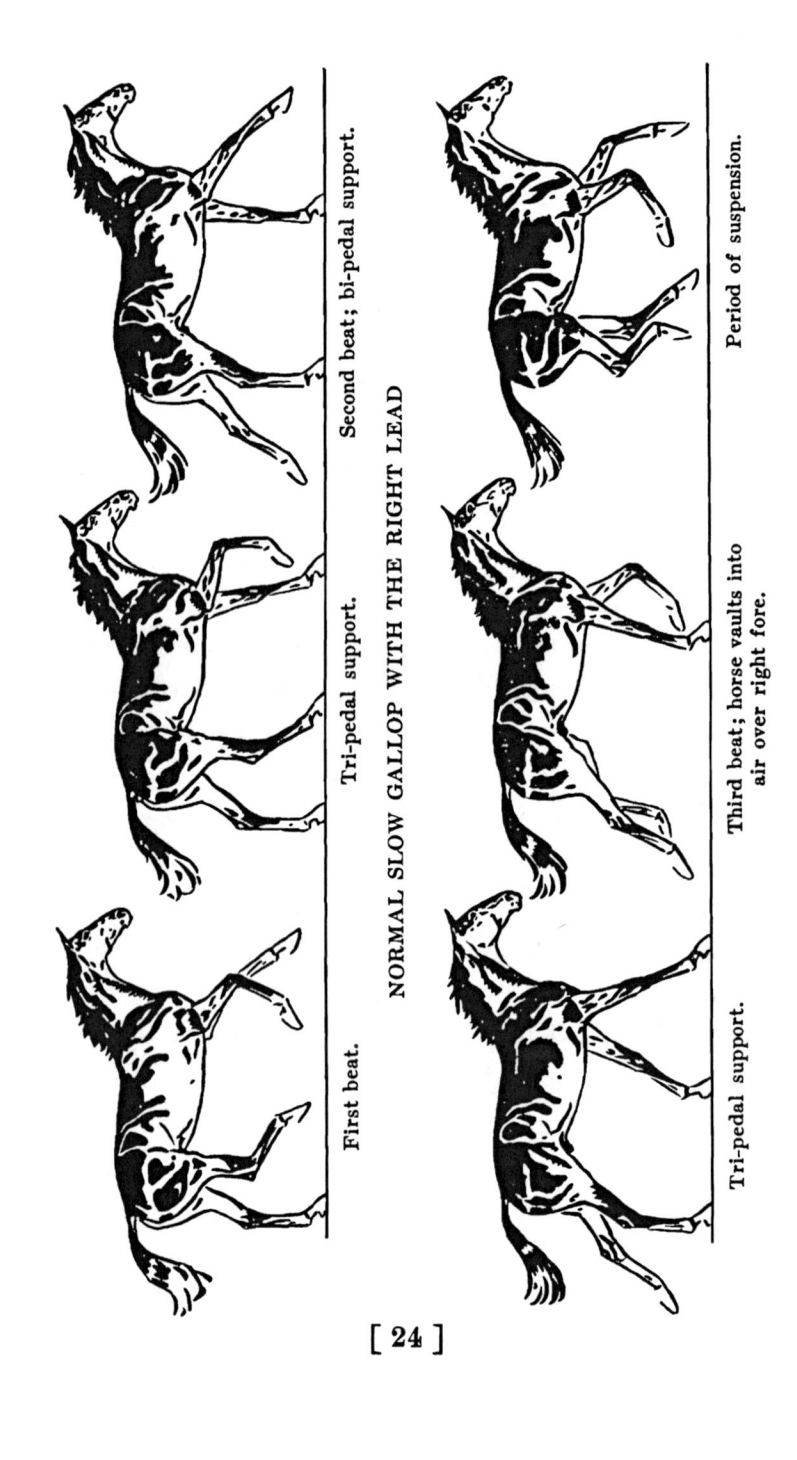

First beat.   Tri-pedal support.   Second beat; bi-pedal support.

NORMAL SLOW GALLOP WITH THE RIGHT LEAD

Tri-pedal support.   Third beat; horse vaults into air over right fore.   Period of suspension.

SELECTION, CONFORMATION AND GAITS

and right hind when leading right) on a broadened base which steadies the equilibrium laterally as the hind legs propel the horse forward.

A good galloper's feet travel close to the ground ("daisy cutter") with little knee and hock action. The hind feet come forward well under the belly with an easy, free swinging of the hind legs and the hock apparently flexes very little. The forehand appears well balanced and light, flowing smoothly along without jerkiness. The shoulder blades and arms appear free and relaxed in their action, while the fore feet reach far out to the front, with fetlock joints supple and springy, as the feet strike earth. There should be no flinging of the fore or hind feet outward or inward when the gallop is viewed from directly in front or behind the horse. A single stride at a gallop varies from about twelve feet at slow speed to twenty-seven feet at top racing speed.

In the case of an unbroken colt that has never been ridden or worked on a longe, he may be observed while at the gallop in a corral or pasture. If he possesses good shoulders and has displayed an excellent walk and trot, his gallop almost invariably will be good.

After studying his gaits dismounted, if the colt is broken to the saddle, the final and most satisfactory test is to ride him. This will tell the tale. Has he a "good front" when mounted? In other words, is there "a lot of horse" out in front of the rider? The front should come from having long, sloping shoulders and long, high withers which run far into the back. The neck should be moderate in length, for a straight shoulder and a long, willowy neck, while giving a lot of front, also place the rider in a most insecure and uncomfortable position.

All gaits should feel free, long and elastic when the horse is ridden, particularly when going down slopes. Galloping down a hill determines whether the shoulders, arms and hindquarters are so conformed as to give natural balance. If they are, the rider will have no apprehension about the horse's falling, for he will gallop almost as easily and smoothly as when on level footing.

If the prospective buyer, after this general examination of the horse and his gaits, is satisfied, a painstaking study of his conformation next should be made. The details to be observed will be analyzed in Chapter II.

CHAPTER II

DETAILS OF CONFORMATION

FOR convenience in studying conformation, the horse may be divided into three sections; the legs, functioning as supports, shock absorbers and propellers; the body, comprising the engine of the machine; the head and neck, serving mechanically as balancer and rudder. These three sections will be discussed individually, by describing briefly and illustrating diagrammatically the more important beauties, defects, blemishes and injuries. A blemish offends only the sight, whereas a defect is either an actual or probable cause of unsoundness.

The Foot
(See Diagrams, Pages 28, 29 and 31)

Examination should begin with the feet and legs. "No foot; no horse" is an adage trite but very true. Probably ninety per cent of all serious disabilities oc-

Location of toe cracks.

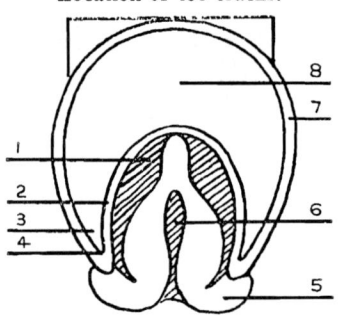

BOTTOM OF FORE FOOT

A good fore foot is almost round; sole concave; frog big and resting on the ground; bars prominent; heels well separated.
1. Lateral lacuna.
2. Bar.
3. Seat of corns.
4. Buttress (junction of bar and sole).
5. Bulb of heel.
6. Frog's cleft or median lacuna.
7. Wall.
8. Sole.

cur in the feet and legs, and of these, about seventy-five per cent are in the fore feet and fore legs from the knees down; the hind members are less susceptible to injuries.

The exterior of the foot is an insensitive horny case, formed by the wall, sole and frog. These insensitive parts merge interiorly into sensitive tissues. Three

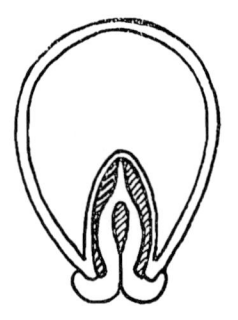

CONTRACTED HEEL IN A FORE FOOT

Source of many troubles. Can be corrected by going barefooted or pathological shoeing.

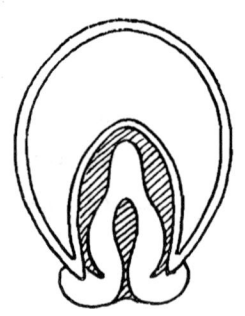

BOTTOM OF HIND FOOT

More elliptical than fore foot, otherwise similar.

DETAILS OF CONFORMATION

DIAGRAMMATIC CROSS SECTION OF FOOT AND PASTERN

1. Seat of osselets.
2. Dangerous seat of ringbone.
3. Toe.
4. Quarter (location of quarter cracks).
5. Heel.
6. Pedal bone (coffin).
7. Navicular bone.
8. Coronary bone (lower pastern).
9. Pastern bone (upper).
10. Cannon.

1. Extensor tendon.
2. Coronary band.
3. Sensitive horn or laminae.
4. Insensitive wall.
5. Insensitive sole.
6. Insensitive frog.
7. Coffin bone (pedal).
8. Sensitive frog.
9. Seat of navicular disease.
10. Navicular bone (small sesamoid).
11. Small pastern bone (coronary, or second phalanx).
12. Flexor tendon (perforans).
13. Sesamoid ligament.
14. Pastern bone.
15. Lower end of cannon bone.

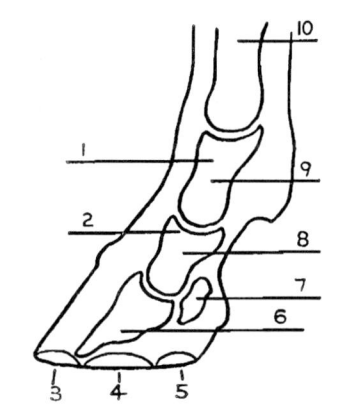

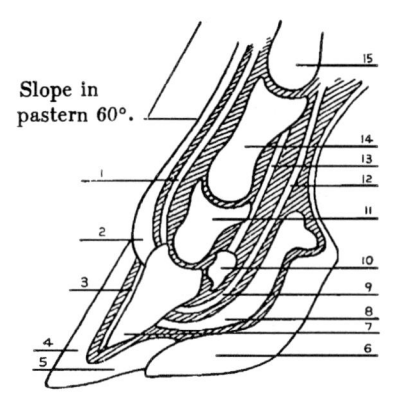

Slope in pastern 60°.

bones form the interior framework: the pedal (or coffin); the navicular (or small sesamoid); and a portion of the lower pastern.

BEAUTIES

Front feet: outline of bearing surface almost round; large enough to properly bear weight of horse.

Hind feet: somewhat smaller than the front; bearing surface more oval in shape.

Front feet should point squarely to front; hind feet, when horse is at rest, usually turn out very slightly.

Heels: broad; well separated by the frog.

Horny wall: smooth; dense; tough; and approximately twice as high at the front as at the heels.

Frog: tough; elastic; large; and very close to, or on, the ground when the horse is shod.

Soles: concave upward; concavity very pronounced in the hind feet.

Bars: prominent; running well forward toward the point of the frog.

Shape of foot: front line of wall, viewed from the side, should be parallel to the axis of the pastern, sloping with the horizontal, at approximately sixty degrees in the front, and sixty-five degrees in the hind feet.

Lateral cartilages: very tough but elastic to the touch.

DEFECTS AND INJURIES

Feet too large, small, oval or narrow.

Contracted feet, or heels; quarter-cracks; toe-cracks; corns; excessively high heels; frogs high off ground; (all these conditions usually are caused by poor shoeing and neglect and generally can be cured by proper treatment).

Flat or fallen soles: (the latter incurable condition

DETAILS OF CONFORMATION

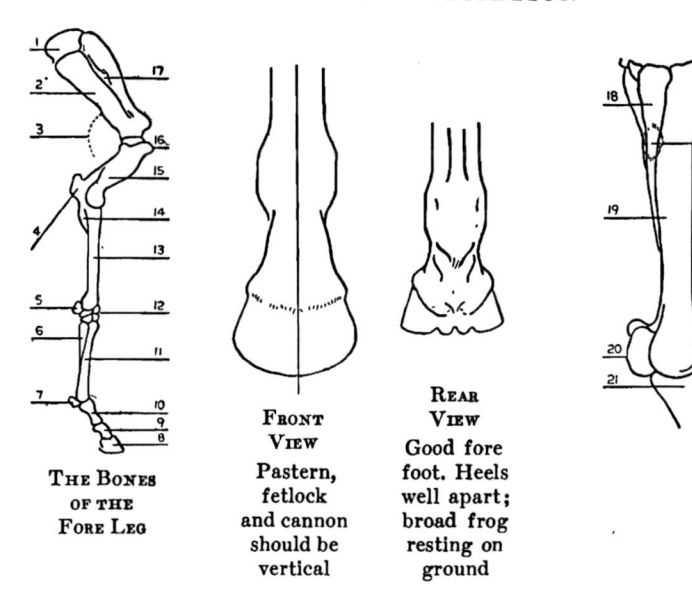

THE BONES OF THE FORE LEG

FRONT VIEW
Pastern, fetlock and cannon should be vertical

REAR VIEW
Good fore foot. Heels well apart; broad frog resting on ground

THE FORE LEG

1. Cartilage of prolongation.
2. Shoulder blade.
3. Scapulo-humeral angle approximately 110° (for good hunter).
4. Olecranon or point of elbow (location of shoe-boils).
5. Trapezium or pisiform bone.
6. Splint bone.
7. Great sesamoid bones.
8. Coffin bone.
9. Lower pastern bone (or coronary).
10. Upper pastern bone.
11. Cannon.
12. Knee or carpus.
13. Radius (forearm).
14. Ulna.
15. Humerus.
16. Point of shoulder (really the arm).
17. Spine of shoulder.
18. Splint bones.
19. Great metacarpal or cannon.
20. Great sesamoids.
21. Upper pastern.
22. Splint.

generally results from laminitis or founder which begins as an inflammation inside the foot). Some horses naturally have flat soles which are weak and easily bruised.

Side-bones are enlarged and ossified lateral cartilages, often caused by injury or poor shoeing (detected either by sight or by feeling the lateral cartilages, which extend up beyond the coronary band alongside the lower pastern bone).

Navicular disease: an injury of the sesamoid bone, which in turn causes irritation and inflammation of the tendons sliding over it. The sesamoid functions as a pulley.

Mealy, soft walls make the foot weak and shoes are kept on with difficulty.

All the above faults, with the exception of those which can be rectified by proper shoeing and care, are serious and demand rejecting as a purchase a horse so afflicted. The foot and its functioning are most interesting subjects for a detailed study, too long and involved to be embodied herein.

Pastern
(See Diagrams, Pages 29 and 35)

The pastern comprises the upper (great) and lower (small) pastern bones. At its top, the upper bone meets the large sesamoid and cannon bones, forming the fetlock joint. Below it articulates with the small pastern bone. The small pastern is partly encased in the foot. In the upper part of the foot it joins the coffin bone and the navicular bone is found just in

DETAILS OF CONFORMATION

rear of the junction. Exteriorly, a rounded band covered with hair joins the pastern and horny wall of the hoof, known as the coronary band (part of coronet). From its interior grow the horny fibers which form the wall of the hoof, much as the nail grows on the human finger.

BEAUTIES

Clean cut; covered with short, fine hair. This appearance is typical in well-bred saddle types.

Wide from front to rear when viewed from the side; thick from side to side when viewed from the front. When these two dimensions are big, the bone and adjacent ligaments are well developed and strong.

Medium in length; if too long, excessive strain is thrown on the flexor tendons and suspensory ligaments, while if too short, the pasterns invariably are upright, making shocks throughout the bony column of the leg violent for both horse and rider. The prime function of the pastern is to serve as a spring-like shock absorber. When too short, it is not springy enough; when too long, it is springy but weak. The slope should be approximately sixty degrees with the horizontal in the front, and sixty-five degrees in the hind pasterns; the same inclinations as given for the front wall of the fore and hind feet.

DEFECTS AND INJURIES

Too slender, narrow, long, short, sloping, or upright.

Ringbone: an exostosis or bony enlargement which develops on the lower pastern bone, and often is partly inside the foot below the coronary band. It usually interferes with the movement of the pastern joint, causing chronic lameness.

Osselets: bony enlargements (often called "high ringbones"), which appear on the upper pastern bones. When they do not interfere with the articulation, lameness generally exists only during their formative period. However, it may be chronic and both ringbones and osselets are a cause for rejection. They come from strains, poor conformation, inadequate diet, and other causes.

Scratches: an irritation and cracking of the skin, similar to chapped hands. These occur underneath the pastern just above the heels. Because of the constant movement in this region, scratches are difficult to cure. Too frequent washing without proper drying is a common cause; the water and soap remove too much oil from the skin.

Grease, or water in the legs: a skin disease causing an exudation of sticky, foul matter. It also affects the fetlocks and cannons and requires a veterinarian's attention.

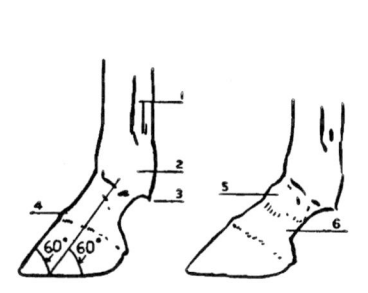

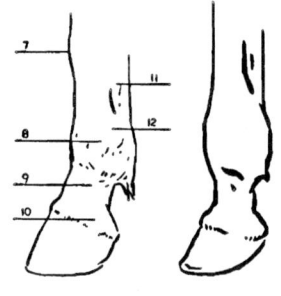

DETAILS OF CONFORMATION

| Good angle to foot and pastern (approximately 60° with horizontal). Pastern and front of foot should be parallel. Foot half as high at heel as at toe. | Pastern too sloping and too long. Heels too low. | Foot too small. Straight stubby pasterns—(do not absorb shocks well and are not durable). Heels too high. | "Cocked-ankle." |

1. Ligament and tendon well defined.
2. Fetlock wide and well defined.
3. Small fetlock tuft (ergot, a horny growth) is in its center.
4. Coronet.
5. Osselet.
6. Location of scratches.
7. Buck shin.
8. Fetlock joint (usually wind puffs first appear on the fetlocks).
9. Upper pastern.
10. Seat of side bones.
11. Tendons not well defined.
12. Poor fetlock (round and puffy). Coarse fetlock tuft.

The Fetlock
(See Diagrams, Pages 29, 31 and 35)

The fetlock joint is the articulation of the lower end of the cannon, the upper end of the upper pastern, and the sesamoid bones. The latter are the pulleys over which the flexor tendons of the front legs and the extensor tendons of the hind legs slide. A small, horny protuberance and a tuft of hair just at the rear of the joint are called, respectively, the ergot and the fetlock tuft. They have no significance.

BEAUTIES

Clean cut; well defined; fine hair and negligible fetlock tuft; thick from side to side; wide from front to rear.

If both pasterns and fetlocks are thick, wide and devoid of puffiness, it is evident that the horse has big, clean bones at the heads of the pasterns and cannons where they meet to form the fetlock. Likewise, it indicates that tendons and sesamoid bones are well developed and strong. Lack of coarse hair and heavy fetlocks evidences good breeding. Clean cut definition reveals lack of wear and tear, and indicates good quality of bone.

DEFECTS AND INJURIES

Thin, narrow, round, puffy, poorly defined, covered with coarse, thick hair.

Osselets (which appear on the fetlocks as well as on the upper pasterns) and bursal enlargements (commonly called "wind galls" or "road puffs") are the usual signs of injuries, strains, hard usage, poor conformation and lack of quality.

Bursal enlargements result from a weakening and swelling of the articular or tendonous synovial (joint-oil) sacs. They normally appear to some extent on nearly all older horses which have been subjected to hard work. If very large, they limit movement of the joint and cause stiffness.

Osselets and bursal enlargements indicate that the machine is partly worn out; in stable talk, the horse is "second-handed." The fetlock should be decidedly wider from front to rear than it is thick from side to side, giving it a rather flat appearance. Round fetlocks, which are not as strong as flat ones, are found generally on underbred horses.

The Cannon
(See Diagrams, Pages 31, 38 and 43)

The bony framework of the front cannon is the great metacarpal (cannon) and two small metacarpal (splint) bones. Metacarpal bones in the fore, correspond to metatarsal bones in the hind legs. The cannon connects the knee and fetlock joints in the fore legs, and the hock and fetlock in the hind. The small metacarpals and metatarsals are rudimentary. Their consolidation with the cannon bone, as a result of an irritation of the bone-covering tissue (periosteum) between them, causes splints. Lameness is frequent in the front legs during the formative period of splints.

1. Extensor tendon.
2. Split bone.
3. Cannon or great metacarpal bone.
4. Extensor tendon.
5. Flexor perforatus.
6. Flexor perforans.
7. Metacarpal ligament.
8. Suspensory or sesamoid ligament.
9. Superior sesamoid.
10. Flexor perforans.
11. Flexor perforatus.
12. Sesamoid ligament.
13. Sesamoid or suspensory ligament.
14. Flexor perforans.
15. Coffin bone.

THE FORE LEG FROM KNEE DOWN

Principal Tendons and Ligaments

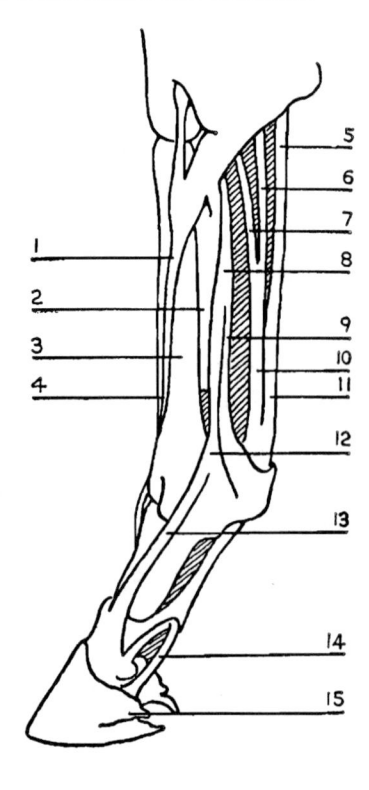

Since the hind legs provide the propelling power and the fore legs are principally supports and shock absorbers, the rear cannons perform far more work in providing impulsion, while the front cannons usually support more weight and resist greater shocks during movement.

The suspensory (or superior sesamoid) ligament holds the fetlock and pastern in a "sling," thus allowing the horse to sleep and rest while standing. In rear

DETAILS OF CONFORMATION

of the cannon and back of the suspensory ligament, are the two flexor tendons, which appear to be one. They can be separated by the finger and thumb when the horse's foot is raised and the bent knee allows them to relax. The metacarpal (or check) ligament, which is attached to the flexor (perforans) halfway down the cannon, also has a very important reinforcing function in the fore leg. It, as well as the flexor tendons and suspensory ligament, is subject to severe strains and sprains, particularly in race horses, polo ponies, hunters and jumpers. A really serious injury to any one of them generally produces a chronic or recurrent lameness. These tendons and ligaments are considered as integral parts of the cannon in its examination and discussion.

BEAUTIES

Relatively short, when compared to the length of the forearm (that segment of the fore leg above the knee) or to the tibia (that segment of the hind leg above the hock). The tibia forms the "leg," properly speaking.

Wide from front to rear; dense; clean cut and well defined; vertical, when viewed from any direction; thick from side to side, when seen from the front.

The tendons, considered independently of the cannons, are designated beautiful when large, neatly defined, clean cut, and well detached from the cannon bone. The total width of cannon and tendons should be the same from just below the knee to just above the fetlock; in other words, the anterior and posterior lines of the cannons, when viewed from the side, should be parallel.

The density, determined by sight and touch, cannot be too great, as it denotes quality and strength. The size of the cannons ought to be proportional to the size of the horse. Cannons, too small, are a serious defect. Many and grave injuries are certain to occur as they are evidently too weak for their tasks.

Considering the fore and hind legs as broken pendulums, it is known that the segments (formed in front by the forearm and the cannon hinged at the knee, and behind by the leg and cannon hinged at the hock) describe arcs which increase in amplitude directly as their lengths increase. However, the speed of oscillation in a particular segment decreases as it becomes longer. Hence, a cannon, short when compared with the forearm, oscillates more swiftly and since it weighs less, with less muscular effort than a longer one. Moreover, it requires less elevation of the knee to allow the foot to clear the ground. These considerations make evident the desirability of relatively short cannons.

Width from front to rear is produced by the ten-

DETAILS OF CONFORMATION

dons' being well detached from the cannon bone, and by the cannon bone itself being wide. Well detached tendons result from well developed knees and big, strong hocks, coupled with wide, strong fetlocks in both front and hind legs.

DEFECTS AND INJURIES

Too long, relative to the forearm or leg; thin, when viewed from the front; narrow, when viewed from the side. All such cannons are manifestly weak.

Puffiness; lack of definition; bony enlargements; enlarged tendons or ligaments, caused by bruises, ruptures, or sprains. These conditions are disclosed to the eye by enlargements, and if recent, by fever found by feeling and comparing the legs after the horse has remained in a cool stable for several hours. When very severe, a strain may completely rupture a tendon or ligament.

All these defects may be very grave. They occur rarely in the hind legs. Badly sprained tendons become "bowed" to the rear. When the suspensory ligament is ruptured the horse "breaks down." Even a very slight enlargement of a tendon or ligament (noted by exceedingly careful comparison of the two legs by sight and touch) should be regarded with the greatest suspicion. The horse should be examined by a veterinarian before a purchase is made. The enlargement of a temporarily cured injury is often difficult to detect.

Splints, common in the front legs, usually develop in young horses from strains or overwork. After ossification has united the small metacarpals to the large cannon bone, and after inflammation has completely subsided, lameness usually disappears. Normally splints are harmless, and only when the articulation of the knee joint is affected, or a tendon's movement interfered with, does chronic lameness occur. The small splint bones invariably unite to the cannon at some time in the life of any horse. This usually causes temporary lameness even when the splint is not visible.

Buck shins (swellings on the front of the cannons) appear most often on young race horses causing extreme soreness but generally dissolve in the course of time with no permanent results.

"Tied-in" cannons are those which are small below the knee or hock compared to the lower portion of the cannons.

The Knee
(See Diagrams, Pages 31, 43 and 46)

The knee, corresponding to the human wrist, is composed of seven bones arranged in two layers and bound together by several ligaments. Three synovial membranes of importance surrounding the joint con-

DETAILS OF CONFORMATION

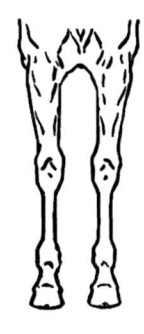

GOOD CONFORMATION
Front feet and legs square, thick knees, cannon and fetlock.

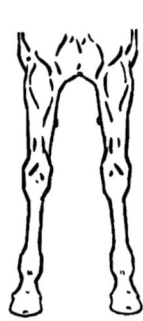

Breast too broad.

Feet too far apart.

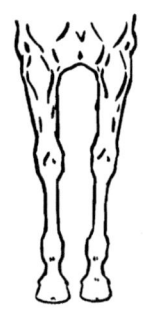

Feet too close.

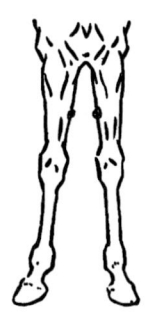

CROOKED LEGS

Splay feet and knock knees.

Good cannon, tendons well detached.

Strong prominent trapezium.

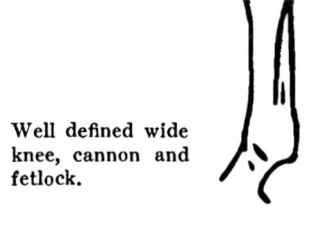

Well defined wide knee, cannon and fetlock.

"Big" knee from injury.

"Tied in" below knee.

Narrow, weak cannon. Tendons not well detached.

tain the lubricating oil. These are subject to injury and enlargement.

BEAUTIES

Well defined, with all bony prominences revealed in a clean cut manner as a result of thin, delicate skin. Thick, when viewed from the front; wide from front to rear. These beauties indicate large surfaces of articulation, strength and stableness in movement. Width and thickness also show that the head of the radius (the bone above the knee forming the forearm) is big and strong.

Well descended (low) as a result of the forearm being relatively long compared to the cannon beneath. The direction of the forearm, knee, and cannon should be vertical, viewed from either front or side.

Prominence of the trapezium (bone projecting out to the rear) is highly desirable. To a careless observer this prominence often makes really good cannons appear "tied-in" (too small just below the knee).

DEFECTS AND INJURIES

Too narrow; thin; crooked; ill-defined; soft appearing.

"Calf knees" (bending backward out of the perpendicular line) usually are associated with lack of substance. Being fundamentally weak and out of line, they throw additional strain on the tendons and ligaments about the joint.

"Over at the knees" or "knee sprung" is a condition either acquired or congenital. The latter cause is less serious, but acquired cases come from inherent weakness and are to be avoided. While undesirable, the congenital cases frequently present no trouble even under very hard work.

"Knock-kneed" horses usually "paddle" (throw the feet outward when moving).

"Bow-legged" ones rarely travel true. Both conditions sooner or later cause lameness under hard work as a result of the additional strain and faulty movement consequent to the legs not being perpendicular.

"Big knees," generally acquired through striking obstacles or falling, often are difficult to reduce and sometimes limit knee action. The bursal sacs, bones, ligaments and tendons may be affected and enlarged in a big knee. Scars on the front of the knees indicate falls. Their unsightliness is also a warning.

Forearm

(See Diagrams, Pages 31 and 46)

The forearm, formed by the radius and cubitus bones, connects the knee with the elbow joint.

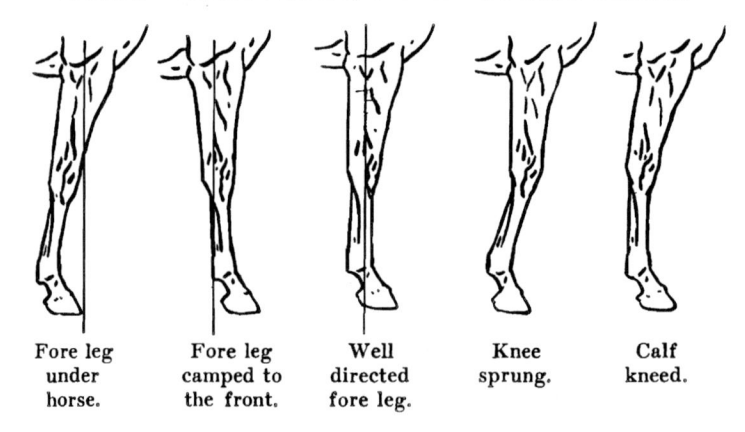

| Fore leg under horse. | Fore leg camped to the front. | Well directed fore leg. | Knee sprung. | Calf kneed. |

BEAUTIES

Long; wide; thick; well directed; muscular.

Through giving the advantage described when discussing the movement of the segments of a broken pendulum under "The Cannon," page 40, a forearm, long compared to the cannon, allows the foot to travel close to the ground and permits great amplitude of movement; in other words, a long stride. While the rapidity of oscillation is less with a relatively long than with a relatively short forearm, the horse with the long forearm takes fewer strides to cover the same distance than a horse with a short one. Also less expenditure of muscular energy is required in moving the whole fore leg.

Being wide from front to rear and thick from side to side, denotes great volume of bone and muscular development.

DETAILS OF CONFORMATION

Verticality, when inspected from any direction, obviously places the forearm in the most favorable position to permit freedom of movement both to the front and the rear, and ease in support when standing still.

DEFECTS AND INJURIES

Too short, narrow or thin. Thin, narrow forearms are an almost certain sign of general weakness. Such a horse has little muscular development and is called "leggy" or "weedy."

The forearm is not subject to many injuries except bruises or cuts from outside sources.

The Elbow

The elbow joint unites the arm (humerus) and the forearm (radius). The cubitus is at the rear of the joint and needs no discussion. The joint is naturally very strong and usually remains sound. When beautiful, it is prominent and stands well away from the chest, resting in a vertical plane parallel to the axis of the body. If deviated outward, the result is a "pigeon-toed" horse. If too close to the chest (tied-in) splay-footedness results. When severely bruised, the resultant swelling is called a "capped" elbow or "shoe boil." The latter name comes from the fact that in lying down, or arising, the elbow sometimes is injured by a poorly fitted shoe which is too long and projects back of the horse's heel. A "shoe boil" usually may be reduced if given consistent and proper treatment as soon as it appears. Occasionally the synovial sac is ruptured, causing grave results which may require the destruction of the horse.

The Arm

The arm (humerus) connecting shoulder and forearm is hidden by powerful muscles. This bone varies more than any other, both as to length and direction, in the various breeds of horses, as well as in those of the same breed. Although seldom sufficiently observed by judges, it is one of the most important features of conformation, particularly in cross-country, jumping and race horses. When evaluating its length both the actual measurements, as well as its length compared to the shoulder blade, must be considered.

BEAUTIES

Long; rather upright; muscular.

Length is essential, for many muscles from the withers, shoulders, neck, forearm, foot and chest are attached to, or run along, the arm bone. Their length obviously is directly affected by that of the arm, and the longer the muscle, the greater is its extent of contraction and potential usefulness. A long arm de-

DETAILS OF CONFORMATION

scribes a large arc, which increases amplitude of movement in galloping and jumping. Actually, it should be greater than half the length of the shoulder and slope at approximately fifty degrees or more with the horizontal. A tendency toward being upright gives the arm extensive movement forward, permitting it to function freely and easily in jumping and galloping across country. The angle (scapulo-humeral) which the arm forms with the shoulder blade should measure almost one hundred and ten degrees for hunters and jumpers, although a smaller angle is desirable when seeking great speed on the flat. This angle, formed at the point of the shoulder, should appear well closed when the horse is standing still, as a consequence of the markedly backward slope of the shoulder—never because the arm closely approaches the horizontal. To check the proper position of shoulder and arm, as well as the angle they form, the following rule is helpful: an imaginary line, bisecting the angle formed by a fairly upright arm and a sloping shoulder, will pass just above the elbow. With a poor scapulo-humeral angle (horizontal arm and vertical shoulder) such as is seen in draft horses and poor types of saddle horses, this line will pass much higher up. Of course the shoulder is never vertical or the arm horizontal—these are colloquialisms of the horseman's world signifying tendencies beyond the average in those directions.

Very rarely an arm too nearly vertical will be encountered. Such an arm produces action too low and "stilty," with a consequent probability of stumbling and little aptitude for jumping.

The space in the angle of the shoulder and arm should be well muscled, but in a hunter, these muscles while strong and clearly outlined should not appear bulky and heavy. In slow draft types, where short strides and intense effort are required, bulky, thick muscles are considered beauties.

DEFECTS AND INJURIES

Too short; too sloping; not muscular.

Shortness limits the extent of stride and decreases the length of important muscles covering the arm. An arm inclined at forty degrees or less with the horizontal is not sufficiently upright, and constitutes a grave fault in a hunter or jumper. Such an arm which appears horizontal, renders the horse heavy and clumsy in front, and invariably is associated with lack of height of chest. It makes difficult the shortening of stride often necessary when approaching a jump, since the horse is perpetually over-balanced to the front. It closes the angle between the forearm and arm (radio-humeral) which condition is undesirable since this angle closes during movement, and therefore should be well open when at rest so as to increase its extent

DETAILS OF CONFORMATION

of play. It is to be noted that the wide opening desirable at rest in the forearm-arm angle is directly opposite to the requirements for a good shoulder-arm angle, which, as previously described, should be well closed at rest. The former closes and the latter opens when the horse moves.

An excessively sloping arm makes a horse short-striding, because it decreases the extent of movement of the fore leg to the front. This limitation also makes him liable to fall when landing after a jump. Fore legs with the horizontal type of arm appear to be set far back under the horse's shoulders. The distance from elbow to stifle is decreased and short appearing. The horse does not "stand over a lot of ground" as he should in order to be stable, well balanced and agile.

Despite the rather general and erroneous opinion to the contrary, comparatively upright shoulders and horizontal arms frequently are seen on very fast race horses, both trotters and thoroughbreds. Among thoroughbreds, they usually are found on sprinters, while in exceptionally fast trotters, they are universal characteristics. Since instability gives the measure of speed, a horse which is always falling over the points of his shoulders is particularly well adapted to racing, but on the contrary is not clever at jumping or cross-country galloping. Also, due to their short strides, horses so conformed perform more work over a certain distance and, other things being equal, become fatigued sooner than those employing the long strides concomitant with an upright arm and sloping shoulder. These facts furnish further condemnation of short races, since the poorly-conformed, short-striding horse often has beaten a well conformed one over a short distance, whereas in a long race, the short-strider would have become fatigued sooner and been mastered by the lightly moving, long-striding type. The success in short races of these poorly conformed horses has had, and is having, a most harmful effect on breeding, since many of them, solely because of their sprinting ability —not because of type—are used as sires and dams. In fact, those chosen for breeding in the majority of cases are far from what is desirable as models for jumpers, hunters or stayers. This is a very great and grave misfortune which already has done much to hurt the thoroughbred's possibilities and conformation. Only long races, and the abolition of those for two-year-olds, promise any amelioration of this truly deplorable condition.

The Shoulder
(See Diagrams, Pages 31 and 53)

The shoulder blade (scapula) is not attached directly to the backbone, but is connected by muscles and ligaments to the withers, neck and ribs. A "carti-

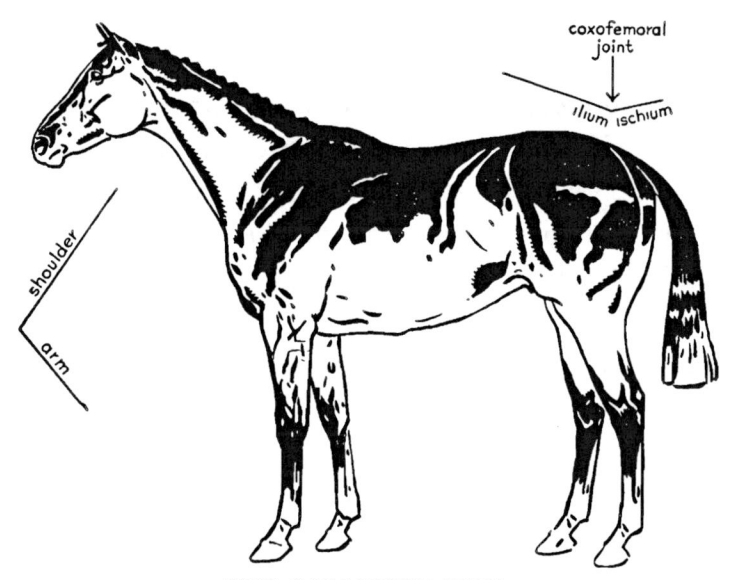

THE GALLOPING TYPE

Sloping shoulder, long, high, well shaped withers; upright arm; long croup and short back; Ischium long relative to Ilium; well directed hind legs. "Standing over a lot of ground."

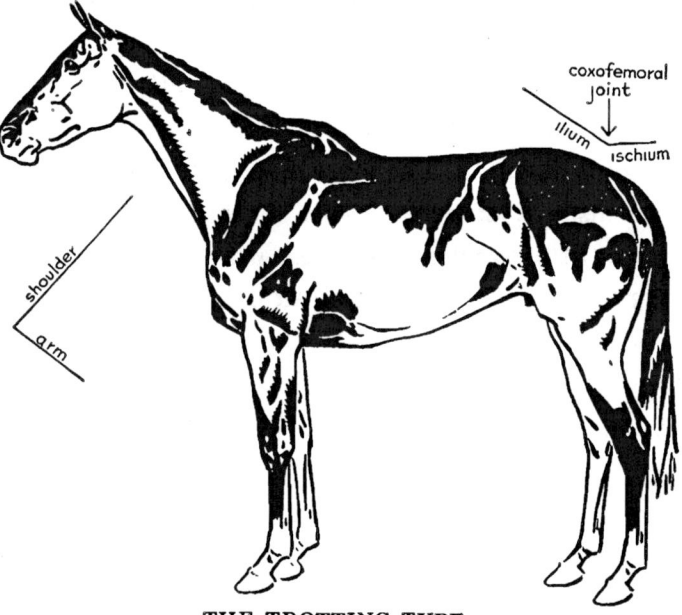

THE TROTTING TYPE

Upright shoulder; sloping (or "horizontal") arm; Ischium comparatively short; hind legs "in back of" the horse.

lage of prolongation" prolongs the upper end of the bone itself, while down the center of the scapula's exterior face runs a bony spine which is an integral part of the shoulder blade. The shoulder primarily is a shock absorbing and supporting agent. The point where it joins the arm is called "the point of the shoulder," although the visible protuberance is, in fact, the end of the humerus.

BEAUTIES

Oblique; long; flat; well placed.

When oblique, the shoulder usually is joined to an upright arm, both being prime requisites for well balanced hunters, hacks, polo ponies and jumpers. Let it be reiterated that this combination permits free, extended strides at all gaits, as well as ease and suppleness in checking quickly and lifting the fore feet. The horse so equipped does not seem to "fall forward" in moving, but remains balanced and graceful, even at fast gaits downhill. The more sloping the shoulder, the more easily it absorbs shocks. It should incline from sixty to fifty-five degrees or less with the horizontal.

Unfortunately, with a well sloped shoulder, the arm is sometimes too horizontal. The great importance of studying the angles and relative lengths of the shoulder and arm as a unit cannot be too strongly emphasized. Often the ensemble appears excellent at a casual glance, but close study will disclose a shoulder too long

"Joe Aleshire"—A Great Jumper
Note the upright position of the arm, great height of withers, slope of shoulders and pasterns, well shaped feet and nicely attached head.

"Joe Aleshire" in action over triple bar and water.

DETAILS OF CONFORMATION

with a relatively short arm, and the resulting stride will be short and choppy.

Seven important muscles which serve to actuate the arm are attached to, or run along, the shoulder. The longer the shoulder, the longer these muscles are, which increases the extent of their action. They should not be bulky, but clean cut, wiry and fine, permitting the outline of the shoulder to be revealed. Coarse, heavy shoulder muscles are typical of draft horses, trotters, and underbred types.

A good shoulder is flat appearing and blends into the neck with no bulging outward at the point of the shoulder or just above it, as is the case in draft horses, in which such conformation provides a place for the collar to rest. The spine of the shoulder blade often is plainly visible on thoroughbreds and horses close to the blood. French authorities say that the horse should be "built into a corner" in front. In other words, he grows broader gradually from the neck and shoulders back toward the croup. Flat, well placed shoulders are largely responsible for this appearance. When well placed, the point of the shoulder is well defined and fore legs are separated by a proper interval, neither too far apart nor too close together. One hoof's breadth between the feet, when the fore legs are vertical and straight, represents an approximately proper interval. Feet too far apart cause a horse to rock sideways when he travels, and are not characteristic of speed. Feet too close together accompany badly placed shoulders and a narrow, weak chest and body. *The spine of the shoulder blade always can be felt, if not seen, and gives the true slope of the shoulder.*

The shoulder should vanish imperceptibly at its upper end through blending into high, well defined withers. When the opposite condition of heavy muscles and projecting cartilages exists, the withers appear low and thick, and the horse is said to have "mutton" shoulders or withers.

An excellent shoulder, as stated, slopes back at between fifty-five and sixty degrees in free moving, well balanced horses. It straightens up to seventy or more degrees in heavy draft types. Thus a good scapulo-humeral angle (formed at the point of the shoulder) measures about one hundred and ten degrees with an arm at fifty and a shoulder at sixty degrees. The rear edge of the top of the shoulder blade should be about a head's length from the point of the haunch (see Diagram, page 78) if the shoulder is sufficiently oblique. As has been mentioned the horse's head is a unit of measure which is useful in testing the symmetry of his various proportions. Horses fed off the ground tend to develop straighter (more nearly vertical) shoulders.

The mastoidal-humeral muscle, which runs in front

DETAILS OF CONFORMATION

of the point of the shoulder and up the neck to the region of the poll, inserts itself at an angle most favorable to efficient action for saddle horses when the humerus, or arm, is upright and the shoulder sloping. This muscle has vast importance in galloping and jumping.

Oblique shoulders permit a well directed neck and normally are accompanied by high and long withers. Superficial judges often err in thinking certain horses have sloping shoulders, through being deceived by the fact that the withers are well placed, high, and run well back. In many present day race horses the shoulder is almost vertical and completely in front of good withers.

FAULTS

Straight, bulging or short shoulders are undesirable, as shown in the discussion of a beautiful shoulder. The shoulder itself rarely is hurt, save through a blow or fall, although race horses, hunters and polo ponies often develop chronically stiff shoulders, limited in their movement, as a result of overwork and neglect when overheated. However this stiffness normally comes to shoulders that are heavy and upright.

The Hock
(See Diagrams, Pages 58, 59 and 60)

The hock, a most important joint, is very compli-

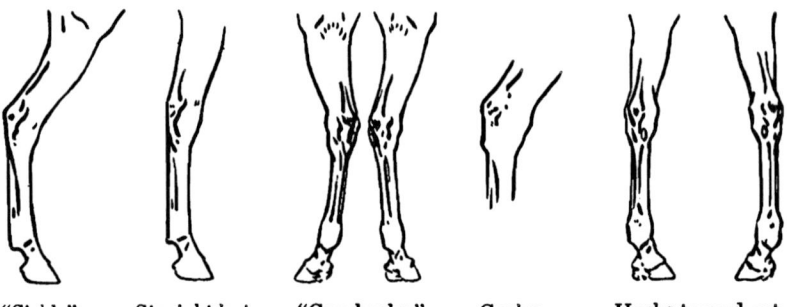

"Sickle" hock. Straight but narrow hock. "Cow hocks." Curby hock. Hocks turned out.

cated in structure. Composed of six bones, it acts as a principal and powerful spring in furnishing impulsion, also serving to some extent as a shock absorber. Connecting the leg (tibia) and the cannon, it is liable to various injuries and merits extremely careful examination because of its numerous responsibilities. It should be inspected carefully from all directions; from

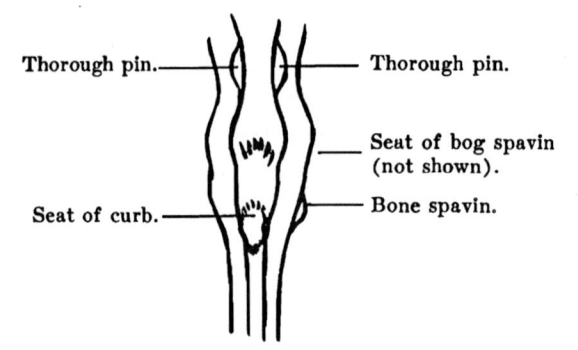

Thorough pin. — Thorough pin.
— Seat of bog spavin (not shown).
Seat of curb. — Bone spavin.

Thorough pin and bog spavin usually occur together and are soft to the touch. Bog spavin occurs on interior, front area of the hock.

DETAILS OF CONFORMATION

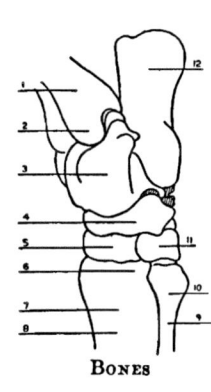

1. Tibia.
2. Tibia.
3. Astragalus.
4. Cuneiform magnum.
5. Cuneiform medium.
6. Seat of spavin.
7. Cannon.
8. Cannon or metatarsal.
9. Inner small metatarsal.
10. Splint bone or small metatarsal.
11. Cuneiform parvum.
12. Os calcis or calcaneus.

BONES

THE HOCK JOINT

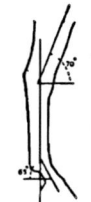

Good direction of rear cannon (vertical). Hind leg (tibia) 70°. Rear pastern 65°.

Interior face of hock.
Locations of spavin.

LIGAMENTS

the sides and from the rear, obliquely from the front, and by sighting between the fore legs. Exact similarity between two hocks is essential. If it does not exist, one hock doubtlessly has suffered a sprain or other injury.

BEAUTIES

Wide, when viewed from the side, both at the top and the base.

Thick, when seen from the front or rear.

Clean cut, with the normal bony prominences well defined.

Dense and powerful appearing; well descended (low)

Point of croup.

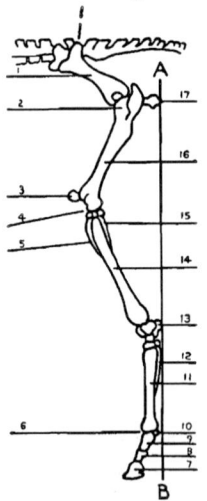

1. Ilium.
2. Hip joint.
3. Patella.
4. Stifle joint.
5. Peroneus.
6. Fetlock joint.
7. Coffin bone.
8. Lower pastern.
9. Upper pastern.
10. Sesamoid bone.
11. Great metatarsal.
12. Small metatarsal.
13. Os calcis and point of hock.
14. Tibia (same slope as femur in opposite direction).
15. Fibula.
16. Femur (should slope at approximately 70° with the horizontal).
17. Ischium (end of ischium is end of buttock).

Perpendicular from point of buttock to ground should be parallel to, and two or three inches in rear of, the back of the cannon. (Line A-B.)

with a large open angle of about one hundred and sixty degrees at the front face, when seen from the side of the horse.

Width and thickness mean strength and power, while well defined, clean cut bony prominences make good lever arms and points of attachment for muscles and tendons.

A low or well descended hock proves that the cannon is relatively short compared to the leg with the same resulting mechanical advantages covered in the discussion of the cannon and forearm (see pages 40 and 46).

DETAILS OF CONFORMATION

A small, sharp angle is very undesirable. It denotes a weak hock, incapable of powerful extension and limited in its forward movement. When so formed, they are called "crooked" or "sickle" hocks. A large angle at the face gives a strong straight hock.

The distance from the haunch to the hock should appear very long, giving great length to the principal muscles that produce the extensive movement of the hind legs in galloping and jumping. Also, the distance from the point of the buttock to the rear point of the hock (formed by the calcaneus bone) should be long and the calcaneus itself, prominent. In a well directed leg a perpendicular line dropped from the point of the buttock should pass one or two inches to the rear of the hock and be parallel to the back line of the cannon. When viewed from front or rear the hocks should be in planes approximately parallel to the median plane of the body and should never deviate outward so as to appear bowlegged.

DEFECTS AND INJURIES

Narrow; thin; high off the ground; ill defined; puffy; doughy; enlarged by unnatural swellings (either bony or bursal).

An exaggeratedly straight hock, if it is narrow from front to rear as a result, is undesirable. A straight hock is a beauty if it also is strong and well developed.

The usual injuries to hocks are spavins and bursal enlargements. A spavin is a bony enlargement generally due to a sprain or injury. A predisposition to spavins is frequently inherited, through faulty conformation. Any puffiness or failure of one hock to correspond exactly in its outline to the other should be regarded with suspicion. When spavins encroach on the articulating edges, or surfaces, of the bones of the hock, they generally cause chronic lameness.

Hocks which are narrow often develop curbs. These appear at the outside and back of the hock in the form of a hard swelling. They rarely produce chronic lameness but indicate weak construction. Curbs may be easily detected when the hock is viewed directly from the side, since they break the straight line which should exist from just below the tip of the hock (calcaneus) down the back of the cannon, to the fetlock.

"Crooked" or "sickle" hocks are accompanied by cannons which are not vertical but slope forward. As stated, such hocks are weak and automatically shorten the horse's strides.

"Bog spavins" and "thorough pins" are bursal enlargements. They generally do not cause lameness, but limit movement when very large.

From injuries, horses develop a "capped" hock. This is a bursal enlargement at the point of the calcaneus usually not involving lameness but very unsightly.

DETAILS OF CONFORMATION

Spavins or other grave injuries to the bones of the hocks, causing severe lameness, often are accompanied by atrophy of the muscles of the croup and hind leg.

The Leg
(See Diagrams, Pages 58 and 60)

The leg proper (formed by the tibia and the peroneus) slopes downward and backward, connecting the stifle and hock joints. The peroneus is a rudimentary bone of little importance mechanically. The gaskin, corresponding to the calf of the leg in man, is the most important part of the leg and should show great muscular development.

BEAUTIES

Long, compared to the cannon; wide from front to rear; rather upright; thick from side to side.

A long leg allows the hock to be well let down, or low, and permits great extent of stride, the amplitude of which results largely from the relatively great length of the tibia when compared to the cannon. Hence, a relatively long leg is a beauty of prime importance.

Breadth from front to rear should exist just below the stifle joint and just above the hock. The gaskin should be very well muscled and the large tendons which define the rear edge of the lower part of the leg, forming the cord of the hock, should be well detached and large.

A leg which inclines only slightly to the rear, measuring about seventy degrees with the horizontal, is directed properly for a hunter or jumper. Too straight a leg rarely is seen. If the tibia is too oblique, the hocks are out behind the horse, so that in galloping too much effort is expended in lifting his mass after the hind legs are engaged under him; the gallop is therefore high, and the stride is short. The loin is poorly supported and quickly fatigued.

DEFECTS AND INJURIES

As seen from remarks concerning beauties, a leg too oblique, short relative to the cannon, narrow, or thin, is undesirable. Injuries are few except from kicks or other external sources. The inside of the leg, being covered only with skin, is easily bruised or cut. Rarely, the tendon running down the anterior face of the leg which connects the lower end of the femur and the upper end of the cannon is partly ruptured, and the leg, apparently broken, dangles about in a weird manner. This injury usually disappears with several weeks' rest.

The Stifle

The stifle corresponds to the human knee and is the

DETAILS OF CONFORMATION

joint between the thigh bone (femur) and the leg proper (tibia). The knee cap (patella) is the third bone forming the joint. The patella is the lower and smaller of the two prominences at the front of the stifle joint. The upper one is formed principally by muscle.

BEAUTIES

Set close to abdomen; turned slightly outward; well developed; prominent.

Size and prominence show strength. Slight deviation outward prevents the joint's striking the belly when the horse is galloping or jumping. The elbows and stifles should be at the same height in a well formed horse.

DEFECTS AND INJURIES

Where the stifles are not prominent, they are weak. If they turn too far in, or out, either "bow legs" or "cow hocks," respectively, result. "Cow hocks," since they turn inward, are too close together. They are easily detected when viewed from the rear.

The most probable accident to the stifle is the slipping out of place of the knee cap (patella) which occurs more frequently in very young horses. The hind member is almost immobilized when the stifle is "out." By forcing the horse to move backward, the knee cap often may be thrown back into position. However, if available, the services of a veterinarian should be sought. External injuries sometimes cause an enlargement of the synovial sac of the stifle, which is difficult to reduce, although lameness may not be present.

The Thigh
(See Diagrams, Pages 69 and 79)

The bony base of the thigh is the femur, connecting the hip joint (coxo-femoral) and the stifle joint. The femur is concealed by the very heavy and powerful thigh muscles. However, through careful study of the horse's skeleton and observing a horse in motion, its direction can be determined by the eye.

BEAUTIES

Upright, approaching the perpendicular; well let down (which means long); well covered with muscles; wide from the stifle joint to the point below the buttock which is farthest to the rear, when viewed from the side; thick, when viewed from the rear as a result of well developed muscles.

The upright thigh is characteristic of speed and is found in horses with low, long gaits, since it allows great extent of flexion and extension in the hind legs. In very fast horses, when observed standing still, the angle of the femur with the horizontal approximates

DETAILS OF CONFORMATION

eighty degrees, the thigh bone appearing almost vertical. For hunters and jumpers, the thigh may well be a trifle more oblique. Length gives long strides and permits voluminous muscular development.

DEFECTS AND INJURIES

Too short, oblique or vertical; lacking in muscular development.

When too vertical—a condition rarely encountered—the thigh has not sufficient play in extension when propelling the horse forward. If too oblique, the engaging of the hind legs under the mass is partly accomplished before the stride is begun. Thus an obliquity of about seventy degrees has been determined by experience and scientific investigation as the best angle for the combination of speed and jumping required of hunters and steeplechasers. If the thigh is too short, the stride is diminished, and of course the great muscles covering the thigh and used in all movements are shorter, with consequent loss of power. A short femur almost invariably gives a weak and crooked hind leg with a sharp angle at the hock. The thigh is measured from the hip joint (which one can learn to locate by a little intensive study of the skeleton and the live horse) to the bottom of the lower prominence on the front of the stifle. The lower prominence is the knee cap (patella). A very sloping croup (goose-rumped) usually accompanies a short thigh. In this case the croup appears short also.

The thigh rarely is hurt, save from exterior sources such as kicks.

The Croup
(See Diagrams, Pages 53, 60, 69 and 79)

The croup is the agent, the duty of which is to transmit all impulsion produced by the hind legs to the spinal column, thus propelling the horse forward. To some extent, it also is a shock absorbing and supporting agent. The ilium, ischium, and pubis constitute the croup's bony framework. These three parts are called the coxa, or pelvis, and form one consolidated bone. At the top point of the croup the pelvis is attached almost rigidly to the spine. Many of the muscles used in jumping and all other movements employ the bones of the pelvis either as levers or points of attachment.

The conformation of the croup and its functions deserve most serious study.

BEAUTIES

Long; approaching the horizontal; wide; muscular; thick.

The apparent length is measured from the point of the hip to the point of the buttock. In a well made horse, this measurement should be a little less than

DETAILS OF CONFORMATION

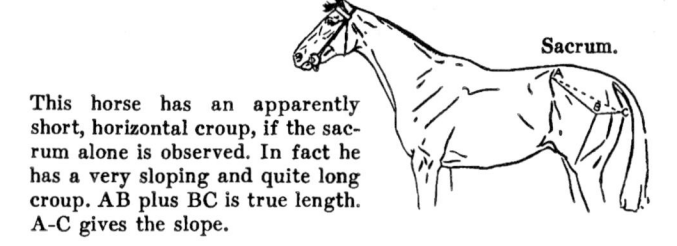

This horse has an apparently short, horizontal croup, if the sacrum alone is observed. In fact he has a very sloping and quite long croup. AB plus BC is true length. A-C gives the slope.

Sacrum.

the length of his head. However, it is to be noted that the croup's true length is the sum of the lengths of the ilium and the ischium, and, as there is an angle between these bones which varies in size in different individuals, the croup must be studiously observed in order to justly appreciate its true length and form. Because of these facts, a horse with a short-appearing and sloping croup often has in reality a long ischium and ilium. With this combination he probably will have great galloping and jumping ability, although he may not have great speed. One may also be deceived concerning the direction of the croup through regarding the upper line of the sacrum (top line of the

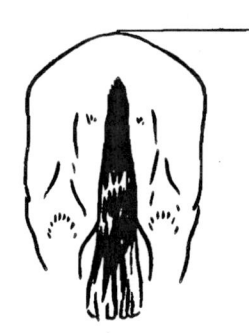

Point of croup.

WELL SHAPED CROUP

Broad hips. Point of croup decidedly higher than the hips. Thick muscular thighs. Beautiful hindquarters for hunter or jumper.

croup) instead of the croup itself. The sacrum may be practically horizontal, while the line of the croup is quite oblique. A croup that veritably is almost horizontal is highly desirable where speed over very long distances is sought. It invariably is associated with an approximately upright femur or thigh, which, as has been seen, permits great amplitude of movement, both in engaging the posterior members under the body and in extending them rearward during the propelling part of the stride.

A most important point to be determined is the comparative lengths of the ischium and the ilium. Their point of union should be well forward, and the point of the buttock (ischium) should project prominently to the rear. This occurs when the ischium is almost as long as the ilium. The nearer these bones approach equal length, the more favorable are mechanical conditions for excellent galloping and jumping. A short ischium compared to the ilium, is, on the other hand, both a typical and desirable beauty in a trotter.

In résumé, the croup should be long, appear fairly horizontal, and have a relatively long ischium. A pronouncedly sloping croup ("goose-rump") is advantageous where intense effort is desired, as in slow draft work. In a sloping croup, the muscles are inserted more perpendicularly to the bones, favoring powerful initial action but having comparatively small amplitude of movement. In hunters and race horses, this great power is not necessary, but amplitude of stride is of prime importance. For steeplechasers and jumpers, a little more inclination of the croup is desirable than is the case when searching for speed on the flat. Few good jumpers are seen with croups which appear almost horizontal.

The point of the croup, which is the upper angle at the backbone, should be decidedly higher than the points of the haunches. This gives depth (measured up and down) to the croup, especially when accompanied by a fairly horizontal sacrum (the part of the backbone running back from the point of the croup to the tail). A croup thus formed gives space for the spreading out, attachment and development of all the massive muscles of the hindquarters.

For hunters and jumpers, the width of the croup when viewed from the rear, should be as great as, or greater than, its length. From the rear, the observer also can note whether or not the point of the croup is markedly higher than the points of the hips and whether the points of the buttocks are, as they should be, well separated. A hunter's croup can be too wide only when it causes the horse to rock sideways or travel awkwardly. Flat-topped, square croups are typical of draft horses and are not adapted to speed, hunting or jumping. The top line of the galloper's croup, when seen from the rear, should be almost semicircular if he has fat enough to round out his hips.

For hunters, the croup should incline at about twenty-five degrees with the horizontal, and when searching for show jumpers a little more inclination is advantageous.

Clean cut, hard appearing and pronounced muscular development of the buttocks, thighs and croup is an absolute beauty in any type of horse.

DEFECTS AND INJURIES

Flat or square; "goose-rumped"; narrow; short; undeveloped muscularly.

The inherent disadvantages of these characteristics were brought out in the discussion of beauties. The croup is subject to few injuries except from external causes. A hip often is "knocked down" as a result of being struck against a door frame. Great care should be exercised in leading a horse through a passageway or into a stall. A knocked-down hip may not affect locomotion, in which case it is only a blemish; on the other hand, it may permanently cripple a horse. From the rear, by visually comparing the hips, one which is knocked down easily may be detected.

Many times the muscles of the croup atrophy from lack of use as a result of some ailment lower down, such as a painful spavin or a serious injury of the foot.

DETAILS OF CONFORMATION

Head and Neck
(See Diagram, Page 74)

As mentioned earlier, the head and neck form a balancer used by a horse in all his movements, particularly in galloping and jumping. Just as a man uses his arms for the purpose of maintaining equilibrium and increasing muscular effort, so the horse employs the gestures of his head and neck.

BEAUTIES

Forehead should be broad and flat. Beautiful eyes are mobile, prominent and set well apart. They should have a clear, bright, limpid, alert, intelligent and frank expression. The eyelids should be delicate and fine. Normally no white of the eye is exposed unless the horse is excited. If the whites of the eye do show, it can be ascertained by careful observation whether it is a natural condition or the result of an excitable disposition.

Well bred ears are rather short, clean cut, active and do not hang sideways (lop eared). Lop eared horses usually are very docile and often too phlegmatic. On the other hand, some are very obstinate. The ears should be widely separated at the base and set forward toward the forehead. They express much concerning the disposition and character of the horse. When the eyes are sullen and the ears often laid back,

Well shaped neck and good attachment of head to neck.

Coarse, heavy neck. Thick throat lash. Impossible to have a good mouth with such coarseness. If so inclined horse will be a low-headed puller.

Permanently distorted head carriage due to over-bitting and faulty training. Horse cannot use head and neck in jumping when held in this position.

"Ewe" or "upside down" neck,—horse will be a "star-gazer."

stubbornness and a recalcitrant disposition are probable innate characteristics.

The front line of the face should be almost straight from the ears down to the nose. A slight concavity of the front line, normal in Arab horses, is preferable to a coarse, bulging "Roman" nose. The thoroughbred is characterized by a head comparatively short in relation to its breadth and depth. This square type of head is quite distinct from the long heads found in gross and poorly bred types. The lips and nostrils should be fine, soft and free of coarse, heavy hair. Too small a head indicates general lack of strength, substance and boldness.

The lower jaws need minute examination. In a good head, the two branches are widely separated near the neck, allowing ample room for the throat and windpipe. The posterior edges of the jaw should set well away from the neck, so that when the horse brings back his nose in flexing to the action of the bit, the jawbones cannot crowd into the flesh of the neck, causing discomfort. A horse with the opposite type of lower jawbone should be flexed very little in training, as the pain soon will render him fretful and obstinate. The interdental spaces on the bars of the jaw inside the horse's mouth, upon which the bit rests, must be felt and looked at in order to discover injuries caused by brutal action of the bit. Often chips are broken off the bone, and after healing, the bars of the jaw are left quite insensitive. The horse, if at all impetuous, probably will be a "puller." Bars too thin and knife-like make a very sensitive mouth. In this case the mildest type of bit is called for. Bars too coarse, broad or flat are insensitive. These normally are found in common, underbred horses.

The teeth should be examined for age, condition and regularity. Space does not permit a full discussion of the teeth. Any veterinary book will give all details.

The beautiful neck is fairly long and well directed (about forty-five degrees in the trained horse when interested and standing at rest); muscular, particularly at its base near the shoulders, and gradually tapering to fineness as it joins the head. Its attachment to the head should be clean cut and refined in appearance. With a very long neck, a light, small head is better, whereas with a very short neck, it is preferable to have a fairly large head. Such conditions keep the balancer adjusted in weight and permit better general balance.

The hair of the mane is soft and fine in well bred horses.

DEFECTS AND INJURIES

Most injuries to the neck and head come from external sources.

Coarse, bulging, exceedingly long and narrow heads

are to be avoided. Small, close-set eyes ("pig eyes") are objectionable, doubly so when accompanied by lopping, coarse or big ears. A heavy, thick attachment of the neck to the head (producing a crowded, fleshy throat line) with the branches of the lower jawbone close together, gives reliable evidence that the horse never can have a light, sensitive mouth. In addition, if he is a rogue, he will be uncontrollable.

Defective necks are too long, low, short or horizontal (the low and horizontal types usually result from upright shoulders); ewe-necked (upper line concave, lower line convex); too slender (particularly at the shoulders, making a rubber-necked horse); swan-necked (too much rounding over of top line). The difficulty of having a balanced horse with a good mouth with any of the above faults is obvious.

The Body
(See Diagrams, Pages 53, 78 and 79)

The body may be subdivided, for discussion, into the withers, back and loin, chest, breast, flanks, and belly.

Withers

The withers are formed by the first six or seven spines of the dorsal vertebrae. Good withers are tremendously important, perhaps the most important feature in a pleasant, clever, balanced mount.

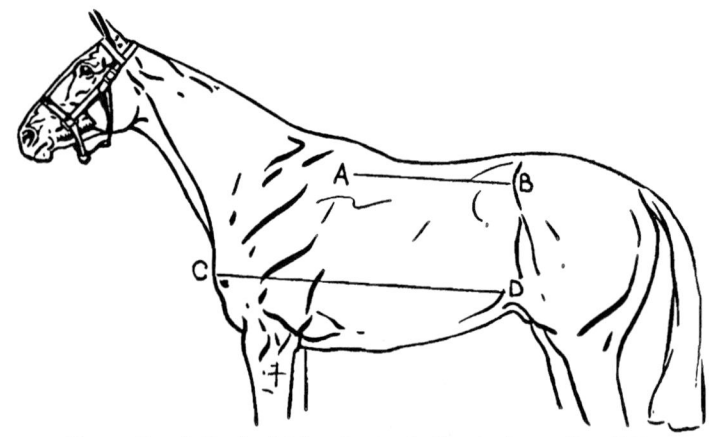

Upper line A-B should be short relative to lower line C-D. A-B runs from rear, upper edge of shoulder to haunch (hip). C-D runs from point of shoulder to last rib. A-B should also be approximately the length of the horse's head.

BEAUTIES

There really are few great hunters, jumpers, polo ponies or race horses, the withers of which are not high, clean cut, fine, long (running well back and gracefully disappearing into the line of the back), thin skinned and well muscled at the base and rear where they join the back. Many of the muscles activating the front legs, as well as those running back to the croup and forward up the neck, are attached to the withers. The length of the lever arm formed by the vertebral spines of the withers directly affects the potential strength and functioning of the muscles attached to them. Well shaped withers automatically hold the saddle in the correct place on the horse's back,

DETAILS OF CONFORMATION

Sway-backed. Pendulous belly (characteristic of windsuckers).

Long, flat croup and well developed thighs.

which in turn allows the cinch to rest in the proper place, just in rear, but not interfering with the movement of the elbows.

DEFECTS AND INJURIES

Low, rounded, or short withers are highly undesirable. When the upper ends of the shoulders are almost as high as the withers, so that the region is bunchy and broad from side to side, the horse is said to be "mutton-withered." Such withers are the cause of poor balance and clumsiness and have none of the advantages attributed to beautiful withers.

Herring-gutted.

Short, drooped croup and weak thighs.

Short withers do not furnish good lever arms and the saddle rests too far forward.

Back and Loin

The withers, back and loin, tracing the "top line" of the horse, are formed by the dorsal and lumbar vertebrae of the backbone. Through the back and loin from the point of the croup are transmitted forces initiated by the hind legs which, as has been previously pointed out, propel the horse forward. If the back and loin are too long, the agent of transmission is weakened. Also the rider's weight soon becomes very fatiguing to a very long back. Nevertheless the back requires a certain length in order that the ribs may extend far to the rear as a result of their being broad, strong and well spaced. Also, length of back gives depth and capacity to the chest.

The line running from the top of the withers should dip gradually to the rear and run gracefully into the back. Thence it should continue almost horizontally through the loin to the point of the croup. In many very fast horses, this line tips rather abruptly upward as it runs to the rear. In seeking a well balanced hunter, however, this upward inclination to the rear, if at all pronounced, is not advantageous. Better balance and better control usually exist when the withers are an inch or so higher than the point of the croup.

DETAILS OF CONFORMATION

This condition accompanies a back and loin that are approximately horizontal.

The well conformed hunter has a back which is rooflike in shape, whereas draft horses have flat, round backs and round bodies. The rooflike back is produced by ribs that slope gradually outward and backward from the spine, rather than by the type which spring out sharply and nearly horizontally and which are characteristic of the round bodied draft horse. Obviously there is less strain from the rider's weight on ribs that slope quickly downward from the backbone, just as there is less strain on the shoulder and coxo-femoral joints when the arm and thigh bones approach the vertical.

The loin, being the space between where the last rib leaves the spine and the point of the croup (or beginning of the sacrum) is unsupported from underneath and therefore is the weakest point of the back. Consequently it needs great muscular development, breadth and shortness.

DEFECTS

A back too short shows lack of depth to chest and often does not allow sufficient space between fore and hind feet for extended movements. One too long makes a clumsy, weak horse "built in two sections." A flat backed, round bodied horse generally lacks speed and cleverness and his front legs are too far apart. A sway back (concave downward) is weak and not suitable to transmit properly the forces generated by the hindquarters. A long, thin, concave or narrow loin reveals weakness. An excessive convexity to the loin (roach loin) usually causes some awkwardness in all gaits and does not permit suppleness in jumping.

Chest

Since capacious lungs are essential to eliminate the toxins generated by muscular work and to purify the blood with oxygen, the necessity of a big chest is evident.

BEAUTIES

Well descended or close to the ground so that the horse appears short legged; deep (from front to rear); broad (from side to side). The ribs should project rearward and have large spaces between them. Since, as described under "Back and Loin," the ribs of the well conformed thoroughbred type of horse slope sharply downward, they must be very long to give the same capacity to the chest that ribs of circular shape will give. (An ellipse has less area than a circle when the long axis of the ellipse equals the circle's diameter.) As they descend, their spread should increase so as to give proper breadth to the chest. If too nar-

DETAILS OF CONFORMATION

row, the horse is called "slab sided" and lacks capacity in both lungs and belly.

The measurement from the top of the withers to the under line of the chest ought to approximately equal the distance from the latter point to the ground. The vast majority of our present-day thoroughbreds are inclined to be "leggy," or "show too much daylight." Even average hunters also have less height to the chest than distance from chest to ground. The width of the chest varies most, in horses of the same type and size, in its middle and rear portions—there is little difference forward near the breast. As already stated, the well built horse spreads out from front to rear.

DEFECTS

Short, narrow, round, shallow chests are to be avoided. Flat ribs (having little convexity) are generally short also and indicate general weakness. Shortness and flatness of ribs are easily discernible in the back or floating ribs. The distance between the last rib and the point of the hip should permit placing from two to four fingers of a man's hand between them. The size of the horse, of course, should be considered. If the distance is greater, the loin will be long and the horse generally weak. At least, he will not be suitable for carrying a heavy rider nor for covering long distances with a light one.

Breast

The breast is roughly what is visible from the front between the arms, lower edge of the neck, and the space between the front legs.

BEAUTIES

Muscular; wide enough to be in proportion to the particular horse; the sternum should be fairly prominent when felt, even though muscles conceal it from view. As several muscles of the neck and fore legs are attached to the front end of the sternum, its prominence adds efficiency to the action of these muscles.

DEFECTS

Excessive narrowness is very undesirable since it usually is accompanied by fore legs too close together; "coming out of the same hole," as the condition is vulgarly expressed. For a galloping horse, an excessively broad chest causes rough, rocking movements unfavorable to smoothness or speed. This breadth does favor stability and in a draft horse is a beauty.

The Tail

The tail should be strongly attached, high up on the croup and well carried (forming a graceful curve and being somewhat raised when the horse moves at the faster gaits). When unexpectedly lifted by the hand, for a moment it should present marked resistance. Weak resistance indicates general lack of strength and stamina.

Flank

The flank, situated below the loin, between the haunch and rear rib, in front of the thigh, and above the abdomen, should be carefully examined, as its appearance reveals many correlated facts. The "hollow of the flank" is the pronounced sunken-in locality just in front of the hip. It is emphasized by poor condition, a slack loin, and a pendulous belly.

BEAUTIES

In the well formed horse, in good condition, the flank appears well rounded out, with the hollow showing very slightly. An excellent flank is short from front to rear just below the hip, or between the hip and last rib. This denotes a short, strong loin and deep, capacious chest, with well sprung ribs, sloping decidedly to the rear.

The movements of the flank should be observed to determine the regularity of breathing. During inspiration, the horse being at rest, the hollow sinks in a trifle and the lower part of the flank expands and settles downward. During expiration, the hollow fills out, the low flank rises, and the false ribs in front of the flank are seen quite easily. These movements should be regular and average about thirteen cycles per minute. Many things, such as condition, age, temperature, etc., affect the respiration. After long, hard galloping, the number may exceed eighty per minute. Normally, when at rest, after several equal breaths, the horse takes a longer one. Also, during exercise the breathing is less rapid than just after the horse is halted. If not broken winded, he should quickly reach his normal breathing rate after exercise, unless the weather is exceedingly hot. For the above reasons, the flanks should be observed at rest and after exercise. Also abnormal conditions in respiration sometimes do not present themselves until the horse has been exercised. The most usual defect is "heaves," an incurable condition, in which the breath is partly expelled, a pause occurs, and a second movement of expiration ensues in order to expel completely the air from the lungs.

DEFECTS

"Tucked-up"; deep hollows; long. All indicate weakness and antithetical conditions to those given under "beauties." Only injuries from external sources come to the flanks.

DETAILS OF CONFORMATION

Routine of Inspection

As suggested in Chapter I, a certain routine habitually followed in examining a horse before purchase will eliminate probable oversights. Often opportunities to inspect him in his stall, on the halter at the walk and trot, on the longe or under a rider at the gallop, will not be found. Frequently a colt may not be sufficiently broken to do any of these things. In the case of an older horse, however, the routine should be carefully carried out and a detailed inspection accomplished.

The order laid down in this chapter, for inspecting in detail, is probably as simple to remember and follow as any other routine. All parts should be regarded from all possible angles; from both sides, from the front, rear, and from oblique positions. Recapitulated, the routine is:

1. Begin at the forehand and examine in order: feet; pasterns; fetlocks; cannons; knees; forearms; elbows; arms; shoulders.
2. Follow the same order with the hind legs, going from the foot upward, through pasterns, fetlocks, cannons, hocks, legs, stifles, thighs, and croup.
3. Look at the head for general shape, refinement, proportions; then study in turn: the eyes, nostrils, mouth, teeth, bars, lower jaws, face, cheeks, attachment of head to neck, ears, poll, and neck.

4. Withers, back and loin in turn.
5. Chest, breast, flanks, belly, and groin.
6. Tail and genital organs.

This examination can only be of value if the contents of Chapter II are understood by the observer. Comparing one leg with the other should be a fixed habit.

If all examinations have proven the horse generally satisfactory, and yet, because of some small enlargement in a tendon, hock or elsewhere, the purchaser cannot be absolutely sure that the horse is sound, he by all means should have the services of a reliable veterinarian. To be absolutely certain that a suspicious, or even unsuspected, condition will not cause chronic lameness, particularly in horses that have been raced, worked hard, or are expensive it is well worth the time and money to have x-ray pictures taken of the front legs from knees down and of the feet. This will definitely decide the matter, and serve as a protection for both buyer and seller.

Examination of Western Horses for Soundness

Where a purchaser is buying horses from ranches in the west and southwest, either singly or in groups, circumstances are quite different from those found at an eastern sale stable or a stud farm. On the ranches many colts may not be halter-broken. The method of inspection *for soundness* used by Major J. H. Dornblaser, who, as a United States Army veterinary officer of marked ability, has examined thousands of horses while on duty with a Purchasing Board, is given below. It was jotted down by Major Dornblaser himself, who kindly permitted the author to publish it.

Routine Examination of Horses for Soundness

The horses will usually be found collected in a corral. They are "roped," one by one, and led out for inspection.

The attendant should be instructed to stand the horse on level ground with all four feet square, and place himself in front of the animal so as not to interfere with the inspector's vision. The inspector should keep his back to the sun and observe the animal from a distance of approximately twenty-five feet, standing, if possible, on the same level with the horse.

The inspection is divided into the following phases:
1. General view of animal at about twenty-five feet.
    Possible defects:
        Obviously not the type desired; large ringbones; curbs; a trifle lame or "favoring" a leg; large sidebones; unsightly scars.

Many will be eliminated in this phase without further examination. In fact, the majority of unsoundnesses are noted during this part of the examination.

2. If the horse passes Phase 1, a more detailed examination of him is made as follows:

(a) He is approached from the near side and his age ascertained by passing the forefinger between the lips from the near side, so that the teeth can be seen. Even "snorty" horses will permit this, although they probably would resent having their mouths opened in the usual manner. At the same time the bars are examined with the finger by running it gently along them, particularly where the bit rests. Putrid odors give evidence of decayed teeth.

(b) The inspector stands directly in front of the horse with the latter facing the sun. The eyes are observed and the fingers flipped near them to note the reaction. (Any peculiarities of the eyes call for a more detailed examination.) The bones of the face are noted for symmetry, trephine scars and evidence of bad teeth. The hand is passed over the intermaxillary space under the lower jaw to detect abscesses and bony enlargements. The inspector now carefully examines the front legs for direction, splints, ringbones, sidebones, and observes the feet. Standing back a little he sights between the fore legs at the hocks, especially noting the usual seat of bone spavin.

(c) Passing to the near side, the poll and withers are felt and the mane brushed to the opposite side if lying on the near side. Stooping down, the inspector

DETAILS OF CONFORMATION

looks at abdomen and scrotal region. Hernias are not infrequent and many young horses are found with a scirrhous cord. Also occasionally a stallion will be presented as a gelding. The fore leg may be carefully examined by sight and touch.

(d) Moving back about five or six feet from the shoulders he again observes the inside of the hocks.

(e) He then steps to a point about ten feet to the side of and exactly at right angles to the hock to observe the hind legs, giving particular attention to curbs.

(f) From directly behind the animal (not too close) he compares the size of the hips. The usual unsoundness is a fracture of the ilium, or "hip down."

(g) From the off side he again observes the abdomen and feels the lateral cartilages, etc., of the right fore if they look suspicious.

The owner is now asked to saddle his horse and walk him with a loose rein directly away from the inspector on a straight line for a distance of about fifty yards; this is repeated at the trot. He is then required to gallop about three hundred yards, making a wide turn so that the inspector can see the horse from the side while in motion; then to bring him back fast, stopping close to the inspector so the latter may test his wind by listening.

The above method is based on examination of from

twenty to three hundred head per day. Certain cases will be found where much more time will be spent on certain parts of the animal. Also thoroughbreds, or other horses that show evidence of racing, should have their legs examined more carefully.

The important thing for the inspector to do is to follow the same routine with every animal. Failure to do so will invariably result in overlooking some very important point.

Inspectors should work quietly and thoroughly but rather speedily. In actual practice it has been found better not to wear white shirts. In examining eyes, the reflection of paper or a white shirt in the eye is very confusing. Also the inspector should avoid conversation while making the examination.

This is admittedly a routine, practical examination. In purchasing a valuable hunter, the prospective buyer should insist upon an x-ray photo of the fore legs. Low sidebones and slight navicular diseases may not always be ascertained by manual or visual examination.

Notes:

1. Horses that have been used or trained for polo should be given especial attention as to condition of the bars of the mouth.

2. Artillery (heavy) types often have sidebones.

DETAILS OF CONFORMATION

3. Thoroughbreds frequently have been raced and may show firing marks and almost any unsoundness in the front legs.

4. Fracture of the hoof is very common in the southwest due to wire cuts on the coronets.

5. Curby hocks are very common throughout the southwest.

6. Always suspect an exceptionally large horse of being a roarer (wind broken).

7. A small flashlight always should be carried for use in examining eyes on cloudy days or toward dusk.

CHAPTER III

HEAD CARRIAGE AND OBJECTIVES OF TRAINING

Objectives

WHEN planning the education of his horse, the owner must have clear in his mind the qualities he desires to develop; in other words, all training must aim at well defined objectives. To begin with, he must analyze "training" in order to understand clearly: *first, what the objectives are; second, what methods are necessary to obtain those objectives.* A trained horse may be defined as one which, through being promptly responsive to his rider's aids under all circumstances met in his normal work, not only when alone but when in the company of other horses, is easily controlled. A program of training, therefore, must be designed to develop gradually this prompt response which can come only from willing submission to the rider's aids. *Willing submission, or obedience, implies great confidence on the part of the horse in his rider; confidence exhibited by calmness, boldness and relaxation.* In addition to this prime requisite of confident obedience, the other important qualities of a well trained mount are *suppleness, balance and agility. Moreover where speed and endurance are required, long, low strides at the walk, trot and gallop are essential. Such strides are economical of energy, time and wear.*

All the above qualities are interrelated and, although more or less hereditary, may be improved greatly by a sound and systematic method of training. Succeeding chapters will set forth a method which, if followed in letter and spirit, is reasonably sure to create or enhance the qualities just enumerated. The method involves step-by-step progress with the objectives, which govern the amount of time spent on each step, always in mind. In schooling a colt, haste not only makes waste, but often results in his ruin.

To reiterate for the sake of emphasis, *the basic training objectives indicative of willing obedience to all demands of the rider are: calmness, boldness, relaxation, suppleness, balance, agility and long, low strides at all gaits;* in all, seven essential characteristics which are the marks of a well trained mount. Since training aims at the perfection of these seven qualities, they must be well understood. Hereafter they will be referred to frequently and their full significance minutely brought out. At this point they will be discussed only sufficiently to show their importance, relationship, and the general method of developing them.

Calmness and Its Relation to the Horse's Head Carriage

Calmness, which from the point of view of pleasure, is the most essential characteristic in a hunter, jumper or hack, is influenced tremendously by the manner in which the horse is taught to carry his head. Since a distorted head carriage causes discomfort and pain, no horse so afflicted ever will render the full limit of his potential ability because under stress and strain, either mental or physical, he will not remain calm. A mount, excitable, nervous or fretful, is forever a source of annoyance; few, if any, of the qualities desired will ever be his.

In addition to being destructive to calmness; suppleness, relaxation, balance and agility as well as long, elastic gaits are either impossible or greatly hampered by a poor head carriage. *Consequently, during all training, it must never be forgotten that the development of a natural, graceful head carriage is of paramount importance.* Any work which threatens to produce an incorrect position must be forsaken temporarily, and such appropriate exercises reverted to as will restore correct head carriage.

Then, too, an excellent mouth is inseparably associated with the proper attitude of head and neck since a faulty or distorted position, because of accompanying discomfort and of peculiarities of the horse's muscular structure, causes general stiffness and awkwardness not only in the neck and poll but throughout the spine and hindquarters. With this general stiffness a responsive, soft mouth cannot exist. To be sure, particularly in polo, some individuals perform well despite an ugly set to head and neck. Certain it is, nevertheless, that they could, and would, perform far better had they been taught to carry their heads correctly. Some horses have such poor conformation that even when riderless they are forced to adopt an ugly position of head and neck for the sake of balance. These individuals should not be purchased, and if one has been acquired, the best recourse, rather than to waste time at training, is to dispose of him. In this connection nothing is more absurd than to buy a horse without having previously made a sincere study of conformation.

Head Carriage and Its Relation to "Accepting the Bit"

While calmness results from a proper head carriage, the latter in turn is entirely dependent on teaching the colt to "accept his bit." Accepting the bit sig-

HEAD CARRIAGE AND OBJECTIVES OF TRAINING

nifies its continuous pressure on the bars of the horse's mouth transmitted from the rider's hands; a light, continuous contact which is necessary to maintain communication, control and guidance. If the horse accepts this support in the correct manner he will not change unduly the position of his head and neck when the rider tactfully uses his reins for any purpose. From the first mounted lesson the colt gradually must be taught to accept his bit calmly and cheerfully. This matter will be dwelt upon at length elsewhere in the book. A spirited, well bred horse which has not learned to accept his bit or, as it also is expressed, "to go on the hand," is not susceptible of control in the hunting field or when going to a jump. He is not considered trained by horsemen who understand the principles of equitation.

The Three Phases in Developing Correct Head Carriage

In teaching acceptance of the bit and developing the proper attitude of head and neck, there are three distinct and successive phases which must be passed through, although in practice they blend gradually into one another. How fast training may progress is primarily regulated by the rider's skill and the rapidity with which the colt is capable of undergoing the work prescribed for each particular phase; work which ultimately will give him a correct carriage of head and neck. There are no short cuts in the training necessary to attain the respective objectives of the three phases. To insure success in the end all three must be passed through thoroughly and well.

First Phase in Developing Correct Head Carriage
TEACHING ACCEPTANCE OF THE BIT

During the first phase the young horse should be encouraged (or required if need be, by means to be explained later) to carry his head and neck naturally. This, in the vast majority of cases, is low and well extended, in which position he next by slow degrees is taught to maintain constant, light contact with his bit. *Of course there should be frequent rest periods when he is allowed to go on long, loose (floating) reins.* Throughout the entire duration of the first phase, when the colt is not being allowed to rest, the trainer keeps the reins lightly stretched and taut. *At the same time he must most rigorously avoid flexing (arching) the horse's neck by too heavy tension on the reins.* If his hands are not clever enough to do this, he is incompetent to train the colt. His constant endeavor should be to gain the confidence of his mount through the softness and elasticity of his hands. In other words, with the neck thrust out horizontally—and oftentimes lower—the colt at first is encouraged and later required to accept a steady, gentle support from the rider's hands, having sure knowledge at all times that no painful, unintentional or angry jerks will come to his mouth. This so-called "normal support" varies from a few ounces' to three or more pounds' tension, and is progressively stronger as the horse's speed becomes greater. Under good training the horse soon learns to seek willingly this support without arching his neck in the middle or near the shoulders. Neither does he poke his nose skyward, a vice called "star-gazing," which is assumed in an effort to escape the bit by a horse that never has been taught to accept properly its support. The amount of support given also is largely dependent upon the natural balance of the horse. A high-withered, well balanced horse wants only a light feel on his mouth; a low withered, high crouped horse generally needs strong support, particularly at speed.

Normal support is never a heavy pull but rather, as previously stated, a light, continuous means of instantaneous communication between rider and horse. The old advice about considering the reins as easily breakable threads is excellent. Keeping this thought in mind the rider quickly grasps the idea of *very light, unvarying and continuous support*.

A STIFF NECK IS DESIRED

Even when halting, although at first by a green colt

it may be executed somewhat stiffly, no effort should be made to compel a flexion of the jaw or the neck—not even at the poll. The tension should be decreased at any signs of such flexion and more tact and lightness used by the rider. *To eliminate the probability of ever developing a soft, over-flexed, "rubber neck," which spells ruination, it is vitally important that the young horse in the first phase acquire a certain stiffness to his neck.* Any raising or lowering of the head, as the tension necessary to slow the gait or halt is applied, must be in this early training period carefully avoided. Several alternating and soft resistances must be set up without "fixing the hands" (as can be done later with a trained horse) and without employing a steady pull against the bit. *Quick halts or rapid decreases in the gait must not be demanded in the first phase, as the head inevitably will be pulled out of place and the painful reactions will teach the colt resistance, fear and stubbornness.*

Conditions Affecting the Readjustment of the Colt's Balance under the Rider's Weight

Depending upon such factors as age, disposition, condition and conformation, a colt takes from two or three weeks to several months to readjust his balance under the burden of the rider's weight. Almost invari-

HEAD CARRIAGE AND OBJECTIVES OF TRAINING

ably, *if allowed to do so,* he will carry his head very low at first and the trainer must refrain from any attempt to raise it unless to prevent bucking or overflexing the neck. Raising the head excessively results in bulging outward the under line of the neck, stiffening the hind quarters, and crushing down the loin. These conditions prohibit both the proper movement and the normal muscular development of those regions. Again let it be stated, *too much importance cannot possibly be attached to allowing the low, extended, natural carriage of the head and neck until the colt has learned to frankly accept his bit.*

As he develops sufficient general strength and energy, and also stiffness to his neck, because of proper training, feeding, exercise and care, the colt also readjusts his equilibrium under the rider's weight, and of his own volition, little by little, raises his head and neck. The methods of training detailed later for the first phase are especially designed to expedite that state of physical and mental development which will permit him, without discomfort or fatigue, to accept his bit freely, bear the rider's weight, readjust his balance, and raise his head and neck to a more graceful and useful position. *The difficult and essential point is to refrain from hurrying this natural but slow process.* A little too much work, a little impatience on the part of the rider, easily may cause irremediable damage to the young colt's physical or mental constitution. This very gradual and unsolicited elevation of the head and neck continues throughout the three phases devoted to developing proper head carriage, and extends over a period of one year or more. The exact angle at which the neck is held depends largely on the conformation of the individual. In a well made and fully trained horse, when trotting, slowly cantering, or interestedly regarding some object, the angle of the neck with the horizontal approximates forty-five degrees.

Importance of the Oscillations of the Head and Neck

For mechanical reasons at the walk and free gallop the head and neck are carried somewhat lower than at the trot or slow canter. At every stride during the walk and gallop the head oscillates backward and forward. This oscillation assists the horse's movements just as the swinging of his arms assists a man in walking, running or jumping. At the walk there is, in addition, a slight oscillation of the head from side to side. At the trot, on the contrary, the head and neck are not only held higher than when walking or galloping, but are fixed in position without material movement of any sort. These facts must be known, continuously borne in mind and utilized in the development of

HEAD CARRIAGE AND OBJECTIVES OF TRAINING

good and educated hands,* without which the trainer never can perfect his horse's education. Thus, when the reins are stretched and a horse at the trot is accepting his bit, the hands should remain practically immovable because, as just stated, the horse's head and neck do not oscillate. If the rider is posting, shoulders and elbows compensate for the body's movements permitting the hands to remain quietly in one place relative to the horse's neck. On the contrary, the hands, through the suppleness and elasticity of finger, wrist, elbow and shoulder joints, should accompany the forward and backward movements of the head and neck at both the walk and the gallop in order to carefully maintain soft, continuous contact of unvarying intensity. It is understood of course that this contact with the mouth continues to be of light and unvarying intensity only so long as the horse goes calmly at the gait and rate desired by the rider. The tension will vary to correct disobedience, to change rate, gait, direction, or to halt.

* Note: "Good hands" are able to maintain soft, continuous contact with the horse's mouth at all gaits. Due to coördination and a good seat the rider, after he has acquired good hands, does not jerk or flop his reins accidentally at each unexpected movement of the horse. "Educated hands," besides being "good hands," are highly skilled in resisting, with exactly the appropriate amount of force, any resistance of the horse; also in immediately softening and decreasing their resistance when the horse ceases to resist. They provide instantaneous reward for good behavior; instantaneous punishment for bad.

Increase of Support on Bit Varies Directly with Speed

As has been briefly mentioned, another important principle to be carefully observed in the education of the horse and the rider's hands, is as follows: *the faster the speed becomes at the trot or gallop, the stronger must be the support on the mouth.* Of course, this rule does not pertain when the horse is allowed to work on a loose rein. After a little training, horses willingly take this increased support at fast speeds since it aids them in maintaining balance. When the gallop becomes very fast and the support quite strong, the rider must exercise extreme caution to continue the soft, elastic following of the horse's mouth. *The increased tension on the reins while at speed must remain continuously uniform, thus allowing the horse to oscillate naturally his head and neck.* Due to instinctive, nervous apprehension there is a tendency to "fix" the hands when at a fast gallop and when jumping. This fixing, or immobilizing, of the hands results in resistance which prevents the horse's use of his head and neck as a "balancer" at the times he most needs it. *Moreover, when galloping, if the head and neck are constrained by fixed hands, an unnatural and distorted position is assumed, which causes stiffness and pain. These destroy calmness, natural balance and agility.* The horse with spirit, so mishandled, becomes a puller or a runaway, dangerous at obstacles and across country.

The error generally committed in attempting to follow with the hands the rhythmic oscillation of the horse's head at the gallop comes from overdoing the hands' movements to the rear. This augments the tension on the reins during the rearward phase of the head's oscillation, pulling it far backward, over-flexing the poll, shortening the stride and bringing reactions of stiffness. During the forward movement of the horse's head, a mental effort should be directed toward exaggerating slightly the forward motion of the hands, thus "feeding out" all the rein possible without losing contact with the mouth. This permits great freedom of movement to the horse, prevents unconsciously pulling him, and instills calmness, since there is no useless hampering of the "balancer" and the stride.

Bracing the hands against the horse's neck is a deplorable habit which soon over-flexes and annoys him. Over a jump, unless the reins are floating in loops, this habit gives the horse, as he extends his head, a blow on the mouth. If the reins are floating, the rider, for the time being, surrenders control. No expert horseman habitually rests his hands on the neck while galloping or jumping.

The normal "feel" and soft, elastic following of the mouth, regardless of the speed, presupposes a light, secure and balanced forward seat.* Such a seat eliminates the normal tendency of beginners—and of many other riders who should know better—partially to maintain their balance by hanging onto the reins. Being "behind the horse," which means being out of balance rearward, makes following the mouth very difficult, and possible only to a rider with great experience. As the old saying goes, "No seat; no hands."

From the fact that the horse's equilibrium is more and more unstable as his speed becomes greater comes the reason for concurrently increasing the support given the mouth. The instability of the horse at speed necessitates a stronger effect in order to influence his direction or rate than when he is well balanced at slow gaits. Therefore sudden, jerky or brutal action on the bit is avoided in demanding changes of pace or direction, if a firm feel is already established when at speed. A firm "feel" never signifies a heavy, leaden *pull*, but an elastic following of the mouth, giving the horse stronger support as his increasing speed renders him more and more unstable toward the direction of movement.

* Although this work deals primarily with the training of the horse, a briefly summarized description of the essentials of a correct forward seat will be found at the end of this chapter.

HEAD CARRIAGE AND OBJECTIVES OF TRAINING

First Phase Coincides with "Breaking" Period

The first phase of teaching correct head carriage covers the same period as that required for "Breaking." Gentling, mounting, longeing, conditioning and putting the colt on the bit, are the trainer's preoccupations during this time.

After the colt is broken to riding, only the simplest movements are required. The three rein effects used are: *the direct rein, which exerts traction to the rear,* and is used only with both hands to slow the gait or halt; *the opening, or leading rein, with which one hand acts toward the front and side,* so as to *lead* the colt to the right or left in changing direction; *and the bearing, or neck rein, with which one rein is pressed against the neck high up and with no traction to the rear,* and is used, after the colt has learned its significance, in place of the opening rein when changing direction. *With both the opening and bearing reins, it is very essential that there be no traction, or pull rearward.* The rein effects are fully described later (see Diagrams, pages 168, 170, 224, 226, 228).

End of First Phase

The colt's conduct will tell when the training of the first phase, or breaking period, is complete. By taking hold of his bit strongly as a result of having gained condition and developed sufficient stiffness in his low, extended neck, he occasionally will attempt to "go through his bridle" by pulling. At this juncture, lest he dominate the situation, steps included in the second phase, to convince him of the trainer's supremacy, must be taken.

Second Phase in Developing Correct Head Carriage

Summarized, there are three steps to be accomplished in the second phase of placing the colt's head and neck. With the initiation of these steps, "Training," in contradistinction to "Breaking," begins. They are for the purpose of gaining more control of the colt through relaxing and suppling the neck and jaw. As he is taught the conventional language of the aids, he now will be required to respond more quickly to demands. The three steps involve: first, relaxing the muscles of the lower jaw so that, in response to any continued tension stronger than the normal support on one or both reins, the mouth opens (called flexion of the jaw); second, softening and bending the neck laterally, particularly in the upper third of its length, by use of the direct rein; third, flexing the neck at the poll very slightly as a result of increased tension on both direct reins.

The lateral flexion teaches the horse to bend his

neck slightly and yield promptly in turning about and changing direction. The softening and relaxation of the jaw and poll are for the purpose of developing springlike actions which, as the horse learns to concede readily to the demands of the rider's hands, lessen the irritation of the bit to his mouth. *The flexion of the poll is taught after the flexion of the lower jaw has become a habit, and must be cautiously and tactfully demanded.*

Dangers of Over-Flexion

To the great detriment of the horse, poll flexion easily may be overdone, causing an exaggerated rounding of the neck. This brings the horse's face to a position back of a vertical plane so that his nose is near the neck or breast. Poor or inexperienced horsemen frequently obtain this faulty over-flexion, *which is not produced at the poll, but in the middle and lower half of the neck.* Such distortion soon renders a horse, when at fast speed, incapable of extending his head and neck naturally into a position where they may be used advantageously as a balancer. As previously remarked, he arrives at this state either through poor early training or later rough treatment by uneducated hands and harsh bits. Since over-flexion automatically shortens the distance through which the mastoido-humeralis muscles (the extensors of the fore legs which run from near the head down the neck to the humerus) can play, the horse exaggeratedly elevates his feet at all gaits and is forced to take many more of his shortened strides at any pace than do his companions which are allowed to extend their necks. Habitual over-flexion first makes a high-spirited horse nervous, next fretful and finally so irritable that he loses all calmness and value. He jigs while other horses walk, gallops when they trot, and runs away when they canter. Such a horse simply has lost the ability to move as nature intended. With a sluggish, over-flexed animal, nervousness may not appear at the slower gaits; nevertheless he will have the short, high, faulty action described, and usually, if possessed of any spirit whatever, will be a "lugger" when in company and when jumping. These poor creatures are truly pathetic. To reclaim them takes much time and skill, and in most cases is impossible.

So while in the second phase training aims toward: 1. relaxation of the jaw in response to demands of one or both reins; 2. obtaining a lateral bending of the upper third of the neck; 3. very slight flexion of the poll in response to increased tension on both reins in halting or decreasing the speed; infinite care constantly must be exercised to avoid exaggerating any of these effects. Paradoxically enough, they all seek to soften to a slight extent that stiffness of neck so carefully built up in the first phase. But the neck, above all else, must not become "rubbery" so that it bends too far when changing direction or turning, nor must it be bent (flexed) to any appreciable extent in the two-thirds nearest the shoulders. Likewise, when relaxing the jaw, the mouth should open easily, but only part way; there should be no continuous, wide gaping. As the rider's hands reward the jaw's relaxation by instantly releasing the additional tension momentarily, the mouth should close and chew softly once or twice as the bit's pressure diminishes. In other words, the horse yields to the bit willingly, and voluntarily reëstablishes normal contact as its pressure decreases.

TONGUE-LOLLING

Of course the fingers must relax the moment the jaw softens; otherwise the horse may acquire the almost incurable habit of tongue-lolling or "balling" the tongue. In the first case he puts his tongue over the bit and sometimes lets it hang out one side of his mouth. In the second case he balls it up far back in his mouth. With either fault the bit rests directly on the sensitive bars of the lower jaw, thereby losing the cushioning effect of the tongue. This condition is painful and the horse will not accept his bit quietly. Moreover, it is impossible to have a soft-mouthed horse with either vice. There are various ways of tying the tongue down but none is very satisfactory.

Third and Last Phase in Teaching Correct Head Carriage

RAISING THE HEAD AND NECK

As work in the second phase nears completion, the trainer easily recognizes the indications. He feels the strength his horse has developed and senses the lightness of balance coming from his readjusted equilibrium. The colt contentedly accepts support from the hands, opens the mouth slightly in relaxing the lower jaw, and flexes slightly at the poll in response to increased direct tension. During the first and second phases the colt, of his own accord, has raised to some extent his head and neck. The amount of elevation depends on the natural inclination of the neck of the particular individual; the manner in which the neck is "set on."

With well balanced hunters, jumpers or hacks, no deliberate effort normally should be made to elevate the head and neck during the third phase. However, where a skillful rider desires to secure greater collection so as to produce more brilliance in his horse for certain purposes, as high-schooling or exhibition in horse shows, he may begin to ask more elevation of the neck and flexion at the poll. These demands are, as

HEAD CARRIAGE AND OBJECTIVES OF TRAINING

is usual in all training, set up gradually. Vigorous action by the rider's legs compels more impulsion from the horse. This impulsion, immediately after it drives the horse forward, is partly contradicted by resistance set up by the hands. Due to this restraint by the bit, the well trained jaw and poll flex, the neck is raised and the hind legs are engaged farther forward under the body. Higher action and more collection result. This technical and difficult subject will be taken up more fully in the later chapters.

DANGERS OF COLLECTION

As has been indicated, high collection should be undertaken only by finished horsemen. The periods of collection should be very brief and it should be thoroughly realized that all preceding work, done for the purpose of producing calmness through developing a natural head carriage, may be quickly nullified by an inexperienced rider in his efforts to obtain a higher head carriage, more flexion and collection. As a matter of fact many experienced riders, in their efforts to proceed too far in collection and high-schooling, succeed in inculcating nothing more than irritability, nervousness and inability to jump or gallop fast across country.

In requiring extreme collection every horse should be allowed to rest by extending the head and neck after each brief period of collected work. Not only should he be *allowed* to do this, but during all his career he *must be tactfully required,* as soon as the hands permit, to extend fully his neck and head in a downward direction and take all the rein possible. If in motion, he should not increase his speed when given this liberty. This is the crux of success in keeping a high-school horse calm and usable as a hunter, jumper or hack, and *it is impossible to over-emphasize its vital importance.*

In the third phase, which corresponds to the latter part of the training period, the horse will be given work over obstacles and many gymnastic exercises to improve his suppleness, relaxation, balance and agility. More promptness in stopping, turning and general responsiveness to the slightest indications will be required.

"PLACING THE HEAD"

In this third and last phase, the head and neck generally will continue to rise to a greater elevation, still without conscious effort on the trainer's part. When, as a result of training, there normally rests at all times a suspicion of flexion at the poll and the face makes an angle of approximately fifty-five degrees with the horizontal when the horse, lightly on the bit, is moving at slow gaits, the head is termed "well placed."

HEAD CARRIAGE AND OBJECTIVES OF TRAINING

Relationship of the Three Phases

In setting forth the above phases in correct head carriage, it has been shown that calmness inevitably is associated with a neck which is fairly stiff and muscular near the shoulders and becomes more flexible and fine in its upper third, and which, after the horse has learned to accept the bit, is carried in a natural, extended position. Intentionally these facts have been repeated and often will be referred to again. For without calmness a horse is rarely of value for any purpose. Even in a race horse, excessive nervousness fritters away his chance of winning. The resultant excitability due to over-flexion or other distortion of the neck is well demonstrated to any careful observer of a large group of horses. In the Army's mounted branches—Cavalry and Artillery—almost without exception the jigging, nervous, difficult horses in any troop or battery are those which have been over-flexed and carry their faces back past the vertical, or which, through never having been taught to accept the bit, remain "star-gazers" with their necks upside down. The same facts are evident at any hunt meet.

Boldness and Frank Forward Movement

Boldness is closely related to calmness. It is also a matter of heredity. However, once he has accepted his bit correctly and calmly, much can be done toward producing boldness in an individual innately inclined toward timidity. *The development of boldness implicates another fundamental principle of equitation; a principle advocated by the great masters throughout the ages, namely: willing, frank, forward movement must be taught to every horse.* Differently stated, the trainer from earliest days must require his horse to move directly forward promptly and freely at the "call of the legs" (use of the legs or spurs against the horse's sides). After he has received a reasonable amount of training, the horse should respond instantly to the slightest pressure from the calves. The moment any horse—either young or old, green or trained—hesitates, sulks, hangs back or balks, he must be attacked instantly by the heels or spurs. This may be done, first by squeezing vigorously, next by tapping sharply with the calves or heels, and last, if the case demands, by determinedly employing the spurs. No compromise should be effected; the intensity of the attack grows until the horse moves freely forward. With a green horse, force just sufficient to get results is used; with a horse that knows well the meaning of the legs, a sudden, severe attack with the spurs will serve to impress the lesson, and have a lasting effect. *The heels, or spurs, always should be used just in rear of the girth, not far back against the flanks as is often done.* Using the legs far to the rear tickles and irri-

HEAD CARRIAGE AND OBJECTIVES OF TRAINING

tates, making horses, particularly mares, restive and fretful.

FORWARD MOVEMENT PREVENTS DEFENSES

Providing he has been taught to move forward promptly at the call of the legs, no horse is able to present a defense which cannot be easily overcome. The only dangerous and serious vices of the mounted horse are balking, running backward, or rearing. To do any of these successfully, he first must refuse to move forward at a free gait. To be sure, it takes a good rider to stay with an accomplished bucking horse even though he goes straight to the front. Nevertheless a bucker is soon, and with comparative ease, "ridden out" by a good cowboy if he is driven straight to the front. Forward movement prevents whirling, "sun fishing," "fading away," and other acrobatics which must be executed more or less in place.

A colt that throughout his training has been forced to move frankly to the front, and has acquired greater respect for his rider's legs and spurs than for anything else in the world, becomes, through habit, more and more bold and ultimately moves across, over, or into whatever faces him. Moving forward at the call of the legs has become a reflex. As a Frenchman said, "The horse must believe God is on his back and the Devil at his belly."

In recapitulation, it may be stated that calmness largely results from good hands which have encouraged and taught correct head carriage, while boldness is produced by tactful, and, when necessary, strong, courageous use of the rider's legs.

Relaxation and Suppleness

When the colt goes calmly and boldly on his bit, the other desirable attributes, *relaxation, suppleness, balance and agility,* are easily obtained. The degree ultimately attained by the particular individual will depend on his conformation, inheritance and the skill of his trainer.

Relaxation and suppleness will be developed through the exercises, soon to be discussed, which are advocated for the second and third phases in teaching correct head carriage, which are included in the training period proper. The work done while mounted in softening the jaw, and in lateral and direct flexion of the poll, simultaneously produces *relaxation and suppleness of the spine, shoulders, loin, croup and all joints*. Little by little the horse gives himself over calmly and confidently to his rider. The exercises are in purpose both gymnastic and disciplinary—developing muscle, suppleness and relaxation, while teaching precise and prompt response to the aids.

Relaxation in the horse, as in the athlete, is economical of energy. *Relaxation implies that only the muscles required for the particular movement are called upon, and expend only that amount of energy necessary for the accomplishment of the movement.* Meanwhile, because of their relaxation, all other muscles are at rest, thus reducing the expenditure of energy to the minimum.

Suppleness, closely allied to relaxation (since the former cannot exist without the latter), develops rapidly under work designed to exercise the spinal column and all articulations. This work comprises shortening and extension of the gaits; movements at all gaits in circles, large and small; serpentines; "shoulder in"; the "false gallop"; frequent changes of gait and rate; half-turns, etc., all of which will be described at the appropriate time. Suppleness must be obtained in the spine laterally and longitudinally, so that the back and loin can bend both vertically and horizontally.

Balance and Agility

Both balance and agility improve greatly with all the correctly executed mounted exercises just mentioned. Here also the degree obtainable is limited by temperament, conformation and aptitude. Jumping and cross-country work over varied terrain, both on a loose rein and with the normal contact, improve balance and agility. Agility in particular is somewhat bounded by nature's contribution of quickness. Some horses are as agile as cats; others are not, and no amount of training will permit them to equal their more fortunate brothers in "handling their feet."

Long, Low Strides

This most valuable trait conducive to economy of energy, comfort to horse and rider, efficiency and speed, needs at present no further discussion. The riding technique and gymnastics for the horse, necessary to develop such a "way of going," will be touched upon later. Suffice it to say, such strides are only possible when a natural head carriage and liberty of the balancer are allowed.

Conclusion

In concluding these generalities on training, it is to be noted that all the objectives are interdependent and hinge one upon the other. They are the guiding lights always to be kept in sight; if one is missed it will be rare indeed that the next is found. *Only a comfortable head carriage will induce calmness. There will not be a comfortable head carriage, relaxation or suppleness unless the bit is correctly accepted.* Since resistance to the demands of the rider's hands causes stiffening of the neck muscles, the exercises conceived to teach relaxation and suppleness cannot be properly

HEAD CARRIAGE AND OBJECTIVES OF TRAINING

executed until the horse softly accepts and obeys his bit. If not properly executed, the exercises do not accomplish their purposes of relaxing and suppling. Incidentally, any horse which resists the bit by stiffening and straightening the poll, automatically stiffens his back and loin muscles. He is awkward, difficult to control and uncomfortable to ride.

Even a naturally well balanced, agile and bold horse is of little or no value until on the hand, calm, relaxed and supple. Boldness, desirable in a hack, is absolutely essential in a hunter, jumper or polo pony. A timid one is forever shying, running out or refusing obstacles, and often attempting to rear or whirl about if suddenly frightened. Forward movement, made instinctive by reflexive obedience to the spurs, will make nearly all horses act boldly. Ultimately they dare not stop, experience having taught them that spurs are more dangerous than any object they may meet.

Thus the seven main objectives of training form the subjects of an outline into which appropriate training exercises are fitted in numbers and types according to each colt's educational needs.

The Forward Seat

Without a good seat there can be no steadiness in the saddle and the body's unsteadiness reacts upon the hands. Consequently the hands can be neither "good" nor "educated."

TRAINING HUNTERS, JUMPERS AND HACKS

The following is a brief summary of all the essential points of a strong Forward Seat. With it, the constant play of hip and knee joints, and an elastic suppleness of the loin, are necessary to maintain balance and security.

1. SEAT: Forward part of pelvic bones rest on saddle; crotch *well back* so as to be deep in throat of saddle; fleshy part of buttocks forced rearward toward the cantle at all times, and never allowed to slip forward under rider. Rider does not sit on buttocks but on inside of thighs and forward points of pelvic bones.

2. THIGHS: Flat; heavy muscles to rear of femurs; continuous contact down to, and including, inner sides of knees.

3. KNEES: Inside of knee bones are snugly against saddle skirts; pushed down as low as possible with stirrup leathers remaining vertical; not allowed to turn outward so as to leave air space between them and saddle; normally do not grip tightly but sufficiently to keep whole thigh softly against saddle skirts. Knee joints almost completely relaxed, except when purposely standing in stirrups; knees increase grip when necessary to keep seat from being displaced forward or sideways as in stopping suddenly before an obstacle, etc.; must not be entirely limp or lower legs will slip too far to rear, heels come up, seat slide forward, and rider hump his back.

4. LOWER LEGS: Inner and upper portions of calves always remain in soft contact with sides of horse; no great effort required to keep them there. Calves squeeze to drive horse forward, and to maintain seat in case of emergency. In latter case, knees also increase grip. When stirrup leathers are vertical, knee joints relaxed, and heels thrust down to absolute limit permitted by relaxed ankle joints, position of lower

legs is correct. Heels should be kept down when squeezing or gripping with calves. Spurs are used just in rear of girth—not far back against the flank.

5. ANKLES: Habitually relaxed, allowing weight transmitted down thighs, through partially relaxed knees, to sink into heels of boots. If trunk is correctly inclined forward at the hips, portion of rider's weight necessarily runs down through thighs and automatically flexes ankles and drives heels down.

6. FEET: Turned out so that upper, inner sides of calves rest against horse. Toes make angle of twenty to forty-five degrees with longitudinal axis of horse. Feet, *home* in stirrups, where they function as lifeless hooks, permitting all weight to sink into heels. For schooling, balls of feet may rest on stirrup treads.

7. HEELS: Thrust far down. Give brace to feet against stirrups if horse checks suddenly, so seat cannot slip forward. Receive all weight coming into stirrups if feet and ankles are correctly relaxed and limp.

8. TRUNK AND LOIN: *Carried in same posture as when standing erect in the "position of a soldier," except that whole trunk is inclined to front from hip joints.*

When fully seated in saddle at halt, walk, slow trot or canter, center of gravity of trunk falls just in front of pelvic bones. *At posting trot or gallop*, center of gravity is approximately over knees, and trunk's forward inclination is greater. Loin is habitually "hollowed out" in its normal, natural position; never remains convex to rear. Buttocks should be well to rear toward cantle of saddle, but due to body's forward inclination *no weight is on them.* Buttocks provide rear counterbalance for the forward-inclined trunk.

Knees, over which trunk and buttocks are balanced, are center of motion when posting, galloping or jumping.

9. CHEST, HEAD AND CHIN: Lifted. Whole body carried lightly. *There should be a feeling of stretching the spine upward and making the body tall.*

10. LENGTH OF STIRRUPS: After some slow trotting *without stirrups* (when seated as prescribed above for slow paces) and with legs hanging down in natural position by horse's sides, treads of properly adjusted stirrups should hang even with center of large bones on inner sides of ankle joints. A little variation in length is inevitable due to difference in conformation of both people and horses. For fast cross-country work or jumping, stirrups are shortened from one to four holes. The shorter the stirrups are adjusted, the greater must be the inclination of the upper body.

11. IMPORTANT POINTS:

a. Any faulty attitude of one part of the rider will cause faults in other parts, thus throwing the whole seat out of adjustment.

b. When the horse checks suddenly, goes down a steep incline, or lands after a jump, the knee joints *should stiffen* a trifle, and in conjunction with the lowered heels, permit the feet to brace the whole body against the stirrups. The knees also should grip the saddle more tightly and the back muscles should stiffen in order to keep the spine swayed (hollowed out). These actions prevent the body's toppling forward, and hold the seat secure.

The above actions are easily accomplished after practice and also serve to prevent the buttocks' slipping forward and the lower legs going to the rear which disrupt the whole seat and involve surrender of balance and control of the horse. *If*

HEAD CARRIAGE AND OBJECTIVES OF TRAINING

the heels are thrust down and the back is kept swayed, the forward inclination of the body, even when checking the horse very quickly, can, and should be maintained.

The rider's knees, when in the position described, are approximately in the transverse vertical plane containing the horse's center of gravity. Hence with the rider correctly seated, their centers of gravity fall approximately in the same vertical line. During movement there is of course oscillation of the centers of gravity of both, but they remain approximately in the same vertical line if the rider is constantly "with his horse."

c. Stiffness should be avoided. As much relaxation should exist throughout the whole anatomy as is consistent with maintaining muscular control of the body, balance, and the seat steadily in place.

12. POSITION AT WALK AND TROT: In order to lessen fatigue to the horse *it is absolutely vital to maintain slight forward inclination of the body at the WALK AND TROT*. This keeps the rider's weight distributed down his thighs; whereas leaning backward or sitting bolt upright concentrates it far back on the cantle which is very tiring, and on long rides or hunts, is absolute cruelty to the horse.

13. LIBERTY OF HEAD AND NECK: In addition to using the correct seat every effort should be made to allow horses *maximum liberty of head and neck*. At the walk in particular the reins should be very long permitting the horse to stretch his head and neck into a low, extended position favorable to long strides and comfort. The hands remain still at the trot; at the gallop they move back and forth with the horse's movements, "following the mouth." Elbows must be partly flexed so as to be soft and elastic.

14. How To Test Correctness of Rider's Position: If the rider is in balance as a result of his upper body's being properly inclined forward he is able at the walk, trot or gallop, *without first leaning farther forward* and without pulling on the reins, to stand in his stirrups with all weight in his depressed heels.

In executing this exercise the seat is raised just clear of the saddle by stiffening the knees but keeping them partly flexed. The upper body remains inclined forward at hips. At the trot one hand should touch the horse's neck *lightly* to assist in remaining in balance. At the walk or gallop the rider, if his seat is correct, should be able to stand in his stirrups without the aid of his hand. A rider who can execute the above exercise at all gaits and without first changing inclination, is in balance and never "behind his horse." The majority of those *not* in this position partly maintain their balance by hanging onto the reins, thus unnecessarily punishing their horses' mouths as well as their backs.

CHAPTER IV

BREAKING

Distinction between Breaking and Training

"BREAKING" may be variously defined. It merges into training proper with no distinct line of demarcation. Here it will be considered as the time necessary to gentle the colt, teach him to work on the longe, bear the saddle and rider, gain strength and generally good condition, and accept his bit calmly with an extended head and neck at the walk, trot and gallop. Having accomplished these purposes in the breaking period, the succeeding period is called "training."

The breaking period includes the first phase of developing correct head carriage. The colt learns to go on the rider's hand but no effort is made to flex jaw and poll. The highly important purposes are to preserve, or develop, a good disposition and to put the colt in such physical condition as will permit without injury the more strenuous work embraced in training proper.

With an utterly unbroken four-year-old, the *breaking* period normally extends from three months to one year. If the colt has been gentled, has had some training and is naturally robust and strong, this time may be shortened to from two to four months. To avoid rushing his education is economical inasmuch as the chance of permanent physical injury is greatly lessened, and the colt remains calm and good-natured if not taxed beyond his ability.

Psychological Principles on Which Training Is Based

The prominent characteristics of the equine mind are: 1. an almost infallible memory; 2. little intelligence (although this varies greatly in individuals); 3. small reasoning power; 4. the trait of mimicking other horses; 5. resentment of unjust punishment; 6. appreciation of rewards when merited; 7. attentiveness. Horses quickly recognize their true masters and seldom try the tricks and defenses that they use when weak riders or novices mount them.

The distinguished French student and psychologist, Gustave le Bon, after having studied the mental characteristics of the horse and various methods of training, was the first to announce that the establishment of a conventional language through the aids, and forcing the horse after learning it to obey that language absolutely, must be based on an application of the fundamental psychological principles concerned in the "association of ideas." The two pertinent ones are: 1. the principle of association by contiguity—"When impressions are produced simultaneously, or follow immediately one after the other, it is only necessary to present one of the impressions in order that the others be brought to mind"; 2. the principle of association by resemblance—"Present impressions revive past impressions which resemble them." Of these two, the first is much more frequently employed in breaking and training.

To help the horse understand each new lesson by combining aids and lessons with which he is already familiar also is a principle of training. As a result of his memory and attentiveness, the intelligent application of the above principle and those of the association of ideas produces astounding results. As an example of attentiveness—when being taught a new and complicated movement in high-schooling, horses often endeavor to execute each air they have learned previously in order to accomplish what the trainer is demanding. If the latter will instantly cease applying his aids and pat the horse on the neck the moment he finally executes, although not perfectly, the first step of the movement required, it will be but a short time until the movement is entirely learned and never will be forgotten. Above all, a horse never must be punished when unable to comprehend what is desired, because of the rider's lack of skill and tact in the use of his aids.

As an elementary example of the principles just quoted, consider a young horse being ridden for the first time. When the trainer desires to halt he applies additional tension to the reins, which causes discomfort to the colt's mouth. The youngster, having no conception of its significance, will introduce various antics to escape the bit's annoyance. If the trainer continuously applies tension stronger than the "normal feel," the colt, after presenting a few defenses such as increasing his speed, pulling, or throwing his head, will halt. *Instantly the tension on the reins should be released.* Thus the colt discovers that coincidentally with his halting the bit's annoyance ceases. After a few repetitions he thenceforward associates the two ideas of halting and escaping the discomfort or pain to his mouth. If the rider applies the increased tension gradually and tactfully, continues it without cessation until the colt halts, and releases it at the exact instant the halt occurs, the lesson is quickly learned, and the amount of tension necessary to secure a prompt halt soon will be very slight. This illustration demonstrates the necessity for instantaneous administration of rewards and punishment. Through such practical application of the principles of the "association of ideas," the horse soon learns to understand the language expressed by the hands, legs, voice, whip, spurs and weight. The rider must always apply these "aids" to demand a particular reaction in exactly the same manner.

Since he has little reasoning ability and only connects simultaneous, or immediately associated, impressions, great patience must be exercised until the horse understands thoroughly what is desired. Thereafter by applying the aids forcefully in cases of indifference, laziness or stubbornness, the impression on his mind is much more indelible. Such a strong impression, correctly administered, is far more valuable than many weak repetitions. But failure to bestow *à propos* reward and punishment, or to employ the aids in precisely the same way, confuses the horse, and training never becomes complete, not because of lack of good will on his part, but because of lack of skill on the rider's. Sad to witness is the brutality to horses sometimes exhibited in the hunting field, show ring, and at polo, which is invariably brought about as a result of poor training and riding. The horses are not wilfully disobedient through temper or stubbornness, but because the incompetent rider's aids transmit an incomprehensible language. Unfortunately some people know so little about equitation that quite unintentionally they severely torture their horses. Were they aware of the unnecessary pain their ignorance causes their mounts, doubtlessly they would be sincerely chagrined. A normal horse, rewarded or punished at the appropriate instant, rapidly gains confidence in his master and gives himself over in the most magnanimous fashion.

Summarized for emphasis, the successful trainer must remember that: *the horse's memory is infallible; he learns by "the association of ideas"; the principal means of communicating with him are through the voice, reins and legs; in order to train him well and quickly the aids must reward or punish at the precise instant, with just the amount of force necessary.*

Punishment or reward bestowed as much as one or two seconds after the provocation is too late. The pupil fails to associate his offense with the punishment, or his obedience with the reward, but instead with whatever he may be doing at this later moment. The principles, while simple in themselves, are very often difficult to apply in higher forms of equitation. However, practice and thought ultimately will make the correct use of the aids reflex actions, even when the horse is working at high speed, as in polo, hunting or jumping.

BREAKING

Care of the Unbroken Colt

In discussing care, let it be assumed that the newly-purchased colt is four years old, partly gentled, halter-broken only, and just installed in his new stable. The first preoccupation is to see that no drastic change is made in his customary diet. His oat ration should not be greatly increased, nor should he be given more than a very small amount of any grain to which he has not been accustomed. If he has been grass raised, after starting with two or three oat feeds a day, of not over one pound each, the amount should be gradually increased at intervals of four or five days. The important subject of feeding is not within the province of this book but an owner not familiar with it should seek, in the interest of safety and economy, the advice of an expert before prescribing his new colt's ration. Moreover, in view of the veterinarians' discoveries concerning osteomyelitis (osteomalacia), it is vitally necessary that horses be fed food containing sufficient calcium. According to the theories, substantiated by the results of practical treatment, a great proportion of all lameness heretofore attributed to a variety of causes is now believed to be due to a diet with an insufficient calcium content. Alfalfa is nutritious and high in calcium, but its feeding must be initiated little by little with horses unaccustomed to it, as too much often causes colic.

Every effort should be made to gain the colt's confidence. Hand feeding and caresses soon accomplish marvels. To eliminate noise and excitement, to stable him near, but out of reach of an old, quiet horse, and to provide a roomy, well bedded stall with hay and water available at all times, add to his contentment. Projections and nails which might cause an injury should be sought for and removed. A box stall is best, particularly if the colt is not accustomed to being tied by a halter, although there are arguments in favor of single tie-stalls. In the latter the colt does not see too much and so does not acquire the stable vices of his neighbors. If nervous he is forced to rest by being tied, and a better bed can be kept under him. Also fewer stall injuries seem to occur in tie-stalls.

Leading

If the colt is gentle, he may be led the day following his arrival about the vicinity of his new surroundings alongside a calm, old horse. These promenades may be gradually increased, from half an hour on the first two or three days, to one hour or longer. During them he is allowed, at first from a distance, to see all the unfamiliar sights. Later he will approach more closely without fear, particularly if the old horse is unafraid. In order to prevent the development of a crooked neck, he should be led equal lengths of time on both sides of the old horse.

Since the colt's muscles are not strong nor his bones firmly set, it is an easy matter to injure him permanently through exercising him for long periods, or allowing him to rush madly about a pasture. Increasing exercise little by little and teaching each new lesson slowly and thoroughly save time in the end, and keep the horse sound. The old maxim about "going slowly" in training, handed down by great horsemen since time immemorial, is constantly violated. In the pleasure and enthusiasm felt in the colt's progress, every owner is prone to overwork him, and the beautiful horses ruined or broken down before they reach seven years of age are the irrefutable proof of the maxim's truth. As has been mentioned, a horse under normal feeding and training is not fully matured until seven or eight years of age.

Accustoming the Colt to the Snaffle

When he becomes quite gentle, it is wise to put a snaffle bit in the colt's mouth once or twice a day while he is feeding. It should be carefully adjusted, neither too low, nor so high as to pull and wrinkle the corners of his mouth. This acquaints him with the bit and eating requires him to keep his tongue underneath it. As a result, when his mounted instruction begins, he will be much less apt to carry his tongue over it.

Care of the Feet

As soon as possible after arrival, the feet should be attended by a blacksmith. If unshod, they should be trimmed and leveled with a rasp, and if the horn is tough and the ground not too hard, it is well to allow the colt to remain barefooted. If he becomes lame, or so "tender" that he shortens his strides, shoes must be put on. Keeping young colts' feet properly leveled and rounded from early infancy on, whether in pasture or under training, is most important. Neglected feet often make splay-footed, pigeon-toed and crooked-legged horses. In addition, thrush easily develops in untrimmed feet. All these conditions lead to chronic diseases and poor gaits. Daily, the careful owner inspects the legs and feet of all his horses, paying particular attention to the young ones. The slightest puffiness about the fetlocks and tendons, or any fever (detected by touching the suspected spot with the palm of the hand and comparing its temperature with that of the same portion of the other limb) is sufficient cause for reducing the colt's work. If the fever or puffiness is at all pronounced, complete rest is essential until the legs and feet are again normal. This matter, constantly overlooked, produces many unnecessary blemishes. Picking up the colt's feet should begin as soon as his degree of gentleness permits.

BREAKING

Grooming

As is often said, "a thorough grooming is as good as a feed." At first, a very soft brush or a rag should be used. Caresses and feeding by an assistant are helpful with nervous colts; also when raising the feet to be cleaned. Needless to say, great patience and gentleness must be exercised in all early care of the colt. Later, grooming with a rather stiff bristle brush should be as vigorous as the horse will allow. It not only cleans and brings a bloom to the coat but also massages the skin and surface muscles.

Longeing
(See Illustration, Page 124)

If after daily leading for a week or ten days the colt is well and apparently growing stronger, lessons with the longe and cavesson may be started. Every horse should be taught this work, which is particularly essential for hunters and jumpers.

THE LONGE

The longe is a cord about thirty-five feet in length preferably of strong, tape-shaped material, which is attached to the cavesson. Tape is less liable to burn the horse's legs or the trainer's hands than is rope, in case the former bolts and breaks loose.

THE CAVESSON

Figure labels: Head stall. Brow band. Metal band. D-Ring to which longe is attached. Padded noseband. Throatlash. Jowl strap. Buckle and strap to fasten noseband under lower jaw.

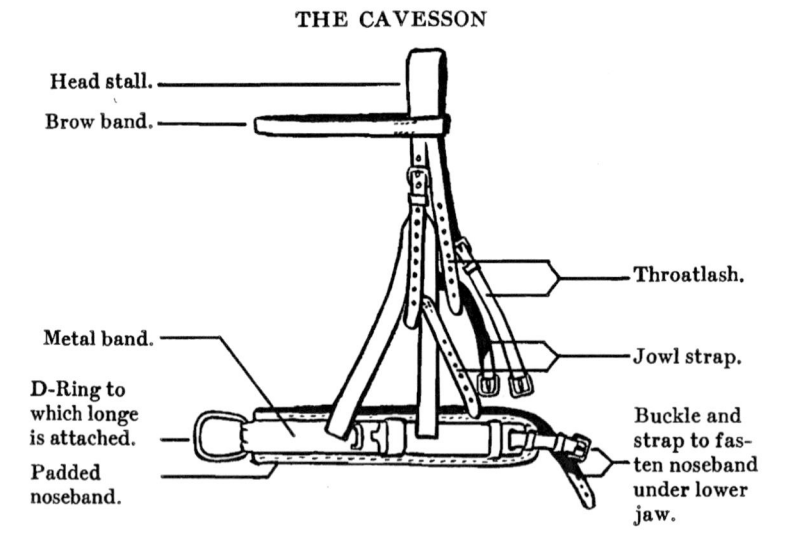

THE CAVESSON

The cavesson has the appearance of an elaborate halter. On top of the upper third or more of its noseband is fitted a jointed band of metal. Underneath the metal portion, to protect the horse's nose from injury, the noseband has a felt or leather pad. Underneath his lower jaw the noseband is adjusted and fastened by a buckle. Directly at the top of the noseband and joined to the middle point of the metal band is a steel eyelet to which a snap on one end of the longe is attached. The noseband should be buckled tightly around the upper part of the nose about one inch below the prominent projections formed by the cheekbones. If fitted too low it may bruise or break the cartilage forming

Correctly adjusted cavesson. Nose band and jowl strap buckled very snugly.

A mild snaffle bridle.

the septum, which becomes bone higher in the nose. A little above the noseband, sewn to the cheek pieces of the cavesson, are two other straps which drop downward and buckle underneath the jaw forming the "jowl strap." Both the jowl strap and the noseband should be tightened snugly to prevent the entire cavesson's slipping around when the horse pulls hard on the longe. This slipping may allow the cheek piece on the side away from the trainer to slide up and injure the horse's eye.

BENEFITS OF LONGEING

Among other benefits, longeing teaches obedience; induces general suppleness of the spine and joints; permits exercise at fairly fast gaits with no weight on the back (greatly lessening the possibility of injury to the legs); gives the first ideas of discipline and authority; prevents the colt's bucking when first mounted (thus again eliminating the probability of harm to his legs); allows training over obstacles; greatly improves balance; and makes it possible for an attendant to exercise a horse when the trainer cannot be present.

HOW TO LONGE

If the colt is circling to the right hand (clockwise) the long end of the longe is held coiled in figures of

eight in the left hand while the lead end, running to the cavesson, passes through the right hand, held palm upward, with the elbow bent and relaxed. If the longe is coiled in circles instead of eights, it may tighten up and seriously burn the trainer's hand if the colt plays up or runs away. A five-foot whip stock with a lash about twelve feet long also is held in the left hand, both stock and lash pointing toward the rear of the trainer and away from the horse. The butt end of the whip stock points toward the horse, as does the left thumb. Held in this manner, the whip is partly hidden from the horse and does not frighten or threaten him except when used to enforce obedience. It always should be carried when longeing, for without it the trainer sooner or later will find himself helpless when the horse disobeys.

In the beginning the colt is led by the trainer who moves alongside, or slightly in front of his head. The trainer should look ahead, not toward him, since for some psychological reason a horse is loath to follow a man facing him. As soon as the command "walk" is learned, the trainer by degrees drops farther to the rear. From this position he endeavors to drive the colt about the circle. An assistant, by threatening with the whip or gently using it on the colt's croup, makes this part of the lesson very simple. Frequent halts are important. "Whoa" repeated in a low, quiet tone is the habitual command for halting.

The first longeing lesson, of not over fifteen or twenty minutes' duration, should be confined to work at the walk, the colt only being taught to lead and the meaning of the commands "walk" and "whoa." With an apt pupil and a tactful teacher, the former will learn to move on a small circle during the first lesson. When moving to the right hand, the trainer constantly places himself opposite the croup so that his whip (when no assistant is present) may be used if necessary to threaten the colt from the rear. In this position, which is the correct one from which to control a horse on a longe, his left arm, if extended to his front, should form a right angle with the long axis of the horse's body and point directly at the side of the croup. The lash is thrown toward the horse by turning the arm and thumb in toward the body. The movement is somewhat awkward but assures all the force necessary in using the whip on a green horse. Any attempt to play up or kick should be stopped immediately by giving horizontal flips to the longe. These flips, which never should be more violent than necessary, cause sharp reactions on the colt's nose transmitted by the heavy metal on top of the noseband and so punish misdemeanors.

If the colt is properly instructed in the meaning of vocal commands and flips on the longe, he will have learned after nine or ten lessons to decrease, increase, maintain his rate or gait, and to halt at the trainer's indications. During this time exercise at only the walk and slow trot is given. A slow gallop should not be required until after at least two or three weeks, and only when the colt is able to gallop without pulling on the longe. Time spent in circling to the right and left should be equalized.

Great care must be exercised not to jerk or pull on the longe so vigorously as to spin the colt partly around on his forehand. This may cause grave injuries, particularly to the hocks. An enclosure or riding hall is the most satisfactory place for first lessons. There the colt is easily controlled in a corner, his attention is not distracted, and he is less liable to break loose and run away. To forestall his getting out of hand and hurting himself, work on a small circle of four or five yards' radius should be continued until he is well disciplined. As previously mentioned, he must not be allowed to buck, rush about, kick or play, as these actions, even though mild, soon become annoying habits and later cause mishaps and injuries. Longeing is only valuable when so taught and executed that the horse always remains obedient and calm.

With a completely green colt, the combination of the work on the longe with the leading beside an old horse gives sufficient exercise for a minimum of two weeks. Nothing more should be attempted and there should be no galloping during this time. In the second week, normally one hour's very slow work per day may be given and two or more short lessons are infinitely more beneficial than one long one. If the colt is undeveloped, thin, weak, or only three years of age exercise at the walk only ought to be continued for several weeks.

Technique of the Longe

There is a considerable amount of technique required in properly handling the longe for it must be adeptly manipulated to attain the best results. It is held lightly stretched when all goes well. The hand resists pulling and yields when it ceases, just as with the bridle reins. If the colt moves away abruptly at the trainer's command or from a flick of the whip lash, the longe must be allowed to slip through one relaxed hand and the loops to uncoil from the other. This avoids a jerk on the nose which would contradict the command of the voice or whip, and only serve to bewilder and frighten the novice. Similarly, when the colt plays up and runs out on a tangent, the longe must be allowed to slip out for a moment and be tightened gradually so as not to whirl him suddenly about on his forehand. The trainer is often forced to run for several yards after the colt in order not to restrain and check him abruptly. As he slows down he should be punished by flips of the longe.

When the longe is let out to its limit, the left hand (if the colt is circling to the right) is braced against the left hip. There should be a loop on the free end of the longe which can be held by the left hand as a final resort in case the horse makes a hard play to escape on the run. With no loop, the longe is certain to be pulled entirely out of the hand.

The trainer will be forced to walk about on small circles or ellipses concentric with those on which the colt travels until the latter is well trained. When no

BREAKING

assistant is present clucking, tapping with the butt end of the whip just in rear of the cinch, and commanding "walk," are employed as means of instigating forward movement during the first lesson. When mounted lessons begin (through the principle of resemblance, in the association of ideas) taps by the rider's heels, replacing the taps with the whip, will be understood to mean "move forward." It must be remembered that to expedite teaching the colt this first lesson, *a single step forward* should be instantly rewarded by pats on the neck, soft encouraging words and sugar or oats (the principle of contiguity, in the association of ideas).

When required to halt, the colt should not face inward toward the trainer, but along the circumference of the circle in the direction he has been moving. By pointing the whip stock at his shoulder, it is comparatively easy to teach him to remain facing in that direction. As soon as he stands fast, the trainer loops the longe in figures of eight in his left hand and speaking in a soft, low tone, slowly approaches and caresses him for his obedience. If allowed to face inward, the colt soon will be doing it of his own volition and once accomplished, it is very difficult to force him to move out in the original direction. If he whirls about and goes in the opposite direction, he should be halted and started anew. Here again, unless the trainer is very experienced in using the longe, an assistant during first lessons is almost indispensable. A colt may be punished and corrected by snaps on the nose for reversing his direction against the trainer's desire. To do this, the trainer advances toward the colt, which usually backs rapidly away, and continues to snap the longe rather violently with vertical flips against his nose until, in attempting to escape the punishment, the colt turns ninety degrees and moves in the proper direction. *At this instant the snaps must cease, tension on the longe be lightened and the colt encouraged by soothing words.*

In ordering the horse to "walk," "trot," or "gallop," the tone of voice has more effect than the word itself. "Whoa" should be pronounced in a very low and soft tone; "walk," "trot" and "gallop," in progressively higher and louder tones. Usually threats with the whip will be needed to make the colt respond when he receives his first lesson at an increased gait. If the voice is used simultaneously with the whip, soon the latter will be unnecessary.

Pulling and Loss of Calmness

If when first compelled to trot the colt pulls against the longe, it is certain that he needs more quiet work at the walk. Pulling is very liable to occur when the gallop is begun. This is due to the youngster's lack of experience and balance in galloping on a small circle; hence if he bores outward, renewed work at a lively trot is necessary until he becomes stronger and more certain of his equilibrium.

This brings up a general rule in training: *if a new lesson provokes resistance and loss of calmness, at once resume preceding and elementary work until the horse again becomes perfectly calm and obedient. Then take up the new lesson again. Resistance and excitement always indicate lack of thorough preparation for the new lesson. This rule should be strictly followed in all training.*

Balance and Collection

After the trot is executed calmly and without pulling, in both directions, the radius of the circle, by slowly letting out or taking in the longe, should be frequently increased and decreased. This simple exercise causes the colt continually to readjust his balance and to supple his spine laterally; meanwhile he develops agility, all of which prepare him for the gallop.

Frequently changing from the walk to the trot, shortening and extending the trot and halting quietly from both gaits inculcate discipline and teach the horse natural collection. He learns to engage his hind legs well forward under his body through these exercises, particularly if he is required to move out very promptly after each halt or decrease in the gait. They also supple the loin in a vertical direction and make the horse "longitudinally flexible." It is the start of an ideal "natural collection," as distinguished from the artificial collection required in high-schooling. It is the only rational form of collection to teach hunters, jumpers and polo ponies, because the horse collects himself without the unnatural distortion caused by brutal action of the bit. Consequently calmness is not destroyed and joints, tendons and bones remain sound. This subject will be discussed more fully later.

THE GALLOP ON THE LONGE

When the colt undertakes the gallop, the longe should be quite long, for, even on a large circle, he undoubtedly will have some difficulty at this gait. The difficulty is announced by his pulling against the longe. The answer to the problem is more work at the trot, until he can canter without pulling.

If the youngster is prone to gallop false (lead with the left foot, for example, when circling to the right) he should be urged into the gallop just as he closely approaches one of the fences or walls at the corner of the enclosure. At this moment the longe may be slack, since the wall guides the horse, and a sudden urging forward with the voice or whip will cause him to take the naturally correct lead. If, on the other hand, the colt is pulling on the longe, he necessarily has a preponderance of weight on his inside shoulder. This lightens the outside shoulder, thereby predisposing him to lead with the outside leg—"gallop false." Sometimes under these circumstances he will gallop "disunited," which means to lead with the left foreleg and the right hind leg, or vice versa.

Any new lesson should be undertaken at the end of the day's work. The moment the colt seizes the idea and executes a stride or two of the movement approximately correctly, he should be brought to a halt, patted, encouraged by the voice, fed sugar or oats, and led to the stable. Many horsemen believe that the horse reflects, for if this procedure is followed, the colt on the following day invariably executes with calmness and ease the movement he managed with difficulty on the day preceding. This rule also applies to all new work after the colt is mounted.

The use of the longe in teaching the colt to jump—which probably furnishes the most valuable type of jumping instruction—will be discussed in Chapter VI.

First Lesson in Mounting

The colt, after having been taught to work well on the longe, may be mounted with little probability of his endeavoring to buck or resist. Without longeing, the opposite results often obtain. After he has been well worked on the longe, mounting is inaugurated gradually by first putting on his back only the saddle, with the stirrups detached. Here again an assistant can be very helpful in saddling and cinching while the trainer holds the longe close to the horse's head and soothes him. At any sign of rebellion a few snaps on the longe, as a result of his previous experiences, will steady the colt. After the saddle is safely on, the colt should be induced to stand quietly for several minutes. When perfectly calm, he should be progressively worked at the walk and trot, being kept on a very small circle. If after a few minutes all goes well and there are no signs of resistance, the stirrups may be attached and allowed to hang so that their swaying against his sides will prevent, when he is mounted later on, any fear of the rider's legs.

After the colt has borne the saddle for several days, the assistant (standing close to the horse, with his knee pressed against the saddle-skirt and his toe away from the colt's side) places his foot in the near stirrup and gradually supports his weight partly in it and partly on the saddle, across which he leans his body. If the colt is frightened and plunges about, the assistant may quickly remove his foot from the stirrup and step clear. The trainer meanwhile attempts to keep the colt's head up by agitating the longe as necessary. If excitement and resistance have greeted the attempt, the colt should be immediately put back to work at lively gaits on the longe. After ten minutes' or more exercise, the attempt should be renewed. It is highly important to prevent the colt's plunging and bucking, for very often young horses are severely or permanently injured in their efforts to throw their riders. In addition, if the youngster succeeds, he is given an idea of his own power, of which it is very wise to keep him ignorant. Furthermore, for months thereafter he will occasionally and most unexpectedly resort to bucking. Patience and the longe will eliminate these misadventures and keep the dispositions of horse and trainer sweeter.

When the assistant's balancing himself across the saddle is no longer resented in any manner, he throws his right leg over the horse and gently seats himself. If this also is agreeably accepted, encouragement by voice and patting on the neck should be lavish, the colt fed oats and allowed to stand for several minutes. In dismounting, the assistant again is careful to depress his toe to avoid its striking the colt's ribs. If the latter has appeared nervous and apprehensive while being mounted, and has indicated by the expressions of his eyes, ears, or actions that he may become violent if required to move forward, nothing further should be attempted during this lesson. The rider dismounts and the colt, after again being reassured by kind treatment, is led to the stable. If this is done, he probably will submit to being mounted with perfect calmness on the following day. On the other hand, colts with very quiet and gentle dispositions may be led about on the longe with the assistant up, on the same day they are mounted for the first time.

At this first mounting lesson the assistant should hold the reins only if they are attached to the two D-rings, one on each side of the cavesson's noseband. Reins attached to a bit should not be held, for the colt's violent movements will invariably cause jerks on his mouth, and at this time it is most undesirable to provoke any fear of the bit.

Mounted Work on the Longe

If, however, all has gone well, the rest is a very simple matter. During the few days following, the colt is mounted by the assistant for about five minutes toward the end of each longeing period, and after being led for a short time, is required by the trainer to walk on circles of progressively greater radii. If his strength warrants it, a few days later the slow trot may be demanded occasionally, but only for two or three minutes. During this mounted work on the longe, which gradually may be increased to a maximum of fifteen minutes, the assistant teaches the horse the significance of squeezes of the legs reinforced, if necessary, by taps of the heels or spurs. If he uses his legs simultaneously with clucking and threats by the dismounted trainer's whip, their meaning is quickly comprehended and the latter two indications may be abandoned.

Improving Disposition by Work on the Longe

Where great energy, excitability and nervousness are natural to the colt, a period of longeing should precede mounted work for several weeks. Only after absolute calmness is evident when the day's exercise begins should this practice be dispensed with.

This longeing preliminary to riding is also of enormous value to older horses with high-strung and nervous temperaments. Their surplus energy may be safely worked off on the longe, and many battles thereby eliminated which would be inevitable were they mounted immediately on leaving the stable. Most horsemen utterly fail to appreciate the enormous benefits of longeing in these cases. It oftentimes will redeem a horse which appears to be hopelessly fretful and rebellious. To mount such a horse without his having been previously longed sets up a vicious circle, for the rider must necessarily restrain the horse's first exuberance and, in so doing, it is impossible to avoid annoying and hurting his mouth. This pain in turn aggravates the nervousness and resistance and matters grow steadily worse. It is well to note that the majority of these fretful and unmanageable horses have arrived at their lamentable condition through having acquired a faulty head carriage as a result of inefficient training. Much longeing, followed by elementary work to place correctly the head and neck and put the horse on the bit, is the logical means of redemption.

As soon as mounted lessons on the longe are cheerfully performed by the colt, the trainer himself mounts and the longe is detached from the cavesson. "First Mounted Lessons," described a little further on, are now commenced. It is advantageous to use at first two pairs of reins, one set attached to the cavesson D-rings, and the other to the snaffle bit. Especially is this true with a high-spirited and sensitive colt, since he may be controlled by the cavesson reins and his sudden shying or other unexpected movements repressed without resorting to the snaffle bit. Not all cavessons are equipped with D-rings but it is a simple matter to have them sewn on.

Common sense dictates when the cavesson may be discarded entirely in favor of the snaffle bridle. With the normal colt, the combination is only needed during four or five lessons.

The Snaffle Bridle

It is presumed that the colt previously has been accustomed to having a snaffle bit in his mouth for brief periods while feeding. Therefore, after two or three lessons on the longe the snaffle bridle is put on over, or underneath, the cavesson. The bridle reins are looped and fastened by passing the throat lash through the loops before buckling it.

A snaffle bit with a mouthpiece (cannons) of large diameter is best employed because of its mild action resulting from the large bearing surface presented to the horse's tongue and bars. A little later two snaffles should be used on a double bridle to accustom the colt to two bits. This combination also gives a large bearing surface, and keeps the mouth soft. A further precaution which prevents the bit's pinching the corners of the mouth may be taken, by placing two circular pieces of leather or rubber, about four inches in diameter, one about each end of the mouthpiece. This device also stops the bit's being pulled through the mouth when the horse resists the effect of one rein during a turn or change in direction. Great care must be taken to avoid hurting or frightening the youngster when he is first bridled.

Diet and Care during Breaking

It must never be forgotten that the two prime preoccupations of the trainer during the breaking period are the building of a sound, healthy, strong physical condition and the development of a calm, gentle disposition. All exercise and work should be intelligently subordinated to the attainment of these two essentials. Daily the colt's legs, feet and general condition ought to be studied and his work regulated accordingly. Also, during this critical period of the undeveloped colt's life, grooming and feeding must be the subjects of unending attention.

The value of grazing for all horses is inestimable, for, as has been remarked, the diet should contain sufficient calcium to nourish the bones, and this element is found in good grasses. In the summer when normally a great deal of water is drunk, additional calcium is received from this source. Nevertheless, green grass in summer and alfalfa in winter should be fed whenever possible to augment the supply. As in the case of all changes in diet, grazing should be initiated by degrees. Beginning with five minutes, the time may be gradually increased until there is an hour's grazing daily. A little salt scattered on the grain is healthful. It stimulates thirst and also replaces the salt which rapidly passes from the body when the horse sweats. This salt in the food should be in addition to rock salt kept in the manger at all times. To provide an ample and soft bed so that he may rest in absolute comfort is obviously important. In cold weather, hot mashes once or twice a week are beneficial.

BREAKING

Another physical phenomenon deserving far more attention than it is usually accorded is the shedding of the coat. This occurs at least once annually and always in the spring of the year, when it is accompanied by a marked general physical depression. Work during shedding time should be decreased and only slow exercise given. Grazing is especially helpful at this time. It can be observed that when horses are transported to different climates the months during which shedding occurs often vary and frequently the coat is changed three times during the year following arrival in a new clime. This is proof of the long period necessary to thoroughly acclimate a horse.

If the owner will study his charges and care for them with the same common sense and solicitude that he exercises in the cases of members of his family he will rarely blunder. Sick, injured, or otherwise afflicted horses need the same care and treatment as do human beings in similar conditions.

Normal Amount of Exercise

Until six years of age, training must be regulated by condition; after that, when moderate exercise has made him hardy and strong, the horse must give himself over to the demands of training. Proper care, schooling and conditioning will make a strong, pleasant riding horse out of a rather second-rate colt, whereas failure to provide those requisites will ruin the best one ever foaled.

It should be remembered that: too much exercise is ruinous to temperament and legs; too little will have equally deplorable results on the disposition and manners, and will invite stable vices such as weaving, cribbing and kicking; there should be some exercise each day. The time for the first lesson on the longe was given as fifteen or twenty minutes. It is gradually increased until at the end of two or three weeks, depending on the individual's condition, strength and aptitude, and weather conditions, an hour's work a day—preferably broken into two half-hour periods— is normal. Providing the colt remains well and gains weight and strength, the entire time for the breaking period will vary from two months to a year. After two months he may usually be given two hours' *slow* exercise per day on six days of the week. *During the first two or three months, for a totally green colt there should be no jumping of any sort and no galloping whatever while mounted.* All mounted work is at the walk with occasional brief periods at the natural or slow trot. The longe is utilized for exercise at a somewhat freer trot, and at the gallop. It usually takes at least a month for the colt's condition, balance and strength to improve sufficiently to make it possible for him to canter on the longe.

BREAKING

The time limits set above apply to *average,* undeveloped four-year-olds with no considerable previous work. The limits may be decreased for those which have been partly broken and are naturally very well developed muscularly. It is a matter calling for determination by the intelligence and judgment of the owner in the case of each colt.

First Mounted Lessons
GENERALITIES

It is far more conducive to good results if first mounted lessons are given in an enclosure such as a riding hall or an arena surrounded by a high board fence. On the other hand, as soon as the colt comprehends and obeys the few simple aids which are applied during the breaking period, he should be taken for daily promenades across country. The fresh air and broken terrain greatly help his physical condition. During these excursions, which are principally at the walk with now and then a very short period at the trot, it is extremely helpful to have as company for the colt an older horse with irreproachable manners, ridden by an assistant. The young one will follow his older comrade quite calmly over terrain which might greatly frighten him, were he alone. The equine attribute of mimicry thus may be profitably exploited.

As a result of the experience on the longe, the pupil,

now wearing only a snaffle bridle, usually can be ridden about the enclosure without difficulty. The saddle, with a soft mohair or felt pad underneath, should be properly constructed with a deep throat in the center of the seat which eliminates any tendency of the trainer to slide backward off the cantle. Needless to say, it should fit well and not touch the withers.

Establishing Contact with the Colt's Mouth

As promptly as possible, after the trainer discards the longe, contact with the mouth is established. The reins are held, one in each hand, with the hands widely separated (a foot or more). The single rein enters the hand between the third and fourth fingers and comes out over the forefinger against which it is clamped by the thumb. Little by little the reins are stretched lightly taut. This must be a gradual and gentle process for the bars and tongue of the unbroken colt are exceedingly tender and the trainer's immediate objective is to teach the horse confidence in the bit's soft support. With a keen, free-going type—termed a "hand" horse— this contact is readily instituted. With the opposite sort which is sluggish or lazy—a "leg" horse—the rider will have to search continually for his mouth and energetically drive him, by use of the legs and spurs, into the habit of seeking his bit. *Almost every green colt, when first mounted, is inclined to wander about aimlessly until, by progressively more decisive action with his legs and maintaining an inescapable chute with the separated reins, the trainer convinces him that there is no escape except to move straight ahead. Only by keeping the reins stretched delicately taut can this wandering about be eliminated.*

Action of the Hands

The fingers, wrists, elbows and shoulders must be soft, flexible and relaxed so that the hands may assiduously follow the backward and forward oscillations of the colt's head at the walk. Softness of hand results from this complete, or semi relaxation of those joints. *Sensitiveness of hand is cultivated by conscious effort.* The hands are placed in any position that is required during breaking and training, or at any other time when the horse must be corrected. When all is going well they are several inches both in front of the pommel and above the withers.

Length of Reins

In all riding, the proper adjustment of the reins as to length may be automatically fixed. They should form a straight line with the rider's forearm; in other words, there is no angle at the junction of the reins and hands. There should be, however, a decided angle at the elbow in order that this joint at all times may be flexible. The upper arm should fall naturally with the elbow a few inches in front of the body, when the latter is correctly inclined forward. When rising at the trot or galloping, the reins must be shortened since the body is inclined farther forward at these gaits and the seat is out of the saddle part of the time. The rider's center of gravity is advanced to a point approximately over his knees.

The Whip

A trained horse, inspired by a strong pair of legs, needs no whip, but with a green colt a light, springy one is most useful in interpreting and reinforcing the action of the legs. It is applied just in rear of the leg itself and simultaneously with the squeeze of the calf or the action of the spur. It may occasionally be used on the shoulder—as usual with only what force is necessary.

The Spurs

During the first few mounted lessons the spurs are used gently and tactfully with just enough force to secure results. *Later on, they must always be used as vigorously and sharply as necessary to insure prompt forward movement.* Their action should be clean cut and determined and the hands should give softly and passively as the colt responds by moving forward.

BREAKING

Under no circumstances should he be checked immediately by the hands after having obeyed the legs. On the contrary, the reins remain slack and the rider instantly pats the horse on the neck as he hurries forward in response to the legs' strong action. These spur attacks are necessary lessons in producing free forward movement which ultimately will become—almost, if not quite—the equivalent of inborn boldness. *After* the caress is administered the horse is gently slowed down and calmness restored. A few moments at the loose rein walk will furnish a recompense for obedience and allow him an opportunity restfully to reflect on the lesson. This action of the spurs, while quick, surprising and determined, must be carefully measured as to intensity according to the colt's sensitiveness. *Most assuredly a strong attack must not be made during the first seven or eight mounted lessons unless deliberate stubbornness is encountered.* However as soon as the pupil perfectly understands the spurs' meaning and fails to respond promptly and generously, their action should be decidedly vigorous so as to invite no misunderstanding. It should force him to the front at a smart trot or canter. The psychological law which indicates this harsh procedure has previously been cited; *an intensified impression serves to provide a much more lasting effect than many weak repetitions.* In view of this truth it is apparent that the habit of tapping constantly with the legs or spurs without securing obedience only encourages disrespect.

The spurs should be very mild, having blunt and round ends to their shanks. For a lazy, underbred animal small rowels which will just prick the skin may be necessary later on. Spurs, except when riding unusually sensitive and responsive horses, always should be worn after the first few mounted lessons. When the spurs are needed, they are needed very badly. The horse must always be conscious of "the devil's presence near his belly."

Objectives and Rein Effects of Breaking Period

To refresh the reader's mind, the principal objectives of the breaking period, after arriving at the point where the colt can be ridden, are to secure: 1. a good disposition (calmness); 2. a hardy physical condition; 3. prompt response to the action of the legs; 4. acceptance of the bit with extended head and neck (*which means to put the colt on his forehand*); 5. obedience to the simple rein effects at the walk, trot and gallop.

Direct, Leading and Bearing Reins

In obtaining the correct set of head and neck during the next two to four months, *habitually only three rein effects, as described below, will be employed.*

First, the two "reins of direct opposition": The effect is simply one of increased tension on both reins to provide opposition directly to the rear for the purpose of halting or slowing the pace. The *single* rein of direct opposition is not employed except in cases of necessity. (See page 223, Chapter V.)

(The *right rein* is used as an example throughout.)

"Opening" or "Leading" Rein: The opening rein is used to turn the horse to the right from the halt or while moving at any gait. It is the effect with which a green colt can be most easily taught to change direction. As it acts in a natural, simple manner, it is one of the first employed. (See Sketch, page 168.)

The right hand is carried to the right and slightly to the front. There is no tension to the rear. It turns the horse's head and bends his neck to the right, throwing the bulk of their weight on the right fore leg. This tends to make him lose his balance to the right, and to move in that direction to regain his equilibrium. If in motion, the horse turns to the right on a large curve, the body following naturally after the head and neck. When using this rein effect, the rider's two legs keep up the horse's movement, usually acting with equal force. However, if a rather sharp turn is desired, the right leg is used more vigorously against the horse's side and a little farther to the rear. This pushes the hindquarters to the left more rapidly, and makes the

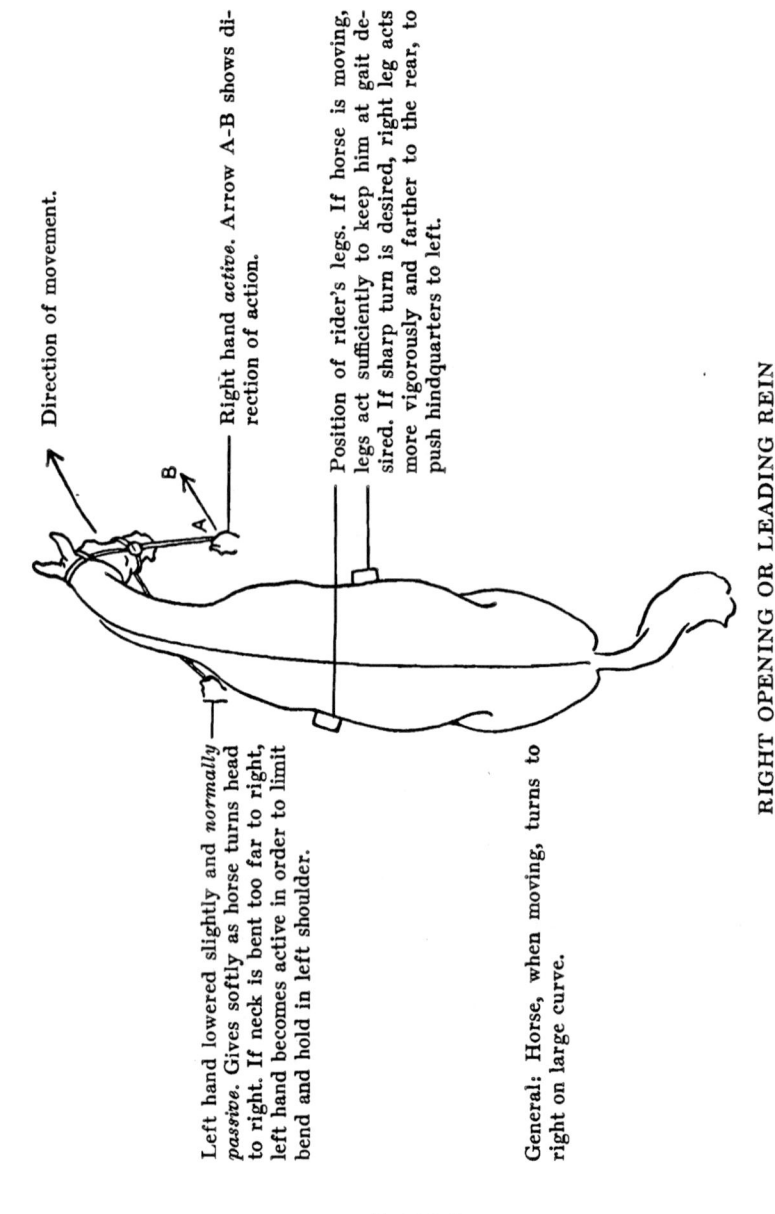

Direction of movement.

Right hand *active*. Arrow A-B shows direction of action.

Position of rider's legs. If horse is moving, legs act sufficiently to keep him at gait desired. If sharp turn is desired, right leg acts more vigorously and farther to the rear, to push hindquarters to left.

Left hand lowered slightly and *normally passive*. Gives softly as horse turns head to right. If neck is bent too far to right, left hand becomes active in order to limit bend and hold in left shoulder.

General: Horse, when moving, turns to right on large curve.

RIGHT OPENING OR LEADING REIN

Sketch 1

curve over which he is moving, sharper. If the horse is at a halt, and the rider does not use his legs, this rein will simply turn the head to the right, and weight the right shoulder.

The left hand, normally passive, should be kept low. Most riders pull on that rein or carry it across the horse's neck, which counteracts the effect sought with the right rein. If the horse bends his neck too far to the right, the left rein intervenes by being fixed at an appropriate length, low and close to the left shoulder, in order to limit the neck's bend to the right.

The effect of the opening rein is to lead the horse to the right front, not to pull him around.

"Bearing" or "Neck" Rein: The right hand is carried just over the crest of the neck and acts toward the left front. The rein, to be effective, should bear against the right side of the *upper half of the neck,* as this part is more sensitive to the rein than that near the shoulders. It is an artificial effect and not powerful, but is habitually used with trained horses to change direction without changing speed, particularly in polo. By using the *left opening rein* in early training, and later combining the *right bearing rein* with it, obedience to the *right bearing rein* alone is easily taught. This is done by using the opening rein to the left front, and when the horse begins to turn in that direction, the right bearing rein is applied. The effects of the two reins

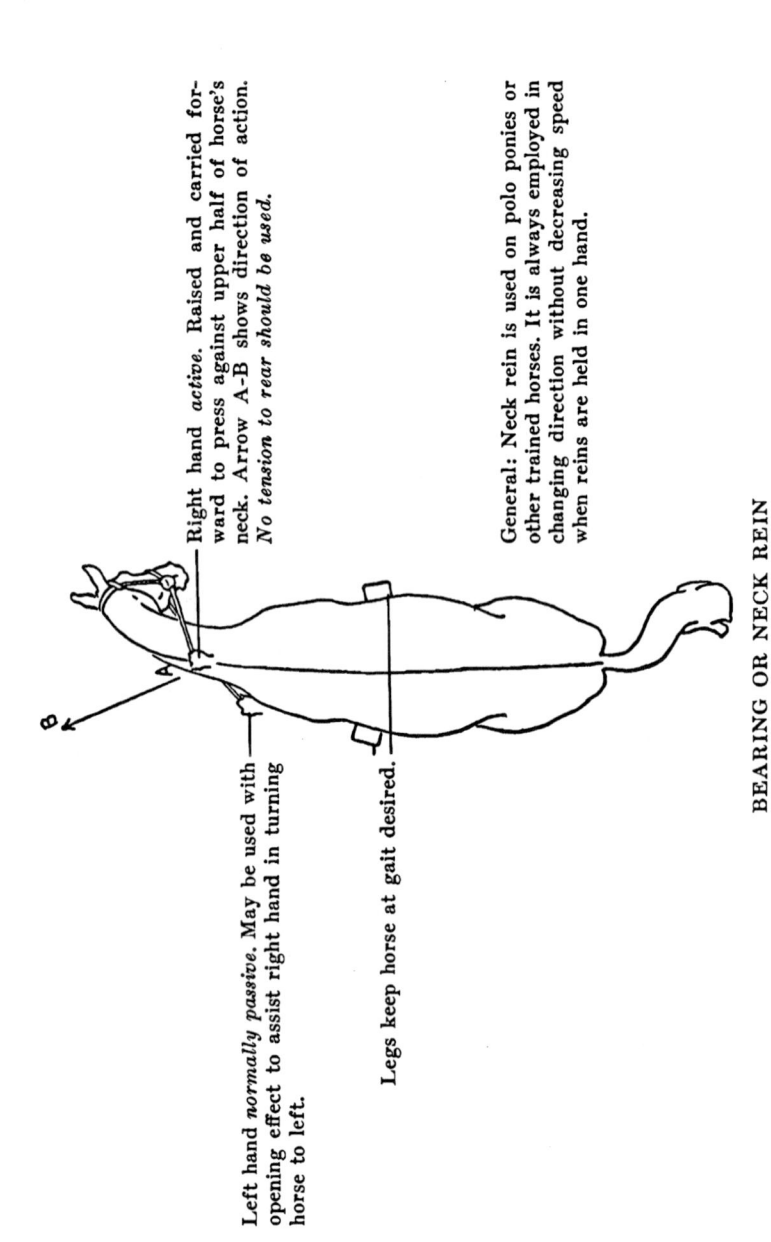

Right hand *active*. Raised and carried forward to press against upper half of horse's neck. Arrow A-B shows direction of action. *No tension to rear should be used.*

General: Neck rein is used on polo ponies or other trained horses. It is always employed in changing direction without decreasing speed when reins are held in one hand.

Left hand *normally passive*. May be used with opening effect to assist right hand in turning horse to left.

Legs keep horse at gait desired.

BEARING OR NECK REIN
Sketch 2

should be alternating as well as intermittent. Soon, through the association of ideas, the colt comprehends, and the leading effect may be abandoned.

The right bearing rein turns the horse's nose upward to the right and forces the bulk of the weight of the head and neck onto the *left* shoulder. While its effect is not strong, if in motion the horse's balance is shifted toward the left front, and he turns on a large curve to the left. The rider's legs normally remain in place, acting only to sustain the gait. (See Sketch.) When working with a green colt their effect should be produced intermittently, when required, each time the left fore leg is moved.

No Flexions Demanded

For the purpose of emphasis it is repeated that *throughout the breaking phase no effort should be made to require vertical flexion of the poll, and every tendency toward a "rubbery," lateral bending of the neck near the shoulders must be combated.* The trainer seeks to keep the direction of impulsion and movement straight into the chute formed by the separated reins— the horse at first being encouraged, and later, as his education progresses, forced by the determined action of the legs, to extend his neck and accept the bit. In other words, *suppleness and complete relaxation at this early period are neither sought nor desired, and under no circumstances should any collection be attempted.* These attributes will be developed by the more difficult gymnastics of the "training" period proper. During the months devoted to breaking, the colt is allowed to accommodate himself to the burden of the rider, to acquire the necessary stiffness to his neck, and to develop his loin muscles, which are pulled upward as a consequence of his low head carriage. In general, during breaking the colt is annoyed as little as possible. To make unreasonable demands would be to ruin his disposition.

The Walk on a Loose Rein

For several months walking provides the major portion of a colt's exercise. In addition to the many benefits already enumerated, it induces relaxation and calmness. *After he has learned to accept his bit and obey the leading and bearing reins, frequent promenades should be given at the walk using, most of the time, a long and floating rein.* All exercises, after being taught on the stretched rein, should be repeated, if feasible, on a loose rein. Across country a long, loose rein adds to the colt's cleverness, calmness and self-reliance.

The Extended Walk

A horseman should make continuous effort through-

BREAKING

out the career of his horse to develop and maintain a long, low-striding walk. This may be done by frequent exercise at the extended walk, in which instruction should start at about the fifth mounted lesson. Attention has been called to the fact that the horse's head moves forward and backward and from side to side at each step at the walk. To accomplish each step he voluntarily ruptures his equilibrium and promptly regains it by moving and planting the appropriate foot. Advantage of these two facts may be taken to lengthen and hasten the strides in the following manner: the rider, by a minute muscular effort of the back muscles, accompanies with his upper body the forward movement of his horse. In other words, the body is not dragged along at each step. The seat and body move to the right front with no perceptible sideward sway as the horse's right fore advances, and to the left front with the left fore. *This is an effortless matter provided the trunk is inclined slightly forward from the hips, the loin hollowed out and the back kept straight.* Slouching or sitting back on the cantle sets up an inert mass which militates against the horse's movement, whereas a rider "going with" his horse at the walk, as well as at the trot and gallop, lightens the latter's task.

The trainer's legs work alternately, the right leg becoming active as the horse's left fore leg advances. The left leg reinforces the right in case of laziness. Until able to "feel" when a particular fore leg is advancing, it can be determined by glancing down to note the point of the shoulder which advances as part of the same movement. At this time, since the shoulder blade pivots on its center, the top of the shoulder is moving rearward.

The well separated reins, held in both hands, are carried forward toward the left front at the same instant that the left fore advances. Their action, assisted by the rider's weight, further overbalance the horse just at the moment when he himself has broken his equilibrium toward the left front and is carrying the left fore foot forward to recover himself.

The rider's left leg acts immediately afterward and the reins are carried across the withers and toward the right front as the horse's right fore foot is advanced. Only the lightest contact while following the mouth is maintained; the relaxed hands and elbows move in a soft, rhythmic manner so that the reins act in combination, one with the "leading," the other with the "bearing" effect. The leading rein becomes slack at each step, while the bearing (or neck) rein is applied nearer the shoulders than is usual when changing direction. Each leg, when active, slides forward against the horse's side an inch or two, the spur being resorted to if the horse is unresponsive. The right leg's effect, when active, is to hurry the horse's right hind leg for-

BREAKING

ward and cause it to engage well to the front under his body immediately after his left fore foot has grounded. The rider's left leg, acting as his right one becomes passive, reacts in a similar manner on the horse's left hind leg. All the rider's aids coöperate to hasten and increase the length of each stride. Increase in length is of prime importance.

In extending the walk, all joints of the colt's limbs are suppled by the great flexion and extension required. While the rider learns to accompany with his hands the oscillations of the horse's head, the horse learns to accept gentle support from the hands. His head and neck are allowed their maximum extension and as low a carriage as he desires. The tendons and muscles are hardened, and general strength increased. It is notable that at the walk, weight is not lost, as is the case when moving at the trot and gallop. This fact suggests nothing but walking for a weak, thin colt.

The extended walk is best practiced on straight lines out of doors, but first lessons are given most conveniently in an enclosure. The rider has the sensation of rolling his horse ahead. In the beginning the exercise is continued for periods of from three to five minutes. *After the horse becomes proficient, very frequent changes from the extended to a slower, or normal, walk should be made.* The instant the slow walk is attained, the horse again should be pushed promptly into the extended walk. Very soon, through expecting to extend immediately after each decrease in speed, he slows his walk by slightly raising his loin and croup in order to engage his hind legs, without noticeable flexion of his hocks, well forward under his belly where they are in a position favorable to moving quickly forward. Thus, soon after mounted work is begun, the first instruction in "natural collection" is given.

It is not advisable to continue the extended walk for long periods at a time as it is more fatiguing for the horse than is the slow trot. The extended walk is gymnastic in nature but also serves to create a longer-striding, normal walk.

Halting

At the first mounted lesson, after the colt has moved about at the walk, a halt necessarily is demanded. The semi-relaxed fingers are closed on the reins and the hands and elbows diminish the amount of backward and forward play used in following the mouth. Thus the hands gradually become more or less fixed in position relative to the rider's body, at the same time retaining a certain elasticity to prevent jerky action. Since during breaking no flexion of any sort is demanded, all actions of the hands, wrists and elbows should be *softly and progressively* executed when setting up increased tension. *The hands resist, in contra-*

BREAKING

distinction to pulling, so that when the colt concedes, they do not fly in toward the body but, instead, instantly relax and move forward to reward obedience.

In the beginning, several successive resistances are set up, the fingers softening momentarily to reward each diminution in the gait. To fix the hands in continuous resistance, as may be done with a trained horse, will break, or over-flex, the poll, which must be avoided. Turning his head *just the least bit* to the right or left and then equalizing the tension on the two reins will expedite the first halt with a contrary colt. This turning at successive halts should be alternately to the right and left, and as soon as he responds readily, the halt is required in the normal manner with his head square to the front.

The head and neck should not be appreciably raised or otherwise displaced while halting. The moment the halt is consummated, all tension is released from the reins as a reward. The rider does not lean backward but remains inclined forward from the hips, increasing the pinch with his knees and the downward thrust of his heels in order to keep his seat from sliding forward onto the pommel. To throw the weight backward interferes seriously with the horse's raising his croup and engaging his hind legs.

A colt low at the withers compared to his height at the croup, or one with mutton withers, or having vertical shoulders, is generally badly balanced and "heavy on the forehand." He should be frequently halted, unless nervous. On the other hand, horses which are reluctant to accept the bit, nervous, fretful, weak and low in the hindquarters, or have poor hocks, should be halted very seldom until, through care and training, condition and strength are improved.

No effort to make the colt stand squarely on four legs at the halt is made for two months. To do so only provokes restiveness. He should be permitted to rest quietly on a loose rein after each halt.

Changing Direction with the Opening, or Leading, Rein

As indicated earlier, the leading rein is used in requiring first changes of direction. Using the left leading rein as an example, to execute a change of direction to the left, the left hand is carried to the left and slightly forward. This action turns the horse's head to the left. *No rearward tension is used unless absolutely necessary.* The effect is to lead him in a turn more or less sharp, depending on how far the head and neck are turned. In cases of intentional stubbornness, tension, as necessary, should be employed to compel the turn.

In early days of breaking, the turn should be large so that the neck is bent very little. If the colt tends to bend his neck too far to the left, it is prevented by lowering the right hand alongside his right shoulder and fixing the hand in position at that point. This also serves to prevent his "popping out his right shoulder." If he responds correctly, however, the right hand gives passively to the front. All actions must be soft and progressive; the half-relaxed fingers are closed after the hand is carried to the position in which it can most advantageously act. When a rein effect is finally understood, there should be firmness and continuity of resistance by the active hand—always tempered by elasticity and a limited following of the mouth to eliminate jerkiness—until the colt obeys, whereupon softness is resumed and the hands again follow completely the movements of the mouth. The effect of the left rein, for example, should be continuous until the colt bends his neck and starts his turn. The fingers and all joints of the arm then relax temporarily, although the left hand remains in place until the turn is completed. The instant the colt begins to disregard the previous effect, the fingers again close. Thus the action is intermittent and each obedience rewarded. After education on the longe, no difficulty in securing prompt response to the leading rein is probable. *This detailed discussion is believed worthwhile, for precision and finesse in the use of the hands require constant thought by even the most expert horsemen.*

Both the rider's legs act when necessary to sustain the gait during a turn. In case the horse bends his neck to the left but continues to move forward, "popping out his right shoulder," the right rein, as just described, is used to limit the bend and the left leg acts to drive the croup to the right. Both legs are used vigorously as soon as the horse is straightened and headed in the proper direction. The action of the left leg in swinging the croup outward to the right also teaches the colt the significance of one leg's acting alone; namely, the displacing, mobilizing or ranging of the croup in the opposite direction. (All three words are used in reference to this pushing of the croup by one leg in the opposite direction.)

By riding in an enclosure for the first few days, the rein effects are quickly taught since they may be applied when approaching the wall or fence. Also, at a corner the change of direction is automatically forced.

Changing Direction with the Bearing, or Neck, Rein

Obedience to the bearing rein is quickly taught through the colt's knowledge of the opening effect. The hand first is slipped along the rein several inches to shorten it. It is then pressed against the upper third of the neck a fraction of a second after response to the action of the opening rein, used by the other hand, has occurred. These alternating effects are employed until the bearing rein alone suffices to insure the turn. The right bearing rein should act toward the left front with no traction toward the left rear. Here again the use of the corners and walls of an enclosure expedite obedience. The right hand, when the rein is pressed against the horse's neck, should be above the crest and not crossed over to the left side of the neck. Hence it must be shortened as advised. The rider's legs function as necessary to keep the horse at a steady pace and to direct his croup.

Reaching for the Bit

Little by little, as he acquires confidence, strength, obedience, and frank forward movement, the average colt will extend his head and neck forward and downward, stretch the reins and maintain contact with his bit. When tired, he frequently lowers and pushes his neck out to its extreme limit for the purpose of resting his back and loin. This instinctive gesture of extension, if not repulsed, gives relief and confidence inspired by the realization that he possesses liberty of his head even though he is controlled by a bit. The "descent of the head and neck," where gently and progressively made from the shoulders down through the neck to the tip of the nose, should not be resisted, but encouraged and followed by the hands which maintain light, normal tension. Later on in training the horse should be required to do this as a relaxing, calming and suppling exercise while at all gaits. There should be no increase in speed as the descent occurs.

On the contrary, when the colt starts the extending and lowering with a quick retraction, or flip upward, of the nose, followed by a violent thrust of the head and neck downward and forward, he should be opposed by tightly closing the fingers of one hand. On the second similar action, the other hand is fixed; on the third, both hands are set. Thus the colt's mouth is more or less severely bumped simultaneously with his misbehavior. Associating his impressions, he will soon cease brutal attempts to jerk the reins out of the rider's hands. Again the importance of setting up no more force than necessary until the colt understands *why* he is being punished, is stressed. The fingers should be closed and set at the limit of downward extension of the thrust in order not to flex the poll or arch the neck.

A long, slender neck, or one very finely attached to the head, requires every precaution to avoid a premature and exaggerated flexion. Excessive softness and flexion of poll and jaw are prone to appear with little or no effort on the rider's part. To avoid them, the tension on the reins must be very light, and the greatest tact used to secure the desirable stiffness of neck so essential to future objectives. Great delicacy of hand is necessary to entice horses with these faults in conformation into reaching for, and accepting, their bits. Methods will be described later.

The Trot

The trot is particularly useful in early work *on the longe,* to improve balance, wear off excess energy and to give strength to the back and stiffness to the neck. Until he becomes quite strong, usually at the end of three months' mounted work, the fully extended trot should not be attempted. This valuable exercise, due to its strenuousness, has no place in the early breaking period, for it may easily stiffen and weaken, rather than supple and strengthen, the young joints.

Throughout the breaking phase only the slow and normal trot are used habitually when mounted. However, to extend the colt more freely than the normal trot late in the breaking period supples the articulations and promotes prompt response to the rider's legs. This should be done when condition permits.

Lengthening the Stride

After a firm, steady feel of the bit is taken, the trainer constantly seeks to increase speed at the trot by securing low, long and regularly cadenced—not quickly repeated—strides. His legs must act almost continuously with phlegmatic subjects. As the objects are to put the colt both on his forehand and steadily on the bit, his head must be carried low. When these conditions pertain, ample play of the joints and greater extension of stride become obligatory in the continual recovering of equilibrium.

In the case of a colt which lacks impulsion or hangs back from the bit, mobilizing the croup outward by predominating action of the inside leg on curves, and in the corners, helps to keep the center of gravity forward. Extremely long, low strides can be attained only by strong impulsion, acceptance of the bit, and perfect calmness. Frequently augmenting and diminishing the speed teaches obedience to hands and legs as well as aptitude in longitudinal shifting of balance.

First Lesson at the Gallop

WHY THE TRUE LEAD PREVENTS INTERFERENCE

At the gallop, when leading with his left leg, the horse carries the croup slightly to the left. This position allows freedom to the advanced left shoulder and, as explained in Chapter I, aids stability by placing the horse's center of gravity and the leading foreleg more nearly on one straight line. As mentioned under "Longeing," a horse circling to the left naturally leads with the left leg (left fore and left hind striking the ground in advance of the right fore and right hind).

During each stride at a slow gallop, the leading legs, while on the ground, are passed by the corresponding members of the other lateral biped. Therefore, centrifugal force, when the horse gallops true on a curve, eliminates the probability of interference (one fore or hind foot striking its mate in passing). In galloping false, since the reverse conditions prevail, interference easily may occur. (See Illustrations, page 24.)

First Gallop Departs

If longeing has been well taught, no difficulty is experienced normally, when mounted, in exacting the first gallop departs. Since the colt knows how to take the correct lead on a circle, advantage may be taken of a corner in an enclosure, where he perforce moves on a curve, to require the first gallop depart. If no enclosure is available, the depart is sought on a circle.

There are two elementary ways of teaching the gallop departs.

First method: Being at the normal trot, a very slightly increased tension is taken on the outside rein (right, if circling to the left) just prior to taking the gallop. A fraction of a second later the right leg is used strongly just a little in rear of the cinch to force the croup inward (to the left). The moment the croup moves over, the left leg comes to the assistance of the right and their combined energetic action urges the horse into the gallop. The right rein's effect is to impede the right shoulder and free the left. Thus with his croup pushed to the left and the left shoulder advanced and freed, the horse is set in a natural position to take the left lead. The rider carries his body slightly to the left front as his legs act.

The usual error in the application of these lateral aids (right leg and right rein) lies in applying too much tension to the right rein. This pulls the head and neck too far to the right and causes the horse to "pop his left shoulder out to the left" to conserve his balance. He thus weights, rather than lightens, it, and so frees the outside shoulder. As a consequence the false gallop (with the right leg leading) is more easily taken. Only the slightest displacement of the head toward the outside of the circle is necessary. When taking the gallop the trainer either should sit tight in his saddle, or post on the outside diagonal and apply his aids just as his seat comes into the saddle.

Second method: The rider, posting at the normal trot on the outside diagonal, takes the same action with his legs as in the first method. In this case, however, he carries both his hands and his trunk to the left and forward just as he settles into the saddle. This action throws the left (inside) fore leg farther forward and over-balances the colt in that direction. The rider's legs give impulsion and hasten the movements of the hind feet so that the horse falls into the gallop. The left rein goes slack and the right has the bearing effect.

Since most green colts prefer to "gallop left," it is wise to start teaching the departs with the right lead. This impresses more strongly the meaning of the aids employed. (If the colt's tendency is to lead right the first departs, of course, should be taken on the left lead.)

From previous training on the longe, the word "gallop" at the instant the aids are applied helps to insure response. The essential point is to employ the over-balancing effect of the weight and reins at the exact instant the *outside* fore foot strikes the ground.

In both methods an effort is made to obtain the depart without unnecessarily extending the trot. Success on the part of the colt is promptly rewarded by pats on the neck. After the departs are expertly executed on the circle, they are practiced when crossing the enclosure, just before arriving at the opposite wall; later, when approaching the corners but before the turn is initiated; finally, on straight lines. Departs from the slow trot are next taught. The trainer must take endless pains to follow the mouth at the gallop from the first stride.

During first lessons at the gallop, all corners of an enclosure are cut short and the colt, since he is not sufficiently well balanced to turn sharply, kept moving on large curves. On both circles and curves he should be given a little additional support on the outside rein. To turn his head decidedly inward while galloping on a curve is unnatural and uncomfortable. It cramps the leading shoulder and provokes resistance. Obviously if the horse is disobedient and runs inward, by "popping out his inside shoulder," his head must be turned inward to force him back in the other direction, by a form of "shoulder in," requiring the indirect rein of opposition. (See Chapter V.)

More refined methods of taking the gallop departs, which are initiated by the hindquarters, will be covered in Chapter V.

Lightness of the Forehand
Serpentines and Zigzags

A simple exercise by which control, balance and agility of the forehand may be secured, should begin as soon as the colt boldly takes his bit and is obedient to the bearing rein. It consists of riding at the walk and trot on broken lines, serpentines, and later zigzags, *while employing the bearing rein only, to obtain the changes of direction.* A serpentine is merely a series of loops requiring the use of the left bearing rein when turning to the right, and the right bearing rein when bending back on the next loop to the left. *There should be no pulling effect on the reins.* Begin by traversing big loops and gradually reduce their size. Use the legs as necessary to maintain a steady rate of speed. A zigzag requires quicker changes of direction and causes the horse to engage his inside hind leg well forward under his body. It is used after the colt is proficient on serpentines.

Since this work lightens the forehand and tends to throw more weight on the hindquarters, especially as the changes of direction become abrupt, there is always a possibility of the colt's dropping back of his bit. Therefore at the end of each exercise, always extend the gait on a straight line and put the horse on his forehand and bit. When any lack of impulsion or tendency to drop back of the bit appears, the bearing rein should be abandoned and the serpentine executed as described under "Reluctance to Accept the Bit," page 203, until frank forward movement on the hand is obtained.

Outdoor Work

At the end of about one week of mounted work the outdoor exercise, so persistently advocated, should begin. Mild slopes are excellent for developing strength, balance and agility. The head, under all conditions, should remain as low as the colt wishes. The horse lowers his head naturally when climbing or descending hills. Halts during promenades, if the colt is not restless, should be frequent. Stopping, dismounting and allowing him to graze improve his disposition and promote calmness. The trainer, while riding at the walk, should pat the colt's neck, flanks, croup and, when halted, occasionally dismount and mount from the off side. These logical and simple things are often neglected with certain colts, and in consequence they never acquire the great confidence of those so treated. At the end of three or four weeks the trot outside is taken up. Unless the horse is overly ambitious and trots too rapidly, he should take the rate most natural and comfortable to himself. The very nervous, ambitious types need only walking, with trotting on the longe, and in an enclosure if mounted, until calmness is attained. While the extreme extended trot should not be attempted during the breaking period, frequent increases and decreases in rate should be practiced on level ground. For several months trotting periods are of about three, and never over five, minutes' duration. When homeward bound, the walk is usually required, particularly with horses which show signs of being stable-bound or are inclined to jig. If started early, they will form the habit of walking quietly when headed homeward.

After about two months, short gallops on level stretches are beneficial. They cover only two hundred yards initially, later up to five hundred.

BREAKING

Faulty Position of the Head

Where, because of poor conformation, high spirits or rebellion against the bit, the colt raises his head too high when increased tension is taken, the rider's hands also move upward so as to maintain the straight line from the elbow to the bit. Instead of releasing the tension, it should be mildly increased and the colt's head held in its high position until, through discomfort, he seeks to lower it. *Tact is required to seize the first, and the exact, instant when the colt endeavors to lower his head.* Thereupon the fingers and elbows must relax and the hands follow the mouth's downward movement. Soon the youngster realizes that raising his head only places him in difficulty, and that comfort exists when the head and neck are correctly placed.

The same theory is applicable to all undesirable displacements of head or neck. If the latter is excessively rounded and the head tucked into the breast, the hands are carried far forward to a position over the poll. From here, one of two corrections may be administered; first, a sharp upward twist on one or both taut reins (euphemistically called a "half-halt") which causes the colt to raise and extend his head; or, second, with the hands fixed and set over the poll, strong resistance is set up and the bit worked back and forth through the mouth (vibrating effect) until, through annoyance and discomfort, he lifts and extends his head into a correct position. In either case he is rewarded upon assuming a correct attitude by prompt reëstablishment of the light normal contact. The "half-halt" and "vibrations" are always executed on taut reins.

Trot Too Fast

Until the colt is confirmed in a calm way of going at the walk, the trot should not be undertaken. Failure to follow this rule often is the cause of his first inclination to go too fast at the trot. When, however, natural energy and fine breeding are the causes, more work on the longe and mounted work on circles in an enclosure, both at the trot, are the best remedies. All this should be preceded by much leading, longeing and riding at the walk.

Very often the real source of trouble in these cases lies in the rider's poor seat; he is not inclined forward sufficiently to be securely and steadily balanced over his knees and stirrups and as a result partly supports himself by the reins, which causes unintentional movements of the hands. Consequently elastic softness of hand and uniform tension are absent, and the horse's mouth is incoherently abused.

When working on a large circle to the left, for example, with a horse which is very impetuous at the trot, the trainer's trunk should be inclined well forward and a trifle to the left. He should post on the outside diagonal so that his seat will come into the saddle as the right fore and left hind feet strike the ground. *The horse should be guided by the leading or bearing rein alone,* since there must be no pulling. If the seat is steady, the rider in balance, and only *the absolute minimum amount of tension on the reins* necessary to remain at the trot is exerted, the colt generally will decrease his speed in a short time. No jerking or pulling on both reins will be of permanent help. Pats on the neck as he becomes calm are in order, and the work on a still lighter rein should be continued. As the days pass and complete calmness arrives, a somewhat stronger support will be accepted without excitement, and ultimately a regulated trot with the normal feel will be possible.

It will be found oftentimes that horses are not, in fact, pulling, but merely seeking to extend their heads and necks. *If the rider will lean forward, ride in perfect balance, cease pulling and follow the mouth,* his horse will become calm and responsive. In the hunting field this frequently is all that is needed to calm apparently "hot" horses. Moreover, the average rider generally pulls on *both* reins in demanding a simple change of direction, when no decrease in gait is desired. He is then talking an unintelligible language to the horse, since extra tension means to check. Yet if the horse does check, his rider urges him onward but keeps on pulling. This unnecessary pulling over-flexes the neck and poll, hampers the horse's action, and soon frantic excitement replaces calmness. The amount of torture of the mouth to which many hunters, hacks and jumpers are submitted is stupendous. Of course only the insensitive, sluggish type of horse submits to this treatment. The high-class mount is either ruined or soon sold to a more skillful, thoughtful horseman.

Kicking at the Leg or at Other Horses

The vice of kicking at the leg or at other horses is quickly obliterated by aggressive action. The moment the kick is delivered, both of the rider's legs must attack with vigor, and continue to do so until the kicking ceases. If the attack forces the horse forward, continuous kicking will stop, whereupon the rider's legs become passive. As a precaution the trainer should hold the pommel of the saddle with one hand, in case pitching and plunging follow the action of the spurs.

With a powerful and stubborn horse whose reactions to the spur are very violent, the longe should be resorted to. The trainer uses his longeing whip to compel the horse to move forward while the mounted assistant, holding the pommel, makes a simultaneous attack with the spurs. This combination soon discourages both kicking and bucking. Whip and spurs cease to act as soon as the colt gives up the fight and the assistant should be quick to pat and encourage him as soon as he moves about the circle quietly. Several lessons should be given by slowing the gait and then using the spurs to increase it, until the horse obeys promptly and without kicking.

Scolding, jerking his head up sharply, and using the spurs vigorously the moment a horse lays back his ears preparatory to kicking a comrade, will soon stop that vice. A red rag in a horse's tail is a sad commentary on his trainer's ability.

"Rubbernecks"

How to prevent the horse's bending his head too far in answer to a rein effect has been described. To briefly repeat: if the head turns too far to the right in answer to the right leading rein, the bending is limited by lowering the left hand to a point near the horse's left shoulder, and tightening the rein when the neck's bend has reached the desired degree. This fault is most apt to occur in long, thin-necked horses. Unless a horse with this type of neck is so complacent that one need never take a strong feel on his mouth during exciting moments in the field, he is rarely of any value as a hunter. To develop a mouth which will not resent a "good feel," and a neck which will not "fold up" when the "good feel" is applied, are functions of sound training. Any well bred, worthwhile horse will "take hold" occasionally. If he can be brought back quickly to normalcy in the hot moments of sport, without rancor, frenzy or distortion of neck, he has a good mouth.

Sluggishness

The lazy colt often develops into an ideal mount. Sluggishness is usually the result of poor muscular development, feeding and conditioning. Little and mild exercise, along with good care and diet, probably will change the apparently lifeless horse into a free-going one, in from four to six months' time. Often colts do not arrive at their potential state of health and condition for eighteen months.

Shying

Leading the colt by a quiet, old horse and later riding him in such company during first mounted lessons, as has been recommended, usually prevent any tendency toward shying. In principle, one should never force a horse directly up to an object of which he obviously is afraid. To do so by pulling on the reins and attacking him with whip and spur will associate in his mind these punishments with the object of his fear, and so make matters far worse. Patient, quiet methods, and tact are required to avoid or cure the habit of shying. Both legs are used to keep the horse moving, at the speed adopted, past whatever causes the shying. Otherwise, as far as possible, all his demonstrations should be ignored and the rein effects are of minimum intensity. If he increases speed, he is not checked immediately but *after* he has passed the source of fright, and then very gently. The trainer should ride past the frightening object often, but to begin with, at such a distance that the colt has no pretext for shying. As the days go by he approaches and passes more closely until the colt ceases to be afraid.

Often shying is due, not to fear, but to playfulness. To ignore both insofar as possible is the best way to make the colt forget. Later on in life the trained horse can be held to his path by compelling him to "shoulder in." (See Chapter V.)

Playing Up

Every well bred, active colt will, from time to time, jump about and play up, notably on frosty mornings. This is an exhibition of a desirable quality and should not be brutally punished. The good rider simply tightens his lower legs and endeavors to push the horse straight ahead at his original rate and gait. If he is successful in this, there is little harm his mount can accomplish. As in shying, the legs must predominate over the hands, but to discourage playing up, which is a subjective matter, the hands are firmly fixed with increased tension until calm is restored. On the contrary, in shying, the hands do not increase their tension until past the fearsome object. When his efforts to bounce about prove themselves futile and he is firmly and surely repressed, the colt is soon bored with the mild discipline connected with playing up and goes about his business in a normal manner. Never punish good spirits brutally, and under no circumstances after play has ceased.

Rearing

When rearing is an accomplished fact, the rider must instantly loosen the reins, lean his trunk forward and wrap his arms about the horse's neck. *The moment after the horse begins to descend,* a quick, severe attack with the spurs should ensue. The reins should be left slack and the horse patted on the neck if he moves forward. Meanwhile the attack continues until a free gallop results, when the horse is brought down quietly to the gait desired, and calmed. The spurs must not be used until the horse's fore feet are coming to, or strike, the ground, and it is wise to seize the pommel with one hand when making the attack so as to avoid jerking the mouth, or being dislodged from the saddle.

If a horse is preparing to rear and it is impossible to drive him forward immediately, his effort is broken up by turning him with the leading rein and the spur on the same side to the right or left before he can halt and throw his weight onto his hind legs; a preparation necessary to rearing. Do not pull on both reins. Horses rarely, if ever, voluntarily fall over backwards. What usually occurs is this: the horse rears, the rider fails to lean forward quickly, loses his balance and pulls the horse over with the reins.

Cracking a bottle of water on top of the horse's head while he is in the air is fraught with danger. Psychologically correct, it can hardly be called equitation. Moreover "forward movement" in response to the spurs is what must be obtained. Its loss is the malady, rearing only a symptom.

Restless, Nervous Types

Horses are born with four general types of temperament: first, the sluggish type, which if also vicious, is of no value; second, the sluggish horse with a good disposition, which may be useful but rarely brilliant; third, the energetic, vicious animal, which is untrustworthy and will periodically display his vices; fourth, the energetic, good natured horse which is attentive and responsive in training and gives himself over with abandon after having gained confidence in his master.

Both of the last two types may be nervous. Hard

work and extreme firmness under a skillful trainer will usually make a useful, but untrustworthy, mount of the vicious, nervous type. His fretfulness and ugly temper must be sublimated by much exercise on the longe, followed by long, hard hours of mounted training. Generally, unless an outstanding performer, he is not worth the trouble. The best solution of such a problem is to be rid of the rascal.

With average horses that are nervous but not inherently vicious, longeing, patience and gentle treatment will accomplish the desired results. With these, the main, guiding idea is to proceed very slowly, doing work at the walk almost exclusively when mounted, until calmness is habitual. When nervousness exhibits itself during first mounted lessons, extreme lightness of hand must be exercised in order to instill confidence in the bit. Once such a horse has learned to go on the rider's hand with extended head and neck, the difficulty is past. To flex the poll aggravates a colt's nervousness. Daily work on the longe, followed by mounted work in the riding hall before being ridden out of doors, should be the normal routine with nervous, excitable horses. Few owners do this, but, as a trial will prove, the results are well worth the trouble.

Ingenuity, patience, gentleness and tact are indispensable in educating a well made, well bred, high-spirited, "going" colt, even when he has an excellent disposition. Longeing, long walks, leading, common sense, carefully avoiding early flexions, finally make these apparently nervous colts into the boldest and best horses. Sadly enough, in poor hands they are quickly ruined. To accustom them to noise, strange sights and circumstances is especially difficult, but the use of kindness and tidbits so that they associate these with the disturbing elements generally will eliminate fear. In the Army, pistols are fired at a distance, after which the remounts are immediately coaxed, or led, up to the firing point and fed oats. Soon they rush voluntarily at the first shot to the location of firing.

Horses that Jig

Shoulder-in (see Chapter V) is the exercise par excellence for correcting the annoying habit of jigging so frequently adopted by fretful horses, the direct causes of which are over-flexion and faulty head carriage. Usually resorted to when in the company of other horses or when returning to stables, it springs from lack of calmness and often calls for more schooling in basic essentials. As has been explained, the horse with an over-flexed neck is unable to make full use of the muscles which extend the fore legs and hence cannot take steps of full length. The consequent inability to keep abreast of the other horses at the walk, or to walk comfortably and freely when anxious to return to his stall, causes jigging. When held back by the rider's reins, nervousness and over-flexion are further accentuated.

By executing shoulder-in on an oblique line (*appuyer*) *on a long rein* with such a horse each time he breaks into jigging, and by maintaining this shoulder-in position until he resumes the walk, this habit finally can be abolished. The trainer should try to anticipate the jigging and compel first the right shoulder-in, and the next time, left shoulder-in, *before it starts.*

Since the cure for jigging lies in bending the neck sideways *without appreciably limiting its full extension,* the passive rein should be as long as possible and used only to a minimum in assisting the active rein to require the walk and maintain direction. At the first walking step, when jigging stops after the application of shoulder-in, both reins are given great length and the horse allowed to walk with a low head and extended neck, with the lightest contact. When jigging is again imminent, shoulder-in is reapplied.

The great extension of the neck, even while bent with one rein, permits long, low steps and leaves one shoulder entirely free. Furthermore it does not cause great discomfort such as prevails when both reins are used to pull the horse's head up and in. Usually perseverance with this practice will destroy any case of jigging provided the horse receives sufficient exercise to keep down his excess spirit. Longeing is very helpful and when the horse accepts his bit with low extended head and neck, jigging will cease.

Reluctance to Accept the Bit

Due to little impulsion, faulty conformation, delicate mouths or sluggishness, certain colts are very difficult to put on the bit. With these it is advisable to do some work *at the trot* on large curves and circles as soon as physical condition permits. The trot involves more impulsion and therefore is better suited to keep the horse on his forehand and in front of the rider's legs. Under these conditions he can be compelled to accept support.

While on the circle, the opening rein of the inside hand (toward the center of the circle) at first predominates, with a slight upward tension combined with the leading effect. The hand is held high, and goes higher if the colt raises his head. The trainer's inside leg (right, if the horse is circling to the right) is used as vigorously as necessary to drive the croup slightly outward to the left. The hind legs then must move on a somewhat larger circle than that travelled by the forehand. The horse, in order to do this, throws an abnormal preponderance of his weight on his fore legs ("puts himself on his forehand") so as to lighten the hindquarters and facilitate their covering more distance than that covered by the fore legs. To do this, he necessarily lowers and extends his head and neck, thus taking support on the right rein. The hand softly gives to permit this lowering of the "balancer," and a pat on the neck with the left hand at this instant helps to make the horse aware of the propriety of his gesture. This exercise is executed while moving on a circle to the right with first the right leading rein and later with the left bearing rein. The colt's head is turned inward on the circle with the right rein; while with the left it is turned outward. In both cases, the passive hand keeps the bit from slipping through the mouth and acts only to maintain direction and prevent an excessive bend in the neck. The bearing rein, also used from a high position, predominates when the left hand is used. After a descent of the head and neck, and support on the bit are secured, the colt is allowed to rest for a few minutes at the walk with a loose rein. Then the work is repeated on a circle to the left hand. Later, serpentines may be used.

In the beginning, the passive hand does very little, and consequently the head and neck may be turned more than is desirable, but after the colt learns to reach down and seek the bit against each rein employed individually, the trainer gradually may begin to take more support with the passive hand also. Before long, equal tension on both reins, first while on a circle or a serpentine, and later on a straight line, may be taken. As described before, the downward gestures in taking the bit should be made in a gentle, tentative manner, the hands elastically following the mouth with very light support. But if the head plunges violently downward, a firm tightening of the fingers of one hand and an inflexible fixing of the elbow joint, so that the mouth is bumped at the end of the thrust, will correct the horse. This disciplinary action is administered by both hands or one only. Accurate timing when immobilizing the hand and elbow to chastise the horse is necessary and requires practice. There is no jerking whatever; the hand simply is fixed in position.

In executing these exercises to put the horse on the bit, the rider's inside leg predominates, but very often both legs must act to sustain the gait and keep the horse on the forehand. Obedience to a single spur and a preliminary step toward shoulder-in are also taught.

Later in the breaking period, another and similar method of securing acceptance of the bit may be employed. The colt is required to take a long, quiet trot followed by a long, slow canter. As he begins to tire, he will lower his head and neck of his own accord and gratefully take support from the rider's hand. Up to this moment, the reins are very delicately stretched, for the colt should seek the bit without effort on the rider's part, except use of his legs to maintain impulsion. This is called "falling on the hand" and is of use after the physical condition of the colt permits considerable trotting and galloping. It is far preferable to the first method, unless the trainer is very experienced.

With all horses, old or young, which are reluctant to accept support, the hands should be held high, and well forward, *so that the reins act in a direction approximately parallel to the long axis of the horse's head* and put the bit, as it should be, in the corners of his mouth. This direction of the reins' tension does not use the head as a lever arm to over-flex the poll and prevent extension of the head and neck, as is the case when the hands are held low and near the withers. The trainer should ride far forward with fairly short reins and carefully follow the mouth.

With older horses an extended gait with strong impulsion should be forced by vigorous action of the rider's legs. If the horse tends to raise his head, the hands, from their high position, vibrate the bit smoothly through his mouth while maintaining a stronger than normal feel. (See "Faulty Position of the Head," pages 191 and 192.) As the head goes down, both the rider's legs drive the horse onward at a little faster rate so as to keep him "in front of the legs." Otherwise he generally follows the downward gesture by slowing the pace and throwing the head upward.

A horse "in front of the legs" is "on the bit." His

center of gravity seems to rest in front of and below the rider's knees, near the horse's elbows. In this condition of balance he remains on the hand and there is a sensation of committed forward movement sustained by great impulsion. This goes to an extreme when the horse becomes too heavy on his forehand as well as on the rider's hand. If the neck has not been over-flexed, such a horse can be quickly placed in better balance by appropriate exercises. One or two sharp "half-halts" (see Chapter V) with the hands high and forward, will suffice to lighten his forehand.

Recapitulation of Breaking

Thus in a period from two months to a year, the gentling, conditioning, longeing, mounting and riding at the walk, trot and canter with the simplest rein effects are accomplished and the horse is said to be "broken." His disposition is stable and friendly so that under all normal circumstances he remains calm. There is still some awkwardness in his movements since no suppling of spine, poll or jaw has been demanded. Some of the stiffness, which every colt when first mounted presents, will have disappeared although relaxation is far from complete. Stiffness causes resistance to the aids but as the colt reëstablishes his natural balance under the rider and relaxes under training exercises, both stiffness and resistance will disappear together. Already he accepts his bit with extended head and neck and has no fear of the rider's hands.

Only the walk has been extended. At the walk and trot, the colt is moderately well controlled on straight lines, circles, curves, broken lines and serpentines. He also canters calmly on circles and straight lines, taking either lead the rider calls for. His whole neck has become rather stiff and when feeling frisky he may occasionally pull, or attempt to "go through his bridle." Above all, strength and condition are greatly improved so that he bears the rider easily, even though somewhat clumsily, at all gaits. In addition, he has been accustomed to being led by the snaffle bridle, or work on the longe, across little ditches, logs and other obstacles. This schooling will be described fully in Chapter VI. The time has now arrived to begin his training proper.

CHAPTER V

Training

Objectives

HAVING laid a foundation of boldness and calmness and commenced the development of long, low strides at the walk and trot, the remaining qualities to be sought during the training period are: 1. suppleness; 2. relaxation; 3. balance; 4. agility; 5. the continuation of lengthening the stride at all gaits. In order to attain these objectives as features of perfect obedience, the horse, without having his calmness and boldness destroyed, must be completely subordinated to the aids. The three additional rein effects also will be taught in this period as gymnastic exercises require their use. The five rein effects are individually designated, in order to have some method of referring to the different actions of the hands and the reactions on the horse. While each effect is entirely distinct and definite in practice, the effects blend into each other and their reactions on the horse may be varied infinitely according to the amount of force employed and the direction of its application.

Suppleness, relaxation, agility and long, low strides are apparent to the layman. "Balance" or "equilibrium" is a hazy expression save to experienced horsemen who have the "feel" of it. "Impulsion," another vague term much used in the equestrian world, is the principal factor in obtaining efficient strides.

Impulsion

As defined in a French manual of equitation, "Impulsion is forward movement submitted to the discipline of the aids and exploited as desired in view of the objective to be attained." Impulsion varies greatly in individuals, and primarily relates to *the manner in which the horse moves.* Excellent natural impulsion is characterized by that ample, supple and springy action of the joints which gives an appearance of great momentum generated with but little effort. It is derived from the hindquarters, with the coxofemoral and hock joints as the prime agents. It has no connection with speed, for, as the French manual also states, one horse at a fast gallop may show little impulsion, whereas another at the walk displays a vast amount. Natural impulsion is easily discernible in a horse on a halter at the trot. His strides, if he has been congenitally blessed with this quality, are long, lithe, springy, effortless and powerful. When moving calmly with a free head, he travels close to the ground and flexes the hocks but little. Some horses, although lazy, have great natural impulsion. Their laziness makes them "leg" horses, heretofore mentioned, because much stimulation is required to provoke their impulsion. When the desire "to go" is associated with impulsion, a "hand" horse is the result. Providing he is well made, of good disposition and physically sound, he is one in a million, and superiority in the work to which he is adapted, be it hunting, jumping, high-schooling or polo, may be anticipated. Yet with such a horse, mistakes in training are costly.

Balance

Obviously all horses are balanced. Otherwise they would be continually falling down! It is a question of degree. Balance involves the factors of weight, manner of employment and amount of muscular energy, and the use of the head and neck as a balancer—upon the freedom of which, when the horse is mounted, so much importance has been placed. In considering the head and neck, their gestures are of first importance, although the position—high or low, extended or drawn in—materially affects balance and the proportionate distribution of weight on the fore and hind legs.

Briefly, good balance means that the horse is able to handle himself quickly, easily and gracefully in changing direction, checking, increasing speed, turning about, crossing difficult country, etc. It is of course greatly affected by conformation. A low-withered, straight-shouldered, high-crouped horse with a plunging back rarely will have it, and consequently will be an unsafe and unpleasant hunter or jumper, although he may serve satisfactorily as a hack.

Three Schools of Thought on Balance

Balance can be immeasurably improved by special gymnastic exercises. However, the artificial form of collection acquired through high-schooling is not suitable to improving the balance of these horses. In high-school collection the hocks are flexed, the croup lowered, the neck raised and the face brought in to an almost vertical plane. As noted heretofore such horses, unless also trained by gymnastics to improve their natural balance, are unable to handle themselves cleverly when given their heads and left to their own devices, and so are practically worthless for cross-country work.

The natural balance, improved by appropriate gymnastics which end in the horse's learning to collect or balance himself, is infinitely more valuable and reassuring out-of-doors to both horse and rider.

TRAINING

There is also another school of horsemanship which advocates almost nothing in the way of improving balance. This is equivalent to asserting that a boxer, football or tennis player, gymnast or any other type of athlete cannot improve his form, balance and ability by practicing selected gymnastic exercises.

The training herein seeks a modified natural equilibrium in between that of the artificial high-school and the other extreme of unmodified natural balance.

Evidently the untrained colt finds his natural equilibrium greatly disturbed when he first carries a load equal to one-sixth or more of his weight. *Hence in the breaking period it is obvious that he should be interfered with only to the absolute minimum necessary for control and to teach him to "go on his forehand."* A horse naturally carries about two-thirds of his own and the rider's weight on his fore legs. During the breaking period, while mounted, he was allowed to adopt his own readjustment of muscular effort with a view toward discovering the easiest way to perform his new and arduous task. However, after his strength and condition have been carefully built up, he can, and should, be aided in bettering his balance by intelligently selected exercises. This seems too manifest to merit argument. Horsemen who have ridden horses trained by all three methods know that schooling which assists the horse in readjusting his natural balance to the rider's weight, makes hunters, jumpers, hacks and polo ponies superior to those trained by the other methods.

Impulsion and balance are related and influence suppleness, relaxation, agility and the manner of moving. Conformation and temperament of course have great bearing on them all.

Agility

Agility, since it is improved by all the training exercises and especially by work across country, up and down hills and over broken terrain, will not be separately discussed. Jumping obstacles of all types, described in Chapter VI, is very beneficial to agility.

Purpose of Training Exercises

As will be pointed out in this chapter, certain exercises are more essential to particular types of conformation or temperament than others. Stiffness, with consequent resistance in the jaw, spinal column, shoulders and croup, is encountered to some extent in all colts. This resistance is not usually the result of stubbornness or vice, but of lack of balance, suppleness and relaxation coming from the colt's difficulty in accommodating himself to the rider's weight and demands. Certain gymnastics are designed to destroy it. Others improve balance inherently bad because of poor conformation and weakness. Again it is called to mind that the exercises themselves are *not ends, but means* by which all horses may be improved, therefore the trainer must analyze each horse and decide which are necessary in each case.

Cardinal Principles of Training

1. The execution of a particular movement means nothing unless the position and gestures of the horse display complete lack of stiffness and resistance.

2. Forward movement always remains a prime consideration. Prompt response to the legs should be demanded time and time again, and always after exercises not involving movement straight ahead.

3. No exercise should be initiated, or continued, until absolute calmness prevails. If, when teaching a new movement, excitement and resistance are met, calmness is first reëstablished; then simple and known movements, leading up to the one which provoked excitement, are rehearsed. After these are well performed, another trial at the new exercise is made, the trainer being sure that his aids are precise and clear to the horse.

4. Any new lesson should be undertaken at the end of the day's work. As soon as some success is obtained, the horse is immediately rewarded and led to the stable.

5. Boredom, caused by repeating over and over an

exercise which the horse has done to the best of his ability, should be avoided. A great part of equestrian tact resides in the trainer's ability to recognize the moment when the horse is *becoming* bored, resentful or tired. Get only one or two more steps of the movement at hand, then stop it for the time being. At some later date when the colt is older and better trained, a battle inevitably arises. The trainer's tact should inform him of the propitious time to accept the challenge and having accepted, he must win decisively, giving no quarter until the colt completely relinquishes the fight. No resentment should be harbored, and kindness instantly should recompense the colt's surrender.

6. With a very young colt, as with a very young child, attentiveness cannot be held for more than a few minutes at a time. Therefore lessons should be brief.

7. To be allowed to walk or stand on a loose rein is a reward greatly appreciated by the horse.

8. The trainer with tact feels from day to day for what new work the colt is prepared but never asks anything beyond his comprehension or which tests his strength and ability to the utmost.

At times training becomes discouraging because progress seems so small and slow. However, if one looks back to conditions a few weeks prior, he realizes that each day has brought some improvement. There are unfortunately many riders who lack the tact and observation to perceive the improvement made and who, in their impatience, are very demanding and energetic. These can ruin horses by the carload.

There is a great chasm between the knowledge of the true horseman who appreciates both equitation and horsemastership, and the ignorance of the person who simply rides for exercise. To the latter, the horse is merely a machine, and to the former the latter is merely obnoxious.

Improving Natural Collection and Longitudinal Balance

The first step in teaching natural collection *while mounted* was taken during breaking, by frequently alternating the normal and slow trot, the walk and trot, and the walk and halt. These exercises are elementary but suitable to the strength and knowledge of the young colt. They should be repeated over and over as soon as he is on his bit, and calm at all times. If restive at the halt, eliminate halting and work mostly at changing from the trot to the walk and vice versa; also at extending and slowing both gaits.

The exercises should be greatly elaborated on as training progresses. But if resistance or displacement of the head develops in halting, or slowing the rate, when working at faster gaits, similar work at slower paces should be resumed; in other words, more preparation is necessary. The halts, changes of gait, and of rate within gaits, are progressively made more difficult as follows: (a) from halt to slow trot, to normal trot, to extended trot, to normal trot, to slow trot, to halt; (b) from halt to normal trot, to extended trot, to normal trot, to halt; (c) from halt to extended trot, to halt. When the horse is fully prepared, he should come to the halt from the extended trot in about six or seven steps, but such tests are not attempted until after at least six months' mounted work. *The prompt moving out after a halt, and prompt increasing of speed after it has been reduced, are essential to teach the horse to collect himself.* Normally he very soon learns to check or halt with his hind legs advanced, ready to spring quickly forward.

After two or three months, these exercises at the trot are carried further embracing similar ones which include the gallop, as: (a) from canter to gallop, to extended gallop, back to canter; (b) from trot to canter, to extended gallop and reverse; (c) from canter to walk and reverse; (d) from canter to halt and reverse, etc., etc.; finally, from extended gallop to halt, to backing and reverse.

Even when halting or checking from the gallop, the head and neck should not be greatly displaced, although they will rise somewhat during a sudden check after the horse becomes well trained and flexes his poll in answer to the reins. Calmness is always the prime essential. If the horse is nervous, slow work and less abrupt changes in gait and rate are necessary. *The strides should be close to the ground when halting, checking and moving forward.* This will follow naturally if the neck is not over-flexed and the head is not pulled high in the air.

Utilized on straight lines to begin with, the exercises are later executed on broken lines, serpentines and circles. On curves and circles, the inside hind leg is forced to engagement still farther under the body as the horse halts or quickly decreases his speed. After a halt, frequent use of the bearing rein should be made upon moving forward so as to change direction quickly, thus improving agility.

Such gymnastics engage and strengthen the hocks; improve balance through rapid shifting of the weight from forehand to hindquarters and vice versa; alternately lengthen and shorten the horse's base of support; teach quick responses to the bit and legs; strengthen the loin and supple it vertically, while general muscular development follows as a matter of course. Gradually the horse learns to extend or retract, and to raise or lower his neck and head in order to assist himself in quickly shifting his balance.

Great care is necessary during rapid increases in speed to prevent simultaneous action of hands and legs. As training nears completion, their actions are very closely associated but never occur at exactly the same instant. It may be necessary in rare cases to continue resisting with the hands, and use the legs to force engagement of the hocks. This is the closest approach to contradictory effects permissible. In these exercises, soft, elastic hands are manifestly necessary.

As discussed in the chapter on Breaking, *quickly halting and slowing the gait are most beneficial exercises for horses heavy on the forehand and bit.* They teach them to shift more than the normal amount of weight to the hindquarters, thus engaging the hocks and lightening the forehand. With these horses, increasing speed and moving out from the halt should be done more slowly. On the other hand, *with those that do not readily accept support from the hand, or that are low and weak behind, the exercises involving extension at all gaits and the maintenance of impulsion are most essential.* Halting and decreasing gaits with this last type of horse should be done gradually.

Common sense and the colt's reactions determine how rapidly this work may progress to the final exercise where, in the course of seven or eight strides, the halt is executed from a fast, extended gallop, and the horse immediately passed into backing. This last step in longitudinal flexibility should not be attempted until the colt is well along in his training period; normally about eight months' time is a minimum with an unusually strong and obedient horse. If poorly done, the exercise has no value and proves that the horse is not properly prepared. Calmness, quick response to the reins, correct placing of head and neck, pronounced hock engagement, and the smoothness felt when a motor car is properly stopped by good brakes, are the tests of an excellent halt from a fast gallop. Obviously such a halt bears no resemblance to the brutal, distorted picture, presented by some cowboys and polo pony exhibitors, in which the horse's head is pulled high in the air, the under line of his neck is bulged out to the bursting point, and the hocks are crushed down beneath a hollowed loin—the ensemble presenting misery incarnated.

Similarly when moving from a halt into a fast speed, while it should be done very quickly, it must be smoothly progressive, just as a good motor car gathers momentum without jerkiness. As the horse's speed increases he is allowed more support to his mouth.

Again the caution is offered: do not progress from one step to the next higher until the first is executed with calmness, suppleness and balance. A slight increase in tension preceded by the oral warning "whoa" or "steady"—depending on whether it is intended to halt or decrease the gait—should effect the desired result.

At this point attention is invited to the futility of repeating "whoa," "whoa," "whoa," when the horse not only fails to halt, but when often the rider has no intention of stopping him. "Whoa" should mean "halt," and that alone. It is a warning and immediately thereafter, according to his age, condition and training, the colt should be brought to a more or less prompt and complete stop.

After the horse's mouth is made, as will be explained later, the fingers close and the hands are fixed in position once only, to decrease the gait or halt. At the instant the halt occurs, the fingers and elbow relax to reward the mouth. The habit of pulling and letting go, time after time, without securing any appreciable response, will quickly ruin any mouth and has no place in equitation. It conveys nothing intelligent to the horse as far as training goes, since he learns to associate the numerous pulls with rushing on as he pleases.

For horses which at speed throw too much weight on the bit and fore legs, the "half-halt" to be described later is the most useful remedy.

Rein Effects

The three additional rein effects, which will be employed in exercises described hereafter, are as follows (the right rein being used as an example).

Rein of Direct Opposition:

The right hand, held normally a few inches higher than the withers, is carried slightly to the right and drawn to the rear to a point where it becomes effective. The hand is then more or less fixed, thus bringing the horse's nose to the right and rear. The neck, perforce, bends to the right as a result, and the weight of the head and neck is thrown on the right shoulder. This impedes the action of the right shoulder and leg, and breaks the horse's equilibrium to the right. Automatically his hindquarters are forced around to the left. If he is at a halt, the action will turn him about in place; fore legs moving to the right, hind legs to the left.

If moving, the horse is forced to turn to the right. If through fear or obstinacy he resists, the right spur should be combined with the effect. The sharpness of the curve is regulated by the amount of tension on the right rein. The hindquarters being forced to the left, the turn is made more or less "on the forehand."

This is a powerful effect and should be taught all horses, as it is irresistible when the right leg, or spur, if necessary, also is used to force the hindquarters to the left.

The left hand gives passively to the front as the head turns to the right. It should not resist the action of the right rein, *unless* the horse bends his neck too far to the right, in which case the left rein becomes ac-

Direction of movement.

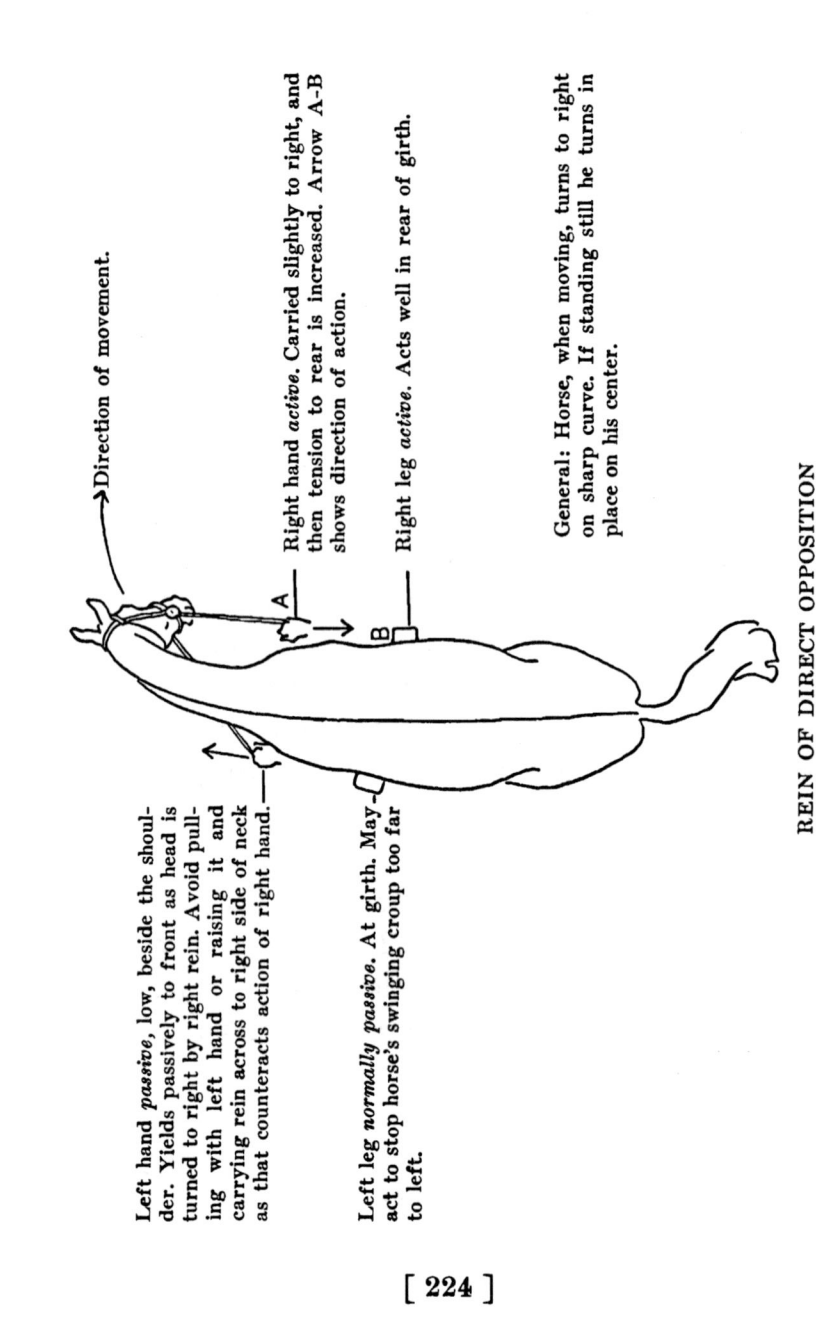

Right hand *active*. Carried slightly to right, and then tension to rear is increased. Arrow A-B shows direction of action.

Right leg *active*. Acts well in rear of girth.

General: Horse, when moving, turns to right on sharp curve. If standing still he turns in place on his center.

Left hand *passive*, low, beside the shoulder. Yields passively to front as head is turned to right by right rein. Avoid pulling with left hand or raising it and carrying rein across to right side of neck as that counteracts action of right hand.

Left leg *normally passive*. At girth. May act to stop horse's swinging croup too far to left.

[224]

REIN OF DIRECT OPPOSITION
Sketch 3

TRAINING

tive and limits the bend as necessary. (See Sketch.) With a horse heavy on the forehand and inclined to pull, the right hand, held high, also should raise his head, thus lightening the load on the shoulders.

Rein of Indirect Opposition in *Front* of the Withers:

The right hand, slightly raised, is carried across the neck to the left, *in front of the withers,* and then tension is applied to *left rear.* (See arrow in Sketch.)

The horse's nose is pulled *to the right and rear,* while the mass of head and neck is forced against the *left* shoulder, impeding its action and tending to break his equilibrium toward the left.

If the horse is standing still, *the rein of opposition in front of the withers* tends to push the shoulders around to the left rear, and the hindquarters, due to the movement of the shoulders, are automatically forced to the right front, the horse turning in place on his center.

If moving, the horse turns to the left, the sharpness of the turn being regulated by the amount of tension on the right rein. In turning sharply to the left, the left rein can also aid by acting to the left rear, and *parallel* to the right rein. As the horse becomes well trained, the left rein should become more and more passive.

Direction of movement.

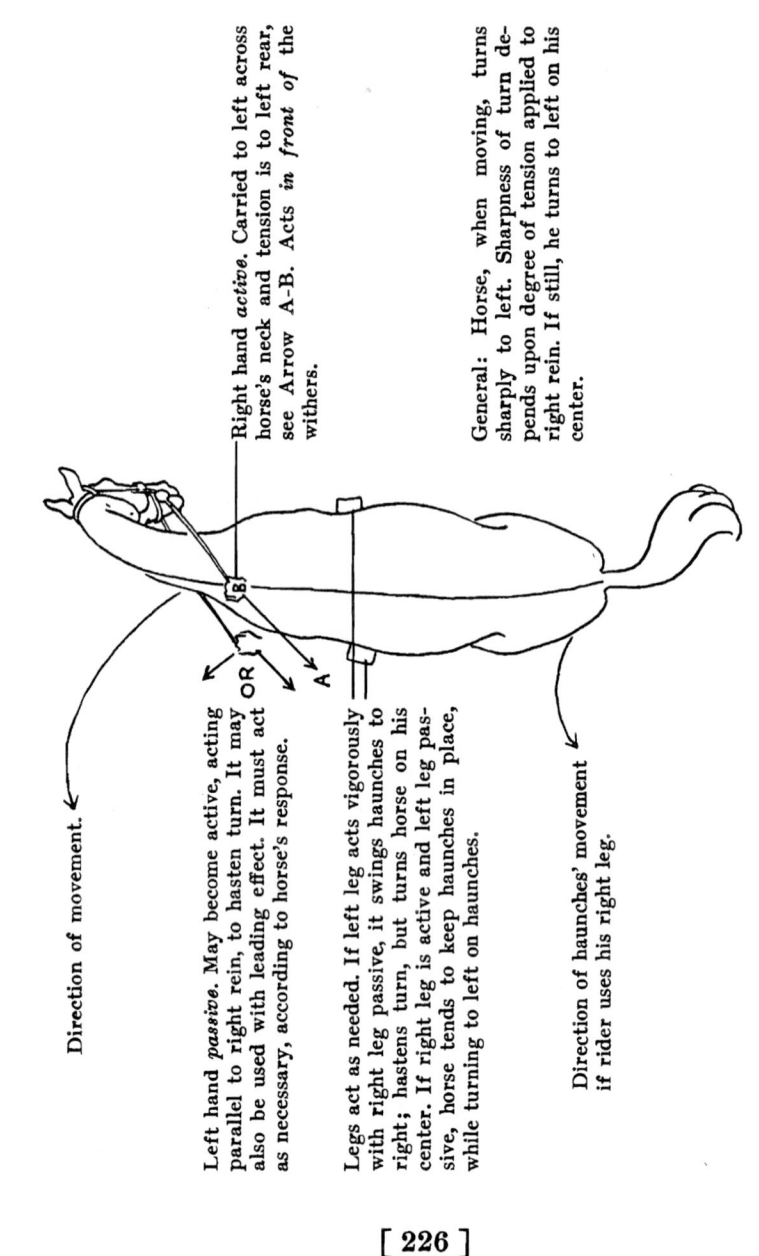

Left hand *passive*. May become active, acting parallel to right rein, to hasten turn. It may also be used with leading effect. It must act as necessary, according to horse's response.

Legs act as needed. If left leg acts vigorously with right leg passive, it swings haunches to right; hastens turn, but turns horse on his center. If right leg is active and left leg passive, horse tends to keep haunches in place, while turning to left on haunches.

Direction of haunches' movement if rider uses his right leg.

Right hand *active*. Carried to left across horse's neck and tension is to left rear, see Arrow A-B. Acts *in front of* the withers.

General: Horse, when moving, turns sharply to left. Sharpness of turn depends upon degree of tension applied to right rein. If still, he turns to left on his center.

REIN OF INDIRECT OPPOSITION IN FRONT OF THE WITHERS
Sketch 4

[226]

TRAINING

The rider can force the horse to turn on his center by using his left leg to push the croup to the right. If, however, he is teaching a "turn on the haunches," the *right* leg acts well in rear of the girth to keep the haunches inside and prevent their swinging out on the turn. This rein effect is used to turn a trained horse when the reins are held in one hand, as in polo.

Rein of Indirect Opposition, in *Rear* of the Withers:

The right hand is kept to the right of the withers, although the rein acts obliquely to the rear and left, toward the horse's left hip. The rider's right leg is active and helps drive the horse's hindquarters to the left. *His head is drawn to the right and rear; the neck and backbone are curved to the right, forcing the mass of the horse against his left hip and hind leg, while increasing the weight borne by the left shoulder, as well.*

The left rein is normally passive, but may act parallel to the right rein, or, more often, as a "leading rein," to assist in moving the horse to the left front. (See Sketch.)

The right leg, and the right rein of indirect opposition in rear of the withers, have a powerful, dominating effect. A moving horse, when "bent around the right leg" by their action, is overbalanced to the left, and must move diagonally to the left front crossing his front and hind legs respectively, to retain his equi-

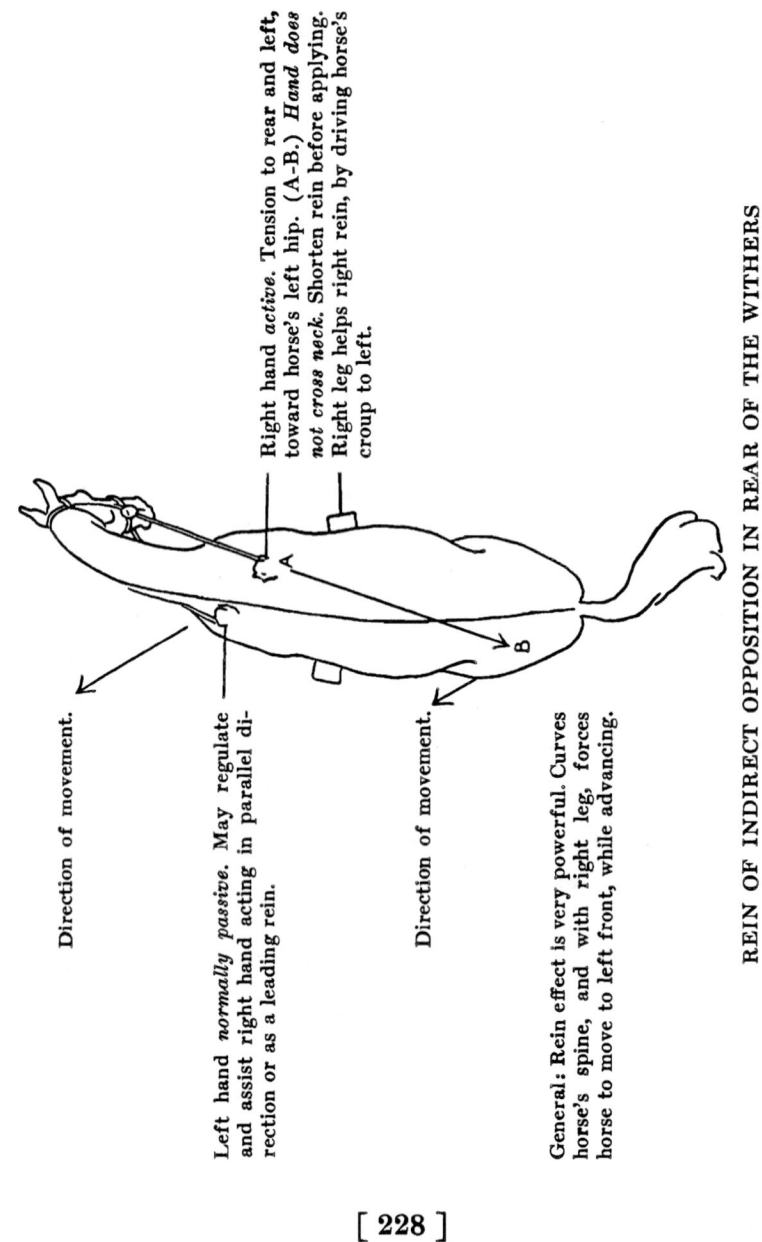

Right hand *active*. Tension to rear and left, toward horse's left hip. (A-B.) *Hand does not cross neck*. Shorten rein before applying. Right leg helps right rein, by driving horse's croup to left.

Direction of movement.

Left hand *normally passive*. May regulate and assist right hand acting in parallel direction or as a leading rein.

Direction of movement.

General: Rein effect is very powerful. Curves horse's spine, and with right leg, forces horse to move to left front, while advancing.

[228]

REIN OF INDIRECT OPPOSITION IN REAR OF THE WITHERS

Sketch 5

librium. It is impossible for a well trained horse to resist their action, or to shy toward the right when these "aids" are applied. His whole body is bent like a bow, the rein and rider's arm forming the tightened string. When moving, he is forced to chase his own balance toward the left front.

The Half-Halt

The half-halt is used to lighten the forehand of horses which, as a result of poor conformation, impetuosity, or physical defects, lean heavily on the hand, or carry the head too low after their physical condition no longer requires it. Even the best trained horses, for one reason or another, occasionally need correcting by means of the half-halt.

It is executed as follows: the fingers are firmly closed on the stretched reins, after which the hands are rotated inward and upward, with the little fingers moving toward the rider's breast. This is accomplished by vigorous rearward and upward twists of the wrists and forearms. The half-halt applies a quick, sharp reaction to the horse's mouth. Since contact with the mouth is not lost due to the taut reins, the reaction differs from a brutal jerk with a loose rein. The effect is to make the horse quickly lift his neck and head, throw more weight onto his hindquarters, thus lighten his forehand and prevent his boring against the bit.

The hands momentarily release all support after a half-halt and then establish the light normal feel. The half-halt may be executed with one or both reins. It is well to change about each time and use it as often as necessary. Needless to say half-halts are not employed against very green colts.

When a horse rounds his whole neck far over so that his face passes in rear of a vertical plane, the hand, or hands, must be carried far forward over the poll when administering the half-halt. This will lift and extend his head and neck, whereas, as explained in Chapter IV, if the hands are low and near the withers, the half-halt, due to the lever arm formed by the head in relation to the neck, pulls the horse's nose closer to his breast. *Half-halts are used to lighten the forehand without decreasing the speed.* They are not concerned with halting.

Extending the Trot

In extending the trot correctly, the horse takes a progressively stronger support on the bit as his speed increases. The hands must provide this support smoothly and elastically, as the strides lengthen in answer to the energetic action of the rider's legs. With practice, the trotting strides become gradually longer, until after several months a maximum extension for the particular horse is attained. Depending on the indi-

An excellent picture of controlled, light and balanced movement.

A trained horse at extended trot. Note balance, calmness, lightness, impulsion and gracefully placed head. With green colts the head and neck should be lower and more extended at this gait.

vidual, there is necessarily more or less increase in the rapidity of the strides, but their lengthening is the objective. The rider feels that the strong impulsion demanded by his legs is allowed to escape through his hands in a regulated, cadenced manner. He also feels that the horse's balance depends largely on the steady, elastic support of his hands. As the horse, through training, becomes relaxed, the flexibility of his poll assists the rider's elasticity of hands in maintaining continuous contact. The support is never a heavy pull.

This exercise confirms bold forward movement on the bit and requires powerful extension and contraction of the hocks and other joints of the limbs. At first it should be practiced on straight lines, later on large curves, serpentines and circles. To post on the outside diagonal, during curves, so as to use the inside leg upon coming into the saddle, throws the horse's croup outward a trifle and helps lengthen the stride, through lowering his head and neck. Where frank support of the bit is not taken, maximum extension often cannot be gained on straight lines. In these cases work on a big circle, with the haunches mobilized as described, expedites improvement.

Since the extended trot is very strenuous, it should be used for short distances and only on soft, level footing. It is purely a gymnastic and disciplinary exercise which, in addition to the benefits enumerated, tends to lengthen and lower the horse's stride at the normal trot.

With a horse "heavy in front," extending the trot should be done very gradually, while decreases in speed, halts and backing from the extended trot should be executed quickly. These combinations, along with half-halts while the horse is extended, will lighten the forehand and by degrees permanently improve balance.

The Extended Gallop

Extending the gallop out of doors is most beneficial to the lungs and muscles. It is started as soon as a few months' work have brought good physical condition. Just as with the extended trot, soft, level footing is necessary and the full extension is worked up to very gradually to avoid strains. As the horse extends he should rest more and more frankly on the bit, while the rider, who should ride well forward with his weight sunk into his heels, follows with his hands the large oscillations of the head. There should be no sudden throwing away of the reins and wild scampering ahead. The horse is required to remain under perfect control, to increase his speed progressively in answer to the rider's legs, and to realize that no initiative in the rate of increase is his. To lengthen the strides is the prime objective.

At first the extensions are over very short distances;

both speed and distance being augmented as strength increases. Many changes of rate from a slow to an extended gallop, and the reverse, enhance balance.

The extensions should be very gradually made with impetuous horses or those heavy in front, whereas the decrease in speed should be quickly performed. The procedure is reversed for horses lacking impulsion, lazy or reluctant to accept the bit.

A brief stretch at the extended gallop opens wide the lungs and so develops them. It is only necessary to go a short distance two or three times a week at extreme extension in order to receive full benefit for the colt. Three to five hundred yards on level, soft footing, will be ample.

Backing

As a general rule, instruction in backing should not begin until the colt, after several months' work, has learned to go calmly on his bit at the extended trot. Dropping back of the bit and legs is the source of all such vices as rearing, whirling, balking and refusing obstacles. Therefore, until perfectly confirmed in bold, calm, forward movement on the bit, no backing whatever is required. Fretful, nervous individuals or those loath to accept the bit should not be backed until their faults are completely corrected.

Unless the trainer is experienced, it is better from

all points of view to back the horse at first while dismounted. This is done by taking a rein in each hand just in rear of his mouth while facing the horse, quietly lowering his head and gently forcing him one step backward. The first step may be expedited if, while working with the reins, the trainer lightly steps on the colt's foot near the coronet until he withdraws it. At the first step, the reins are slackened and the colt's neck patted. Do not pat the face; no horse likes it.

Backing is of no value unless quietly and correctly performed. *To prove calmness and relaxation, the steps should be long, low, regular and slow.* Thus done, it is an excellent disciplinary exercise and as a gymnastic, supples greatly the spinal column, coxo-femoral and hock joints. The head should be very low so that the hindquarters are lightened. Backing with the head held high is a severe strain to the loin and hocks of even an old and thoroughly trained horse.

Preparatory to backing while mounted, the horse's head is first lowered, and he is pushed up lightly against the bit. The rider's legs then continue to act gently until the horse is on the verge of stepping forward. At this instant the legs become passive and while balance is still unstable, the reins compel the horse to step backward. In this manner, backing is initiated by forward movement. Only one or two steps should be required at the first lesson and the number

Backing with low head carriage. Correct method with green or partly trained colts.

Backing. Correct head carriage for *trained* horse while backing. Rider's body is inclined forward.

TRAINING

slowly increased on following days. Later, backing on circles and broken lines, which supples the joints still more, may be undertaken. In doing these exercises the reins are carried to the right (or left) and, just as balance is disrupted sidewards, additional tension requires backward movement.

The secret of teaching willing and calm backing lies *in rewarding each step by momentary relaxation of the fingers.* The forward inclination of the rider's body must be maintained in order to free the horse's loin of weight. The hands and legs do not act simultaneously. After pushing the horse up against his bit the legs remain passive except when their use is necessary to keep the croup from deviating to the right or left, or to stop the backward movement. The knees pinch the saddle more tightly and the heels are forced down to prevent dislocation of the seat. When the legs close to stop the backing, the fingers relax entirely.

If, after the horse's head is lowered into a correct position and the mouth softened, he resists the reins and stands fast, a single rein may be used to turn the head a trifle to one side. Then with equal tension on both reins, another effort to move him backward is made. If, for example, the head is turned to the right, the tension tends to force the left hind leg back and to the left (technically speaking, the right shoulder is opposed to the left haunch). When a step is obtained, although not directly to the rear, reward is prompt and the exercise is repeated with the head turned to the left. Later backing directly to the rear without resistance is easily obtained.

Hurried, quick steps demonstrate nervousness and fear of the bridle. Such a horse is not on the hand and should be at once urged forward by the legs. When calmness again prevails, he is halted, *backed one step only,* and moved forward immediately at the walk. If still nervous, what is needed is sufficient training to put him calmly on his bit before again attempting to back. This may be a question of days or weeks.

Half-Turn in Reverse
(See Diagrams, Page 237)

The half-turn in reverse may be used: 1. to teach obedience to the action of a single rein of direct opposition (this is simply traction, or resistance, to the rear with one rein, see Diagram, page 224); 2. to teach displacement (mobilization) of the croup relative to the forehand in obedience to the action of one of the rider's legs (for example, the croup should move to the left when the rider uses his right leg alone); 3. to lighten the croup at the expense of the forehand; 4. to aid in putting a horse on his bit; 5. to bend and soften the neck laterally; 6. to assist in flexing the jaw; 7. to begin instruction in shoulder-in (see page 253, Chap-

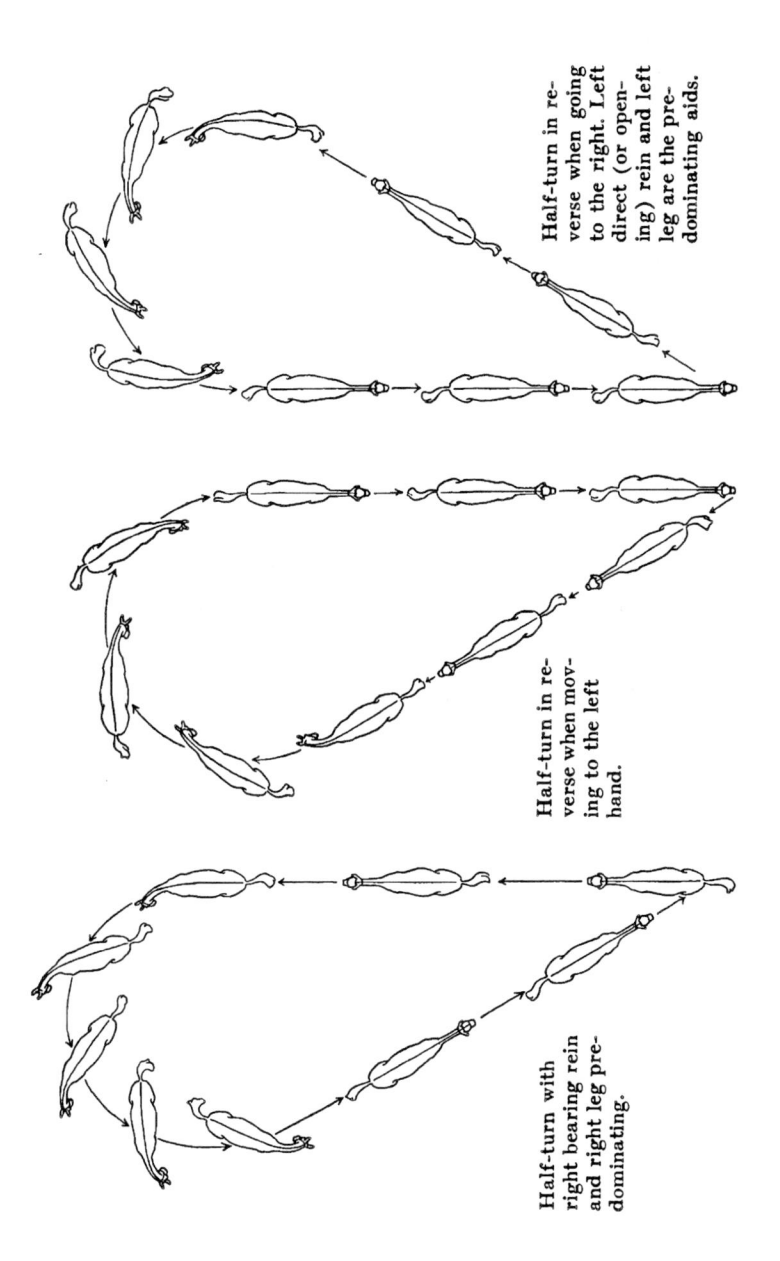

Half-turn in reverse when going to the right. Left direct (or opening) rein and left leg are the predominating aids.

Half-turn in reverse when moving to the left hand.

Half-turn with right bearing rein and right leg predominating.

ter V); 8. to supple the spine laterally; 9. to assist in flexing the poll; 10. to teach the "turn on the forehand."

Thus it is seen that: horses not definitely ahead of the legs and on the bit from any cause whatever; those stiff and resisting in jaw, poll, neck or spine; or those which, from ignorance, stiffness or willfulness are disobedient to the action of a single leg, may be improved by this simple exercise. While originally designed for use in an enclosure, the half-turn in reverse can, and should, be practiced out of doors. Assuming, for simplicity in discussion, that it is performed *while marching to the right hand in an enclosure,* the half-turn in reverse is executed as follows: at any selected spot while moving forward on a straight line, the horse is directed (by the bearing or opening rein) on an oblique of forty-five degrees. Upon arriving at a point varying from one to ten or more yards to the right of the wall (or of his original path) the trainer turns his horse to the left on a half-circle back to his original line of march. Upon reaching it, he will be going, of course, to the rear in relation to his original direction. The turn-about, upon leaving the oblique line, is started by using the left (inside) leading rein which, as soon as the horse begins to turn, is changed into a direct effect of opposition by traction to the rear. (This effect may be further strengthened, if the horse's shoulders bear in toward the center of the arc, by changing from the direct rein to that of indirect opposition in front, or in rear, of the withers. See pages 225 and 227.) The rider's left (inside) leg also becomes active as the turn begins and ranges the haunches to the right (outward). The right (outside) rein gives passively until the head is turned sufficiently inward, whereupon it assists as necessary, usually with an opening effect, to keep the horse on a semicircle and prevent his cutting in toward the center of the arc.

The left direct rein (a lateral effect) can compel the horse's neck to bend to the left. The bend, or too sharp a turn, to the left, can be limited by the right rein. The left (inside) leg, if used vigorously, can compel obedience and force the croup outward over a larger arc than that traversed by the forehand. This results in a lightening of the croup and resultant weighting of the fore legs, which, in turn, causes the horse to lower his head and neck. If both the rider's legs sustain impulsion, the horse, in the condition of balance in which he finds himself, is forced ahead of the rider's legs and onto his bit. As he learns to do the exercise calmly, the spine also will be bent laterally and suppled accordingly.

Vibration of the bit while on the semicircle, combined with the action of the inside leg, hastens relaxation of the jaw. As usual, the moment the mouth opens, the fingers cease resisting for a moment to reward obedience. After the mechanics of the exercise are taught at the walk, the slow trot is generally the most satisfactory gait for the practice of this exercise since impulsion is more easily maintained and the rider can sit steadily enough to apply his aids with precision. If the seat is insecure it is better to post at the trot or do the exercise at the walk.

If the trainer fixes and resists with both hands momentarily toward the right rear, while the neck is bent laterally, flexion of the poll is induced.

The fingers should soften as the left fore crosses in front of the right while on the half-circle. The inside leg is used intermittently in mobilizing the croup and acts just before the left hind foot leaves the ground in order to make it pass across, and in front of, the right hind. In more advanced stages of training, this exercise may be used while at the false gallop.

With a little thought and practice the rider can learn to apply his aids at the moment when their action is most effective. Each obedience to action of leg or spur immediately is rewarded by a cessation of the action until again required—just as the fingers soften to reward the mouth's concessions.

Turns and Half-Turns on the Forehand

As a half-turn in reverse is diminished to its minimum size, it becomes a "half-turn on the forehand." Executed at the walk, one fore leg marks time approximately in place while the other fore leg and the croup circle about it. Properly done, it is an excellent gymnastic and develops perfect obedience to a single leg. The horse necessarily learns to concentrate his weight on the inside fore leg while the other three legs are very mobile. The easiest method of executing the movement to the left follows: while executing a half-turn in reverse, the radius is greatly reduced, and increasingly more mobility is required of the haunches. Finally the oblique is eliminated and the horse brought to a halt for a fleeting instant. At that instant the left direct rein (or indirect rein in *rear, or in front,* of the withers, according to how the horse reacts) is used to oppose the left shoulder to the croup. The left rein's action also turns the head a trifle to the left while the rider's left leg at the same time pushes the croup to the right. The right rein, by tension to the right rear at first, assists the left rein in holding the left shoulder opposed to the croup. It then is used with a bearing effect to keep the weight of the head and neck on the left shoulder. Both reins soften at each step in time to permit the right fore leg to cross over in front of the left, but at the next instant when the left fore starts to move toward the left front, the right bearing rein changes again to a direct effect to the right rear.

Thus, combined with the left direct rein at each step it prevents the left fore's advancing. The left fore consequently marks time more or less in place in the regular cadence of the walk as the right fore circles around it.

The rider's left leg acts, as the right fore foot advances, to persuade the left hind (which moves immediately after the right fore) to step across in front of the right hind. In résumé: the right fore leg must have freedom to cross in front of the left fore; the left fore must be allowed to start its step, then be checked by the reins at the same instant the rider's left leg presses the croup to the right. The reins act: 1. both more or less to the right rear; 2. left softens and right uses bearing effect; 3. both again to the right rear. Of course, tension and direction vary infinitely according to the horse's conformation and reactions.

The rider's right leg limits the croup's displacement and sustains impulsion. Normally if held lightly against the horse's side it will perform its duties.

The movement should appear smooth, free and cadenced, not stilty and jerky.

The art of correctly executing the turn on the forehand rests in the intermittent action of the aids, and in the correct balancing of their intensities, so that they blend into a singleness of purpose. Rhythm and smoothness constitute the beauties.

TRAINING

Half-turns in reverse and the gallop false are similar exercises. The same aids predominate and the effects on the horse's balance and movement are almost identical. Long, relaxed strides are necessary with both to supple and balance him. Both tend to lower his head and put him on his forehand.

A half-turn on the forehand faces the horse about one hundred and eighty degrees. A turn on the forehand is through three hundred and sixty degrees.

The Half-Turn
(See Diagrams, Pages 237 and 244)

The half-turn, also originated for use in a manège, may be utilized as well out-of-doors. Its purposes are: to gain, through obedience to a single leg, both control and engagement of the hindquarters; lightness of the forehand at the expense of the hindquarters; control of the forehand by the rein of indirect opposition both in front and in rear of the withers; to teach the turn on the haunches; to improve general agility.

In executing *a half-turn to the right,* for example, the horse is required to leave the path on which he is travelling and traverse a half-circle to the right. The radius at first should be large, but as the horse gains experience, it may be gradually reduced until executed with one hind foot marking time in place, called the "half-turn on the haunches." There are two types

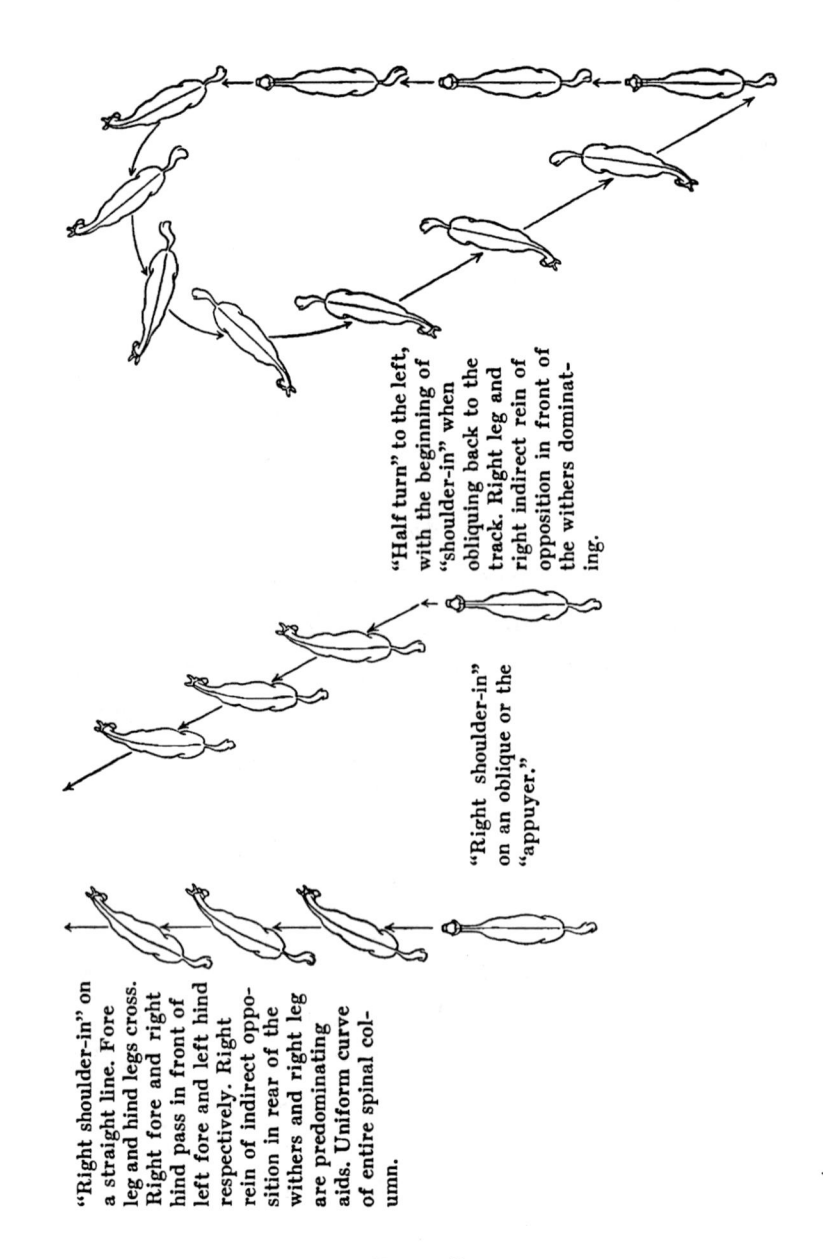

"Right shoulder-in" on a straight line. Fore leg and hind legs cross. Right fore and right hind pass in front of left fore and left hind respectively. Right rein of indirect opposition in rear of the withers and right leg are predominating aids. Uniform curve of entire spinal column.

"Right shoulder-in" on an oblique or the "appuyer."

"Half turn" to the left, with the beginning of "shoulder-in" when obliquing back to the track. Right leg and right indirect rein of opposition in front of the withers dominating.

[244]

of half-turns on the haunches which will be explained below.

In leaving the track, the rider's outside (left) leg, used a little in rear of the cinch, predominates in order to hold the horse's hind legs engaged under his body during the entire half-circle. As a result they travel over an arc smaller than that described by the fore legs. To facilitate this movement the horse lightens his forehand by throwing additional weight on his haunches, and tends to raise slightly his head and neck. The left bearing rein initiates the half-turn and is assisted as necessary by the right opening rein. In the event that the horse fails to respond readily to these effects and swings around on too big an arc, the left bearing rein becomes the left indirect rein of opposition in front of the withers (see page 225, Chapter V); while the right opening rein becomes one of direct opposition with resistance toward the right rear (direct rein). After completing the half-circle the horse is straightened between the legs and reins, and ridden on an oblique line back to his original path, upon reaching which he is travelling to the rear, relative to his original direction.

This exercise, as stated, may be practiced by using either the left bearing rein or the left rein of indirect opposition in front of the withers. The latter effect usually is called for when the half-turn becomes sharp on a semi circle of small radius, similar to a turn on the haunches as executed by a good polo pony. The rider's inside leg assists in controlling the croup and maintaining impulsion.

Turns and Half-Turns on the Haunches

To execute the half-turn on the haunches to the right, the radius of the half-turn is reduced until the fore legs turn one hundred eighty degrees about the right (inside) hind foot which, as a pivot, marks time in place. It is accomplished as follows: the horse is brought almost to a halt; the right rein, with an opening effect, leads the forehand to the right, but during the first step of the right fore foot, it changes to a direct effect to the right rear, and is reinforced by the left rein's traction to the right rear in front of the withers (rein of indirect opposition in front of the withers). Thus the two reins swing the right fore out to the right with no advance, and oppose the left shoulder to the right haunch which prevents the right hind foot's advancing. As the right fore swings to the right, the rider's left leg, in rear of the cinch, pushes the left hind in front of and across the right hind. The rider's right leg, an instant after the left has acted, resists in order to prevent the right hind's stepping to the right. The tension on the reins is softened momentarily in time to permit freedom to the left fore as it

THE TURN ON THE HAUNCHES TO THE LEFT, OR PIROUETTE

Left hind foot is raised and put down on same spot. Right fore has just crossed in front of left fore.

Horse pivoting on left hind foot which marks time in place.

steps across *in front of* the right fore (otherwise it may interfere with, or move in rear of, the right fore). The left rein is used with a bearing effect during the left fore's step across.

In résumé: at each step of the right fore, the right shoulder is restrained and the foot swings as a result of the reins' resistance, to the right and rear. In other words, they first overbalance the shoulders to the right and then oppose them to the croup. At each step of the left fore, the tension on both reins is lightened so that it may be free to step in front of the right, and the left bearing effect replaces the left rein's effect of indirect opposition. At this same time the rider's left leg becomes active and its effect, of pushing the left hind across in front of the right, is checked and limited by the rider's right leg in time to hold the right hind in place. These actions, occurring at each step, are barely visible to the onlooker, since the movements of the legs, hands and fingers are slight.

A turn on the hindquarters, still more valuable as a gymnastic, is started while backing. Executed, for example, to the right, the horse pivots on the *outside (left) hind leg, with the right hind circling around and in rear of it, while the left fore steps across and in front of the right fore.* The aids employed are similar to those in the half-turn on the haunches previously described, where the *inside (right) hind leg is the pivot.* The main difference in the aids in the second exercise is that the rein effects are stronger *so as to back the horse around the pivot.*

This exercise, when the horse is soft and relaxed, supples and engages the outside (pivot) hind leg more than any other. It is only taught after backing is perfectly executed, and is led up to by backing around a circle with the haunches held engaged toward the circle's center.

If one step is well executed (this applies to the turns on the forehand as well) the horse is halted and caressed. The exercises may be fairly well taught in a few days if the hands and legs are used so as to *actually aid* the horse's movements. Inability to use the aids as indicated, at the appropriate moments, confuses the horse, causing him to resist, interfere, and become nervous.

Comparison of Half-Turn and Half-Turn in Reverse

Both the half-turn and half-turn in reverse, as has been seen, teach, to some extent, obedience to the action of a single rein and single leg. The former, however, is primarily an exercise designed to lighten the forehand at the expense of the hindquarters, while the latter weights the forehand, puts the horse on the bit and lightens the hindquarters. The half-turn in reverse should be taught first, and may be employed early in the breaking period with colts which are reluctant to accept the bit. The half-turn, on the contrary, is partly the answer to the problem presented by a horse heavy and over-balanced on the forehand. Either mobilizing or engaging the haunches may be performed on complete circles. However, the half-turn and half-turn in reverse have more instructional value for young horses as they require a change from the dominating effects of a single rein and leg to straight ahead movement. This brings responsiveness to delicate changes in the aids and repeats the basic lesson of frank forward movement. Work on complete circles is taken up when the horse nears the completion of his education.

"Appuyer" or Shoulder-In While Obliquing

In the half-turn to the right, for example, advantage may be taken of the movement back to the track on an oblique line to keep the horse's head turned outward with the left rein of indirect opposition in rear of the withers, while continuing the action of the outside leg so as to make him cross his fore and hind feet with his body set obliquely to the line of movement. This is a mild form of shoulder-in, called in French, the *"appuyer."* (See Diagrams, page 244.)

Both the half-turn and half-turn in reverse, when executed out-of-doors, may be interchanged as to execution. For example, on the half-turn, the haunches may be thrown outward, while on the half-turn in reverse, they may be engaged. In an enclosure the wall interferes somewhat with this reversed procedure whereas it aids in the execution of the movements in the normal manner first described above.

Circles
Suppling the Spinal Column

Work on a circle, particularly at the gallop, is the most effective exercise for suppling the spinal column. As the colt becomes well balanced, the speed at the trot and true gallop on circles should become progressively faster. This makes the horse agile and clever at fast work. Circling at slow speeds is no longer difficult and has little further value. Also the circle should be gradually reduced in diameter without decreasing the speed. On the other hand, the speed on circles at the *false gallop* should be very slow, since this requires excellent balance and great suppleness, and is much more difficult for the horse than if moving quite fast.

If a horse cuts into the circle *with his shoulder leading,* it is accomplished by either an increase or decrease in speed. *If by an increase,* restrain him and carry his shoulders outward in front of his hindquarters with both reins, the outside one acting with direct opposition and the inner one with indirect opposition in front of the withers. They remain approximately parallel to each other. If he is stubbornly disobedient, require shoulder-in of the inside shoulder and push him outward onto his circle with determined action of the inside leg. Raise the inside hand high when using the rein of indirect opposition to prevent cutting in on a curve. Upward tension, or a half-halt, takes weight off the disobedient shoulder. If he cuts into the circle *over a shoulder by decreasing the speed,* drive him with both legs and carry the shoulders over in front of the croup with both reins, as in the preceding case.

In general, in all types of resistance where the croup is deviated, the forehand should be carried over in front of the hindquarters by the rein effects just described, rather than by attempting to push the croup over in rear of the forehand with one leg. The latter action destroys impulsion and provokes other defenses. Moreover direction of movement should be governed by the forehand.

If the horse *carries his croup inward on the circle* (or a curve) the rider, as a result of not riding forward in balance, is probably pulling on the reins too heavily. If the horse *throws his croup outward on the circle,* the speed is probably too great for his strength and balance, and should be reduced.

Horses heavy in front should be required to work on circles with the haunches in; those behind the bit and

Shoulder-in at trot; horse moving on straight line directly toward camera; entire body oblique to line of movement and bent in an arc about rider's left leg; left fore in process of crossing in front of right fore. Left leg and left rein of indirect opposition in rear of withers dominating aids.

Appuyer or shoulder-in at trot; horse moving obliquely to his right front; spinal column bent around rider's left leg; head turned away from direction of movement. Note crossing of hind legs. Best of all gymnastic exercises.

lacking in impulsion with the haunches ranged outward. The false gallop is an excellent exercise for the latter types.

Keeping the horse's head turned inward while working on the circle is occasionally beneficial as a gymnastic and disciplinary exercise, but should not be insisted on normally except at the false gallop. It is unnatural, impedes the inside shoulder, shortens the stride and instigates resistance. Generally a show jumper is greatly annoyed if his head is pulled inward. Consequently he will pull and have less time to concentrate on the obstacles. His spine should be kept straight in turning corners if he is attempting to cut them, and the rider's legs must keep him up to his bit, so that his hind legs will not be "sprawled out" to the rear when he faces the next obstacle. In doing this, however, the rider should "stay forward."

Shoulder-In
(See Diagrams, Page 244)

One of France's most brilliant horsemen of former days, Guérinière, stated that shoulder-in, because of its many virtues, ought to be the first lesson and the last lesson in training. However, it is a little easier to lead up to this truly great gymnastic by half-turns in reverse and half-turns as preparatory work. Therefore, as soon as the horse is proficient in ranging his haunches on half-turns in reverse and serpentines, and will cross his fore and hind feet when obliquing to the track in completing half-turns, instruction in shoulder-in should begin.

Taking right shoulder-in as an example; the horse is bent symmetrically throughout his spinal column, from poll to point of croup, around the rider's right leg, and moves toward his left front with his body set obliquely to the line of motion. This requires him at each step to cross his fore and hind feet, respectively. The movement is obtained by: 1. shortening the right rein; 2. beginning a turn to the right with the right opening rein; 3. just as the horse's forehand is led off the straight line which he has been following, the leading rein is changed into a rein of opposition *in rear of the withers,* which acts in the direction of the left haunch (see Diagram and description, page 228, Chapter V); 4. at the same instant, the rider's right leg is carried back a few inches and used to force the horse's croup to the left; 5. the left rein, with combined opening and direct effects, assists in conducting the horse in his oblique attitude along the same straight line he has been following; 6. the left leg aids the right as necessary to sustain impulsion.

The horse thus is bent around the rider's right leg so that his right shoulder is inside the curve made by the spinal column. Obviously his right fore and right hind legs must cross over in front of the left fore and left hind, respectively. If the rider is unsuccessful in obtaining shoulder-in along a straight line, further preparatory work in mobilizing the haunches, and in schooling with the rein of indirect opposition in rear of the withers, while moving through the corners of the enclosure and on half-turns is necessary.

Work at the *appuyer,* which is merely shoulder-in on an oblique line (described on page 250, Chapter V), should precede shoulder-in on a straight line. In this, the spine is not bent so markedly nor do the legs have as much difficulty in crossing. *Appuyer* and shoulder-in on circles should be used as preparatory exercises to shoulder-in on a straight line.

The benefits of shoulder-in are manifold. If the horse is required to carry his head in a low position, a soft, relaxed lateral bending to the right of the well extended neck occurs. Alternate resisting and relaxing of the fingers, which is necessary to keep the horse oblique to the direction of motion, combined with vibrations (see "Vibrations," page 262, Chapter V), will secure complete relaxation of the jaw, as well as a slight flexion of the poll as the horse gives himself over entirely to his rider. The crossing of the fore legs involves a raising, and an unusual swinging, of the whole right fore leg across and in front of the left fore, necessitating suppleness and relaxation of the right shoulder and knee. Also the horse is required to obey the rider's right leg and to bend his whole spine laterally as he moves in a sidewise direction. To cross his right hind over the left hind calls for engagement of the former far forward under his body. This supples the joints of the hind leg, particularly the coxofemoral and stifle. The horse, in working at right shoulder-in, is over-balanced to the left because of the attitude forced on him by the aids, and consequently is compelled to chase his own center of gravity in order to maintain balance. When fully trained, a shying horse can be pushed into an object which frightens him by applying shoulder-in to the shoulder away from the object.

Shoulder-in, although here described while moving on a straight line, may be practiced on curves, serpentines and circles. The horse's curved attitude, and not the particular direction in which he moves, constitutes shoulder-in. His spine is bent like a bow, with the rider's arm and rein functioning as the bowstring and his inside leg as the arrow bending the bow. As it is most difficult to execute on a straight line, this movement is taught last.

The principal points to be observed in right shoulder-in are: shortening the right rein and making the rein of indirect opposition in rear of the withers predominate so as to bend the whole spine (to do this the right hand should be held low and near the top of the shoulder-blade); limiting the bend of the neck with the left rein so that it is uniform with the curve of the backbone; maintaining impulsion; endeavoring to keep the neck low, well extended and relaxed and the jaw soft with frequent flexions; using the right spur just before the right hind starts to cross the left; stopping the exercise before the horse, through boredom, shows resistance. As always, the rider's fingers and legs act or become passive as required: to break any resistance; to maintain the correct position; to follow the prescribed path; to reward obedience.

In right shoulder-in at the walk, the fingers relax as the right fore crosses the left fore, since this difficult movement of the right shoulder requires its freedom. They tighten more or less as needed at the instant the left fore steps to the left front, which prevents the horse from moving on a curve to the right. Just at the time the fingers tighten, the rider's right leg, or spur, pushes the right hind across the left hind. Since the right hind moves immediately after the left fore, the action of the rider's leg is timely. At the trot, similar timing of the aids is essential, remembering that the diagonals move simultaneously.

Shoulder-in is obviously almost universal in its relaxing and suppling results. *Taught first at the walk, as all exercises should be when feasible, it is most ef-*

ficacious later on when executed at a free, long-striding trot. The long strides and impulsion make agility, relaxation, suppleness and good balance imperative. At the gallop the exercise obviously is confined to left shoulder-in when the horse is leading right; right shoulder-in, when leading left. The work has no value unless his position is correct and all resistance is absent. He should be utterly relaxed and contentedly obedient.

Where a rider's inexperience makes it advisable, advantage may be taken of a wall or fence to give first lessons in shoulder-in. In so doing, the horse's head is turned toward the wall so that he cannot escape obedience. Great care, however, must be taken to prevent the crossing of the right fore and right hind *in rear, instead of in front,* of his left fore and left hind, respectively. The wall should be utilized only at the walk for interference easily may occur. Moreover the horse is controlled largely by the wall and not the aids.

Each horse develops, on one side or the other, certain stiffnesses and resultant resistances, or vice versa. If, for example, he stiffens his neck and jaw to the left front, he generally increases the resistance by thrusting his left hip to the same side. The quick remedy is shoulder-in. In this case, left shoulder-in is indicated, but in practice it will be found that some work at right shoulder-in will also be beneficial. This exercise is immeasurably helpful in breaking up all such resistances and a few steps at shoulder-in will reveal to the rider who mounts a strange horse, where the resistances lie—whether in the croup, jaw, shoulder or elsewhere.

It is an excellent idea at the beginning of each day's work to require a few steps of shoulder-in at the walk shortly after leaving the stables. Complete relaxation of the jaw, neck and spinal column are quickly obtained. This puts the horse in a pleasant mood and he becomes calm, obedient and agreeable in the work to follow.

The False Gallop

The false gallop—leading with the left leg when curving or circling to the right, or vice versa—lengthens and lowers the stride; supples the spine; lowers the head and neck; puts the horse on the bit; and improves balance and agility. It is begun by riding on broken lines composed of very long, large curves, so that there will be neither interference nor attempts to change lead or gallop disunited. The left direct rein, with the hand held low, is employed to control the left shoulder, if circling to the left with the horse on the right lead. This rein effect when combined with the predominating action of the rider's left leg (which is required to sustain the false lead with the hind legs) bends the horse's spine slightly to the left. As he gains experience and balance on broken lines, a figure-of-eight, initially described with very large loops, is traversed. This results in the false gallop on one loop and the true on the other. Calmness and success may be quickly attained if the rider, in addition to the aids just mentioned, allows great liberty to the loin, by sitting well forward over the inside shoulder, and to the head and neck by following the mouth. He also should encourage a low head carriage. As the false gallop is difficult insofar as balance is concerned, the average colt finds it necessary at first to maintain a fairly fast speed. Later, the speed of the gallop should be decreased in order to get the greatest benefit from the work. Even with an experienced mount, the circles and figures-of-eight normally should not be too small as these provoke a tendency to gallop with short, stilty strides and so defeat one of the objects in view. The false gallop should be perfected before making any effort to teach a change of lead. It is more valuable for horses reluctant to take the bit than for those heavy on the forehand.

Flexion of the Jaw

It will be recalled that the second phase in producing correct head carriage includes: relaxing the lower jaw; bending the neck laterally; and obtaining a slight flexion at the poll. These flexions were discussed in

Chapter III, page 110, under "The Second Phase in Developing Correct Head Carriage," but were all purposely avoided throughout the breaking period. During the training period proper, they are usually brought about almost imperceptibly by the relaxing effects of the various exercises already described; if not, methods which will now be discussed will secure the necessary softening of jaw, poll and neck.

Suppling of the jaw while dismounted, still practiced by some high-school experts, is entirely unnecessary for the average, modern, outdoor horse. These flexions were perhaps essential when few horsemen owned thoroughbred horses, or those close to the blood. For the most part, riding horses of those days were coarse, thick-necked and poorly bred. Moreover, they were continuously held to slow gaits suitable to the airs of the high-school, for there were no equestrian sports requiring great speed. The slow, collected gaits, and training of former times are unsuitable to modern, outdoor riding.

General lightness and relaxation in a horse may be easily recognized by observing his jaw during slow schooling. When those qualities exist, the lower jaw relaxes without resistance, and the mouth opens part way and softly closes at each demand which involves a well marked resistance of a hand, or the hands, to the jaw.

The importance of this relaxation of the jaw muscles lies in the fact that when the mouth is held tightly shut against the action of the hands, muscular reactions occur elsewhere, which stiffen the poll or spine, or both. When both jaw and poll are relaxed, suppleness and relaxation of the back, loin and hocks follow automatically.

Oftentimes the colt's jaw will have relaxed as a result of the simple work performed during the breaking period. However, if no resistance has been encountered while breaking, only the opening, bearing, and two direct rein effects should have been used in order to build stiffness of the neck. Therefore unless the two direct reins have unintentionally brought about flexion of the jaw, the mouth will have become habituated to remaining closed, and the neck and poll, to remaining rather stiff.

Vibrations

Simple vibrations while at the walk or trot, on a circle or curve, particularly if combined with a predominating effect of opposition of the inside rein, so as to turn the horse's head inward, will cause decontraction of the jaw muscles. As noted previously, vibrations, produced by the opening and closing of the fingers, slip the bit very gently backward and forward through the mouth. There is no roughness or jerkiness in the action and all tension is relieved from the reins, momentarily, the instant the colt's mouth opens. If the rider's hands cannot "feel" the giving of the jaw he must move his head into a position where he can see it. The flexion, when first taught, is obtained if possible without any concomitant flexion of neck or poll.

Shoulder-in, half-turn in reverse, backing, increasing and slowing the speed, changing gaits, and halting also aid in relaxing the jaw. As described for the work on circles, vibrations should be employed during these movements in case the jaw does not soften.

Division of Supports

Division of supports refers to holding, for example, one snaffle and two curb reins in one hand while the other hand "plays" with the second snaffle rein. Any other combination may be used, such as one curb rein in one hand and the three other reins in the other, or two curbs in one hand and two snaffles in the other. Playing with the bit, by closing and relaxing the fingers of one or both hands, while employing various combinations of divided supports, generally breaks up set resistance of the jaw which is instinctive when there is a steady pull against the bit.

This relaxation of the jaw, like all other flexions, may be easily overdone. The jaw should not become a limp spring, and when the trained horse is at great speed it usually remains closed. It is only at slow and very balanced gaits, when the horse is lightly on the hand, or when he is being quickly checked from speed, that the jaw should become relaxed. No horse will keep a soft jaw unless he is well ridden. When bridled with a brutal spade bit, such as is often seen in the "modern west," the jaw, because the tortured mouth is open, appears soft. The horse is actually "behind the bit."

The fingers must be taught to open part way, and the elbow joints to relax, the instant the jaw and poll flex in answer to the opposition of the hands. Until these reactions occur automatically and unconsciously, the rider cannot make or maintain a perfect mouth.

Lateral Flexion of the Neck

Half-turns in reverse, circles, serpentines, changes of direction and the false gallop, all, when demanded by the predominating effect of a single opening, or direct rein, quickly bring a lateral bending in the upper third of the neck. As the direct tension to the rear is applied with one hand, the other gives passively to the front and only becomes active when necessary to prevent an excessive bend in the neck.

When training is complete, this bending of the neck by a rein of direct opposition is not often employed in equestrian sports. However, it is to be borne in mind

TRAINING

that if, for example, a horse refuses to turn to the right, it is only through the combination of the right rein's pulling his head around and the right leg's forcing his croup to the left, that he can be *compelled* to turn to the right. As soon as turned, both the rider's legs can drive him forward. These lateral aids (right rein and right leg) and not diagonal ones (left rein and right leg, for example) must be resorted to when battles arise. If a horse has been properly instructed in the effects of lateral aids, he always can be dominated, whereas the diagonal aids, being more or less artificial, can rarely force obedience from an obstinate and unruly brute. *Therefore all horses should be trained to bend the neck and turn promptly, with no sign of resistance, in answer to the direct rein—both for gymnastic and disciplinary benefits.*

When the direct rein is used *in cases of rebellion*, the other rein must be entirely passive; otherwise the horse throws his weight against the latter and is assisted thereby in his efforts to disobey.

Flexion of the Poll

Flexion of the poll is taught only after flexion of the lower jaw and lateral bending of the neck are well understood. This flexion, like flexion of the jaw, generally appears, without particular effort on the rider's part, as a result of such exercises as extending and slowing the gaits, halting, broken lines, half-turns and shoulder-in. After the breaking period is completed and training has been in progress for one or two months, the colt's head and neck normally will have risen to a higher natural carriage as a result of improvement in condition, strength and balance. If, however, he has not begun to flex his poll after learning to relax his jaw, this flexion is quickly taught as follows: 1. push the horse into a slow, strong, and cadenced trot; 2. fix the hands steadily in place and close the fingers so as to resist the mouth immediately after the horse gains impulsion in answer to the legs; 3. an elastic vibration may be added by the resisting fingers in order to relax the jaw completely, which helps to bring a nod at the poll; 4. reward promptly the first flexion however slight, by relaxing the fingers and elbows, and sustain, with the legs, the same rate at the slow trot; 5. keep the reins fairly high, forming, as usual, a straight line with the forearm, *for the flexion in the upper part of the horse's neck* will present itself *above the line established by the reins*. It is therefore apparent that the hands must not be held low, near the shoulders or withers, since this causes, rather than a correct flexion at the poll, a distorted arching of the lower and middle neck, with a consequent overburdening of the forehand.

After these oppositions of the hand to the mouth at

the slow trot bring a prompt nodding of the head, so that the face moves back into an almost vertical plane, they should be practiced at faster rates and gaits until at these also there is an equally prompt concession of both jaw and poll. At extremely fast speeds, flexibility of the jaw is not to be expected, although some remains in the poll. The speed, in early lessons, should not be changed in demanding poll flexion except when necessary to bring it back to the rate previously established in case the legs' action provokes a momentary increase.

After flexion and obedience in first lessons have been obtained, always allow the horse to extend his neck and head immediately by relaxing fingers and elbows, while maintaining light contact with the mouth.

With stubborn cases, shoulder-in, half-turns in reverse, serpentines and circles, during which the neck is also bent laterally while utilizing the method just described, expedite obtaining flexibility of the poll.

With a colt of generous disposition, well on his bit and bold in forward movement, the flexions may be first demanded at the walk. However, as the horse necessarily stiffens his spine and neck while at the trot, there is much less danger, when working at that gait, of his falling back of the bit or becoming over-flexed. As poll flexion becomes a reflex on the colt's part, the trainer, in order to utilize its softening effects when decreasing the gait, or halting, merely continues to keep the fingers closed and resisting after the first flexion occurs, until, with the poll remaining flexed, the desired change in speed, or the halt, is obtained, whereupon the fingers instantly must relax.

When training is completed, a quick halt, with a correct flexion of poll and jaw, from an extended trot or gallop should be possible in a few strides with but a *single* closing of the fingers and fixing of the elbow and hand. In early training, however, it is a matter for the tact of the trainer to determine how many separate resistances of the hands are required to check or stop a young horse—always remembering that a soft, over-flexed neck is an abomination, and that, until it has acquired the desirable stiffness, no flexions are demanded.

Horses with thick, gross throat lashes, short necks or poorly attached heads, should not be asked for much flexion of the poll; in bad cases none should be sought. Many heavy-necked horses apparently become mechanically wind-broken from over-flexion. Poll flexion also must be cautiously required of horses having long, slender necks lest over-flexion, rubber-neck and nervousness result.

Placing the Head (Ramener)

Placing the head constitutes the last step in the second phase of developing a correct head set and links the second and third phases together. When carried to an extreme it gives an exaggerated set to head and neck useful only in the realm of high-schooling.

Better balance is always associated with the gradual and natural rise in the habitual attitude of the head and neck. As it occurs the poll develops a small permanent flexion which brings the face, when the horse is in hand at moderate speeds, into a plane more nearly perpendicular to the ground. When the horse is at fast speeds, the bend at the poll decreases and the face becomes more nearly horizontal as the neck and head are extended and lowered. In other words the balancer extends as the horse's base of support lengthens. On the other hand, when slow speeds cause a short base of support, the horse raises and retracts his balancer. In this latter position the face normally approaches an angle of forty-five degrees with the vertical, and becomes almost perpendicular when the gait is quickly decreased or a sudden halt required.

The tension on the snaffle is broken into two components of force, one lifting or lightening the forehand and the other stopping forward movement. If the curb chain is properly adjusted, when tension is applied to the reins the branches of the curb bit form an angle of approximately forty-five degrees with the line of the horse's mouth. If his face is also at forty-five degrees, the curb reins will be working most effectively, since they form an angle of approximately ninety degrees with the branches of the curb bit.

The ramener, which is intimately connected with poll flexion, means the normal set of the head at forty-five degrees and the flexibility of the poll which brings the face into an almost vertical plane when the horse is closely in hand at slow gaits, or when a check or halt is made.

As a rule, when a graceful placing of the head does not result from the intelligent selection and use of various training exercises, great caution ought to be exercised before attempting to force the horse to flex his poll greatly or change his natural head carriage. If the ramener obviously causes discomfort and nervousness it should be abandoned, for the horse's conformation is undoubtedly faulty in certain respects.

Three General Methods of Resisting the Bit

While the horse's resistances to the bit have been touched upon from time to time, it is well to compare them, and to have the remedy for each one clearly in mind.

For the first resistance, effected by contracting the jaw muscles and rigidly shutting the mouth, the cure is the combination of vibrations of the snaffle and the "division of supports." Both have been explained.

The second resistance comes from a stiff poll which invariably is accompanied by stiffness of back and loin, and consequent failure to engage the hind legs at demand. The work described under "Flexion of the Poll," page 265, Chapter V, is the cure. Briefly stated, the rider, after first stimulating impulsion with the legs, combats the horse's defiance by closing his fingers and fixing his hands in resistance against the mouth. If well done, this is certain to relax the poll.

The third defense is offered by the horse's throwing too much weight on his forehand. This may originate from poor conformation, a naturally very low and heavy carriage of the head and neck, or a general arching of the neck, particularly near the shoulders. Half-halts (see page 229, Chapter V) are necessary to lighten the forehand in those cases. If two resistances present themselves at once, an appropriate combination of two remedies must be employed.

The rider always should analyze his own technique, for the aforementioned resistances may be caused by heavy or unsteady hands, sitting too far back on the saddle which distresses the horse's loin, or inappropriate and severe bits.

The Gallop Depart

The crude method of taking the gallop depart prescribed for use during "Breaking" is employed only because the colt's lack of education in the aids makes it necessary in order that he may reap, as early as possible, the great benefits derived from exercise at the gallop. During that period, he is thrown off balance to put him into the gallop. As training advances the rider senses when the colt understands the aids sufficiently to learn a more graceful manner of taking the gallop. Since it is only necessary to impede one shoulder, while freeing the other, to induce the desired lead, the aids applied must be conceived with that idea in mind. It may be observed that a well trained horse normally goes into the gallop from the trot by quickly carrying forward and dissociating one hind leg from the fore leg of the same diagonal. This permits settling an abnormal amount of weight on the haunches and springing from them into the gallop. Therefore, as soon as the horse obeys the indirect rein of opposition in front of the withers, a gallop depart off the hindquarters, with the lead desired, may be taught.

To take the gallop with the right lead, put the horse at a quiet trot on a circle to the right. Both hands, with the reins well separated, are then carried a few inches to the left. The tension on both is increased to throw an abnormal amount of the weight of the head and neck onto the left shoulder. The rein effects should be smoothly and progressively brought into play and the tension increased only the minimum amount necessary to react momentarily on the left shoulder. A fraction of an instant after the reins act, and before the speed of the trot is diminished, both the rider's legs urge the horse forward into the gallop. The hands immediately relax and move to the front, provided the horse responds, to allow the escape of the first galloping stride with the right lead.

The right rein's tension is applied upward as well as to the left and rearward, in order to further lighten the right shoulder, and later on when the horse learns its meaning, to serve as a distinct and individual indication that the right lead is desired. If he fails to respond to these aids but seeks to trot faster, the leg aids are relaxed until calmness and regularity of gait are restored, when the attempt is renewed.

In first lessons the left leg predominates and acts a little to the rear so as to command some displacement of the haunches as this is the aid to which the colt has been accustomed. When he grasps the significance of the new rein aids, the left leg may gradually cease its predominating action and be used in the same relative place and with equal intensity as the right one. This eliminates any tendency to throw one haunch too far out of line in taking the gallop. However, no attempt to compel a gallop with the croup directly in rear of the shoulders should be made. This is neither natural nor beneficial, although it is considered very important in high-school work. The horse should never be made uncomfortable, except for an intelligent reason.

To take the trot from the gallop, simply oppose the leading shoulder with the direct rein on the same side, and with the indirect rein of opposition in front of the withers with the other hand. One leg can assist by pushing the croup straight behind the forehand. Thus the aids to take the gallop depart are merely reversed in order to return to the trot.

When the departs are readily taken on circles and curves, they next are taught on straight lines. *Just before* reaching a curve where a turn is obligatory is a favorable spot to take the first depart on a straight line. Ultimately the departs are taught from the walk, halt, and backing. Lifting one rein a trifle as described above, and promptly easing the hands as the gallop starts, soon make correct departs easily obtainable.

Change of Leads

The change of leads during the period of suspension in a gallop stride, while not essential to the training of a hunter or jumper, nevertheless promotes discipline and agility and is oftentimes very useful. There is no difficulty in teaching the change on a straight line, without unnecessary switching of the croup from side to side, provided careful preparatory work is done. Proper preparation requires perfection in the false gallop and in the departs from the walk, halt and backing before trying the change of leads.

In beginning this instruction, the figure-of-eight may be used profitably in the following way: after nearly completing one loop, the horse is brought to the trot for a few steps and, with the aids just discussed, put into the gallop *with the other lead* as he enters the second loop. The number of strides at the trot are reduced as rapidly as progress allows. After reaching a point where only one or two trotting strides are taken, this same work of taking first one lead and then the other with only one or two trotting strides intervening is repeated on a straight line. All work is then repeated with the gallop departs taken from the walk.

When both leads are taken with equal facility on a straight line, with only a step or two at the walk intervening, the first lesson in actually changing leads is undertaken by again utilizing a large figure-of-eight. Since the hind legs experience more difficulty in changing than do the front, the rider must be exceedingly careful to keep his weight well forward and partly in the stirrups during the change so as to lighten the hindquarters. If galloping on one loop of the figure-of-eight with the right lead, the rider, just prior to entering the loop where the left lead will be the true one, gently carries his hands three or four inches to the right. The right rein is prepared to act with direct opposition, and the left with indirect opposition in front of the withers. A stride before the change is to be sought the fingers are closed and additional tension is gradually applied during the period of suspension in order to confine the right shoulder. The rider's calves are tightened at this same time so as to prepare the horse for their strong action a moment later when the change is actually demanded. For a fleeting instant just as the horse comes to ground in the next stride, the resistance of the rider's hands is emphasized. Instantly thereafter the two legs act vigorously with the right one predominating farther to the rear in order to insure the change by the hind legs. This may cause a little apprehension on the horse's part which tact and less vigor soon can eliminate after the change is learned. There thus exists a brief flash of time during which the hands resist both the impulsion just produced by the rider's legs and the movement of the horse's right shoulder. This opposition of the hands to the legs occurs just as the seat comes strongly into the saddle, at which moment it is easy for the rider to use his legs as indicated. Immediately thereafter, during the next period of suspension, the hands soften, allowing the impulsion to escape along with the slipping forward of the left fore and hind past the right lateral biped.

If the horse makes a successful change the aids are

abandoned, pats on the neck bestowed, and after being allowed to gallop a few strides he is brought to a walk and permitted to rest on a long rein.

Gradually the necessity for predominating with the one leg disappears and equal stimulation by the two, in conjunction with the rein effects described, will secure the change. However, the outside (predominating) leg should be promptly called to service, and used convincingly, whenever the horse, after knowing how, becomes lazy or careless and fails to change behind. If he becomes disunited in early lessons, the trot is resumed, the true gallop renewed and the trial repeated with more energetic leg effects.

Softness and elasticity of hand are necessary to avoid excitement, yet firmness is essential. As in the gallop departs, lifting the left hand a trifle as the change from right to left lead is made, will help clarify the rider's desire.

There is another method of employing the legs in changing leads or securing a gallop depart. *In this, the left spur is used just in rear of the cinch when seeking a depart with the left lead or the change from the right to the left lead.* It is a very artificial method usually practiced in high-schooling. In theory this action of the inside (left, in this case) spur is supposed to hasten the movement forward of the left hind leg to its correct position in advance of the right hind; a position, necessitated by the change to, or the depart with, the left lead. It is further helpful in keeping the horse's croup straight. As a refinement this method is useful in augmenting high collection, and in maintaining the horse's body rigorously straight, both of which are virtues in high-schooling. However, the use of the outside leg to procure a depart during first lessons, and equal action of the two legs later on, are very much preferable for outdoor horses since these methods take advantage of natural inclinations and keep the horse contented.

The pernicious custom, frequently seen in high-schooling and elsewhere, of striving to hold the horse's body on an absolutely straight line while at the gallop, and the even more ruinous one of habitually bending the spine and neck outward to conform to the curve being travelled, shorten the stride, cramp and annoy the horse. These faulty methods are to be carefully shunned in the practical training of outdoor horses.

After the changes of lead are easily secured at the junction of the loops on the figure-of-eight, they are soon obtainable in milder changes of direction and later on straight lines. As proficiency arrives, changes with fairly long and loose reins should be practiced so that the horse learns to obey with little restraint or assistance from rein effects.

In speaking of changes of leads, it is well for the

horseman to know that when his mount changes leads on a straight line of his own accord during a hard ride, it is a sure sign of fatigue; just as forging—striking one hind foot against the fore foot on the same side—proves that the horse at the trot is becoming tired.

The Double Bridle

It is impossible to lay down a definite rule as to when training in a double bridle, with bit and bridoon, should commence. As a matter of fact after correct training in a snaffle bridle, many horses of quiet temperament can be successfully hunted or hacked with this alone. For training in jumping and for horse-show jumping, nothing but the snaffle bridle should ever be utilized. It is impossible for even the best of riders to keep a horse unafraid of a Pelham, or bit and bridoon, over a succession of big jumps.

On the other hand, while hunting, many horses are too warm-blooded and high-spirited to be controlled by the average horseman with a snaffle alone. Others are either so coarse, or unresponsive when tired, that a fairly strong bit is required now and then when checking quickly to avoid an accident.

With hot-blooded types, the only rule that may be given concerning bits is to employ the mildest type of either Pelham, or bit and bridoon, with which the horse can be controlled. Except during hunting and polo the snaffle bit alone is sufficiently powerful to control any well trained horse. Yet, regardless of how light the mouths of certain ones may be, it is wise to teach all horses to execute, first with a Pelham and then with bit and bridoon, all the gymnastic and balancing exercises described in Breaking and Training. At first the curb chain should be left off.

Meticulous attention always should be given to the careful fitting of bits and the proper adjustment of curb chains. A curb bit which is a trifle too wide of mouthpiece or too long of branch, or a curb chain one link too tight, will excite, or make disobedient, a horse that has been going perfectly with properly fitted and adjusted bits. The more finely bred, delicate and better conformed the horse is, the more mild and carefully adjusted must be his bits.

The half-moon Pelham, without the curb chain, is particularly useful for "putting on his bit" a colt which is inclined to carry his head too high. The lever action produced by the branches of the chainless bit react downward, through the crown piece of the bridle, on the poll and tend to lower the head and neck. In all cases when the curb chain is first attached to the bridoon or Pelham, it should be adjusted very loosely. Thus adjusted, it quickly brings about relaxation of the jaw, whereas a tight one invariably creates stiffness, for the horse dares not let go of a tightly chained bit, and sets his jaw against it. Nothing is more destructive of disposition, head carriage, mouth and general efficiency than a curb chain so tight that it causes the bit to "stand stiff." On the other hand, although he may pull, no horse will be ruined by a chain so loose that it lets the bit "fall through." Putting felt or leather around a curb chain, as is often done with polo ponies, is another unwise practice since it usually teaches disrespect for the bit. A curb chain of proper width and correctly adjusted needs no covering. A narrow curb chain, or a bit with cannons very small in diameter, be it snaffle, Pelham or curb, will annoy and often ruin a good mouth. Many of the horrible contraptions seen in the hunting field, show ring and at polo, are almost unbelievable in severity and lack of intelligent construction.

The trainer must decide when a particular colt is frankly enough on the snaffle to warrant putting on a bit and bridoon or a Pelham. Above all else, he must avoid over-flexing the neck, poll or jaw, lest the penalty be complete destruction of all the good results produced by careful training with the snaffle. As soon as the double bridle is worn, the colt should be taught, precisely as he was with the snaffle alone, to extend his head and neck while accepting light support from the new bits. Allowing him to lower and extend his head and neck gently and take more rein as the fingers and elbows relax, should be frequently rehearsed. If an inclination to arch the poll greatly or drop back of the bit appears, it is an ample indication that the bridle or the hands are too harsh. Either the hands must act more delicately, or work on the snaffle alone be resumed. All effects with the curb bit should be exceedingly light since they are much more severe than those of the snaffle.

The old high-school theory about the snaffle's being an "elevator" of the head and the curb a "depressor" is superficial. Either the curb or snaffle may be used by a good rider either to depress or elevate the head and neck, depending upon the position and action of one or both hands.

High-Schooling

It is not within the province of this book to discuss high-schooling. This art is of very great benefit to a horseman inasmuch as he learns to diagnose and destroy quickly all resistances presented by horses. However, since high-schooling calls for high knee and hock action, and a rearward balance developed by an extreme ramener and great collection, it is not essential to the training of a hunter, jumper or hack.

Collection is taught by ever more closely associated effects of the hands and legs. The latter inspire impulsion which the hands check and regulate so as to

Two-tracking at trot. Horse moving on an oblique to his left front; head turned in that direction. Note crossing of right hind in front of left hind.

Two-tracking on right oblique at trot; fore legs crossing; right rein and left leg dominating (diagonal aids).

transform what naturally would be long, low steps into high action and slow gaits. These are inefficient in outdoor work and a horse so trained does not have his center of gravity sufficiently far forward for fast galloping and jumping. When continuously held to collected schooling, a horse soon lacks balance, agility and calmness *when extended at speed* across country. When the rider attempts to give him the support required by fast galloping, the horse over-flexes his neck, is unable to stride long, and becomes frantic if naturally keen and in company of other horses.

Only a horse with a hereditarily calm disposition, and so expertly trained that his instinct to extend the head and neck and go calmly on the hand at fast gaits is never destroyed, can become both a finished high-school horse and a hunter.

Official photo, Olympic Games, Los Angeles, 1932

View showing several obstacles of the Prix des Nations Course, Olympic Games at Los Angeles, California, 1932. The jumps ranged from 4' 6" to 5' 3" in height.

CHAPTER VI

Training the Horse to Jump

A MONTH after breaking begins, or as soon as the colt goes well at the walk and trot on the longe, he should be led across poles or small logs laid flat on the ground. Sugar and oats fed to timid colts immediately after obstacles are crossed, have a tremendous influence in creating calmness and boldness. This applies both to the colt, and to the older horse when the latter is being schooled over big and strange obstacles. Leading is not only the best way to start jumping lessons, but is often useful later when, during hunting or hacking, it is wiser to lead one's mount over some tricky little barrier than to jump it. In leading, no difficulty whatever will be found if the height is built up gradually to eight or ten inches. The colt at first should be required to *step* across and *not jump* the obstacles. In the beginning they should be low enough so that in stepping over them *he does not bump his legs.* The ideas in mind are to give him confidence and to teach him to lead over unusual places, and it is well worth the trainer's time. Later, after learning to jump on the longe, leading over obstacles high enough to require jumping occasionally should be practiced.

In this leading, the obstacles, wherever possible, are rigidly fixed; otherwise heavy poles, hexagonal or octagonal in shape and having sharp edges which will hurt the colt if struck, are used. This rule applies to all future training in jumping. Hedges, or obstacles easily knocked down teach carelessness and disrespect. Small ditches, from one foot to two and one-half feet wide, are led across concurrently with the instruction over upright obstacles.

Jumping on the Longe

Generally after about six weeks' schooling, but only when the colt has perfect manners at the walk and trot, his instruction over obstacles while circling on the longe may begin. As always, obstacles are practically rigid, and the end away from the trainer is enclosed by a high wing. (See Illustration.) In all early instruction in jumping, every advantageous device which may prevent refusing, running out, or becoming excited, ought to be utilized. In other words, if the trainer takes ample time and uses patience, ingenuity

Rider opposite croup so that whip may be used from in rear of horse. Longe lightly stretched; coiled in figure-of-eight. Sloping pole from standard near trainer prevents longe from catching on upright.

and common sense, bad habits need never be acquired by the horse. For this reason, an assistant should be on hand when first lessons over obstacles on the longe are given. He follows the colt from in rear, and by use of voice and threats or light touches with the longeing whip, prevents hesitation and refusals. Whenever any excitement or apprehension appears the obstacle should be lowered. Above all, both on the longe and later when mounted, calmness and the same gait should be maintained. Loss of calmness, in any training, proves lack of sufficient preparation.

When longeing over an obstacle, the trainer moves up and down the long axis of an ellipse, which permits the colt to approach and leave the obstacle on a straight line. This is important, for in early training he should not be required to jump while moving on a curve. From the bar on the ground, the height is increased inch by inch, but with the colt still being required to approach at the walk. From experience in leading, he normally will continue to step over, and not jump the fence. However, when the height has been increased to twelve inches or more, occasionally he will bump his legs or stumble, in stepping over the bar, narrow box, "chicken coop" or other obstacle. If these are rigid, or heavy, and sharp-edged, sooner or later the colt, while continuing to move at the walk, in order to avoid the painful bumps will decide to jump. Every effort is

TRAINING THE HORSE TO JUMP

made to keep him moving calmly at the walk *after jumping* as well as while approaching. As soon as he jumps while walking without excitement, the height may be progressively increased up to two feet, or possibly higher, depending on the manners and natural ability of the individual. The increase should be made very slowly; one or two inches every three or four days. This careful preparatory training requires patience, but as stated before, it will prove most profitable.

The jumping on the longe should take place at the end of the day's work when the colt's "edge" is worn off. If he is fresh he inevitably will "play" and discover undesirable tricks. Great care to avoid overdoing the practice and generous rewards for good conduct soon produce adroitness and calmness. The time spent jumping while going to the left and the right hand on the circle should be equalized. Constant variation in type, appearance, height and eventually breadth of obstacles employed is most desirable. *However, the use of a take-off bar on the ground to increase breadth is not recommended.* It is unnatural and requires so much study during the approach that it interferes with the development of good form. An efficacious device for making a horse "stand back" at his take-off will be described later on. In-and-outs should be employed as soon as calmness and skill permit.

Well conducted lessons in jumping on the longe are the quickest and most efficient means of making a calm jumper. This implies that the horse is well disciplined and obedient on the longe before any jumping is undertaken.

Danger of Longeing over Broad Obstacles

In connection with breadth, it is very dangerous, even with experienced horses of great jumping ability, to longe over exceedingly broad obstacles. Breadth and unusualness of appearance often may puzzle or intimidate a horse as he studies the obstacle during his approach and cause him to decrease his speed. If his slowing of rate is sudden and marked, it is practically impossible to prevent it with voice and whip. He then either may refuse or, because of insufficient impulsion to carry him over, fall into the obstacle. Even though he receives no injury, *falling into an obstacle* generally brings loss of courage for a long period of time even to a very bold horse. Striking an obstacle, but falling clear of it, never has the same *demoralizing effect* which follows a fall into it. The trainer, when mounted, by use of his spurs when approaching a very broad obstacle, usually can compel sufficient impulsion to clear it.

Amount of Jumping To Be Done

In jumping, more than in any other phase of training, horsemen are prone to proceed much too rapidly, thereby pushing the colt beyond his ability. The latter then loses his confidence, courage and form. To restore them all is usually impossible. Always the thought should be kept in mind that much practice over jumps well within the horse's ability finally produces that prime requisite—good form. As good form is slowly and carefully perfected, the jumps may be broadened and heightened inch by inch and a fearless jumper developed. He then will stand well back on his take-off; jump without decreasing his speed or putting in short, pecking strides; describe a long, graceful parabola of flight over the obstacle and land smoothly "going away." The moment any timidity, nervousness, rushing or lack of form is evinced, training over smaller jumps should be resumed.

When training a *green* hunter or jumper, young or old, practice two or three times a week over ten or fifteen moderate obstacles is ample. With an *experienced* old one, wise horsemen do very little jumping until two or three weeks prior to the show, or other event, in which the horse is to participate. At other times, work over *five or six obstacles once a week* is enough schooling for such a horse, and none of these should be up to the height the horse is capable of negotiating. Of course, when preparing him for competition, one or two of the obstacles should be a few inches higher and broader than those to be encountered, but when he jumps them well *once* it is time to stop work. If he does the whole course well except one or two obstacles, he should be jumped over those he failed on and then sent home. If the size frightens him, the obstacle should be lowered and built up gradually along with his confidence. Unfortunately, this routine usually is not followed. Most hunters and jumpers are ruined by too much too-high jumping, not by too little.

Normally the four-year-old green colt should not be asked to jump higher than three feet while mounted, and not over four feet on the longe. *The principal test, in order to determine whether any horse is fit to jump on a particular day (after his legs and feet have been inspected by sight and touch for enlargements and fever) is accomplished by trotting him on hard, level ground. If any sign of stiffness or lameness exists, under no circumstances should he be required to jump.*

First Jumping Mounted

After about two weeks' jumping instruction on the longe, mounted work over the same obstacles that were employed for leading and longeing may begin. When mounted, the trainer, beginning at the walk, rehearses thoroughly all work previously done on the longe. This is done despite the fact that the colt, when on the longe, by this time may be cantering over small ob-

Good balance of horse and rider over five-foot fence. Note absolute freedom of horse's head and neck.

AMERICAN OFFICER
Display of excellent form by both rider and horse.

stacles about two feet high. The points of most concern, when mounted work starts, are: allowing absolute liberty to head and neck; maintaining the same speed and gait before and after passing an obstacle; and approaching the center of each obstacle perpendicularly. The rider should hold with one hand either to the pommel, or to a strap around the horse's neck, in order to prevent being displaced and so alarming and hurting the colt through jerking his mouth or jolting his back. *The reins, without exception, should be loose and floating when the colt actually crosses the obstacle.* In fact, the reins should be floating *at all times in these early lessons.*

If a certain horse, either when mounted or on the longe, does not learn to jump smoothly *at the walk* after the obstacle is set at a height of fifteen or more inches, but instead persists in hopping over, first with his forehand and then with his hindquarters, he should be put over it at the trot. The speed of this gait will make it necessary for him to jump, rather than to hop one end at a time. While this elementary mounted work at the walk takes place, longeing continues over higher obstacles. In other words, training on the longe and at liberty is always more advanced and difficult than that which is carried on concurrently while mounted. No increase in the height of obstacles, used either in the work executed on the longe or while mounted, should be attempted until perfect calmness exists in the work at hand. Calmness is demonstrated by the colt's approaching and leaving the jump on a straight line and with no increase or decrease in speed. Thus work at the trot, both mounted and on the longe, begins only when absolute calmness exists at the walk. Consequently, the time to commence jumping at the trot varies in each case. The mounted colt often should be very gently halted, while approaching, or just after clearing, an obstacle; then patted and rested.

Jumping at the Trot

Jumping at the trot is very beneficial for it *necessitates entire relaxation of the spinal column* and teaches clever use of the hindquarters in propelling the horse over the obstacle. Here too, the pommel, or neck strap, always should be held in order to avoid falling out of balance to the rear with the evil results mentioned above. At the trot this is very necessary, for the reaction of the horse's jump on the rider is violent. Jumping, while at the trot, all types of obstacles, which have been gradually heightened to about two and one-half feet, should continue until perfect manners are habitual. If excitement develops, jumping at the walk is resumed. Only after all goes perfectly at the trot does the trainer attempt jumping at the gallop. In leaving the obstacle the horse is not permitted to turn continually in one direction. The trainer's imagination ought to keep the pupil expectantly attentive and allow him no initiative.

Jumping at Liberty

Work over obstacles at liberty is excellent practice for both colts and older horses, provided an elliptical pen is used. (See Diagram, page 296.) The great disadvantage of a straight jumping chute lies in the fact that colts almost invariably develop the bad habit of rushing their jumps. With the elliptical pen, the rather sharp turns at the ends not only prevent rushing but also improve the horse's balance. In it, every type of obstacle may be introduced to the horse. Moreover, much experience may be gained with far less chance of leg injuries than when the horse is handicapped by the rider's weight. *For young colts, jumping at liberty should be postponed until calmness over small obstacles at the walk and trot, both on the longe and mounted, is obtained.* To teach jumping at those slow gaits before taking a single obstacle at the gallop, normally will eliminate any tendency to rush. An able horse so instructed, and capably handled, ultimately will be exceedingly clever and brilliant because no excitement will interfere with his cool, experienced judgment.

As soon as conduct at the trot makes readiness for

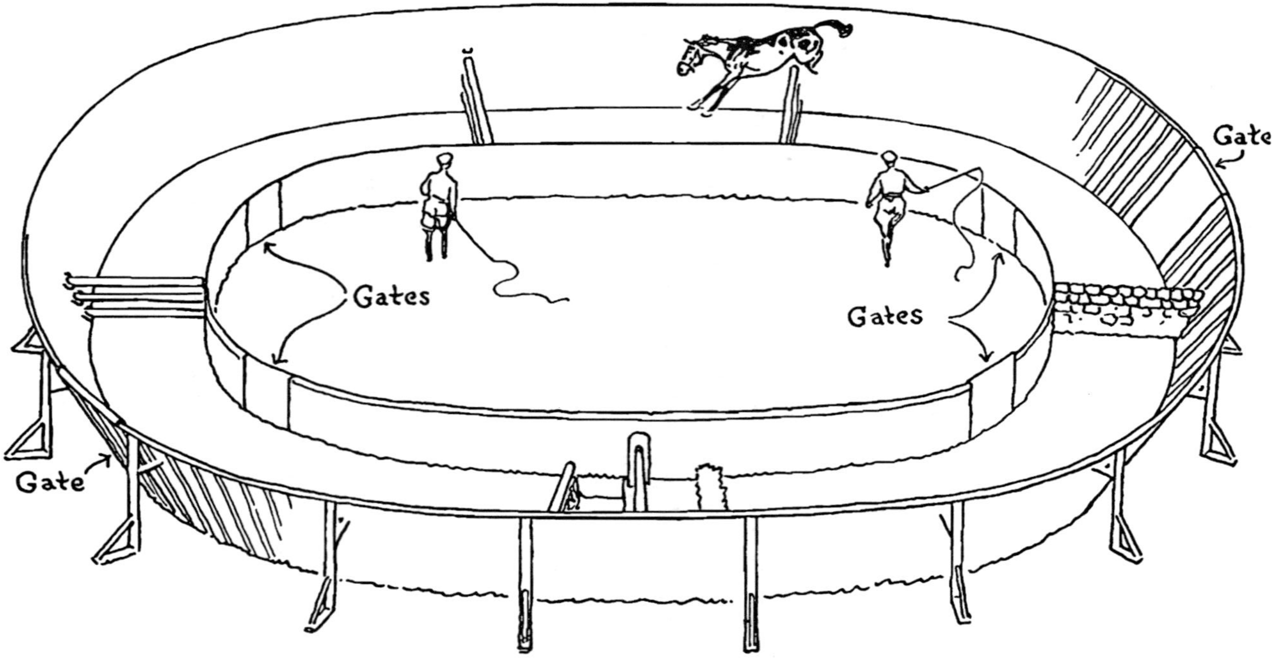
Gate
Gates
Gates
Gate

jumping at the canter evident, work in a Hitchcock or elliptical pen may be advantageously begun.

Jumping at the Gallop

Normally three or four months from the time breaking begins, the colt's strength and balance warrant jumping at the canter on the longe. Therefore, at the end of five or six months the colt may be expected, with the trainer up, to jump in good form at the canter. The obstacles ought not to exceed two feet in height. It is wisest to limit the height for the mounted work of four-year-olds to three feet. Many will boast that their horses at that age have cleared five feet. However, the advice just given holds good if one has only one or two colts to expend and desires sound six-year-olds.

The trainer's weight is a vital factor in early jumping. If much over one hundred fifty pounds, great caution must be taken to avoid injury to the colt's legs, and the greater part of his jumping should be done on the longe. The heavy trainer, however, may longe his colt over obstacles with a light assistant riding. This, incidentally, is a sure way, if the assistant is given no reins, of preventing harm to the mouth.

The Arrangement of Obstacles

From the day leading over the poles laid flat on the

ground begins, the arrangement, color, shape, type and spacing of obstacles constantly should be varied. With a little imagination this can be done with a very limited number of obstacles available by using blankets, ropes, chairs, buckets, hay bales, branches, etc. The spacing and arrangement may be infinitely diversified. This training, at first thought, may appear to be more essential for a show jumper than a hunter. Nevertheless the latter will be a far safer, bolder and more clever horse in the field if he receives a similar education.

In-and-Outs

In-and-outs, with frequent changes in spacing and type, furnish the most effective means of developing agility, judgment and balance, over and between jumps. Again it is pointed out that this training—being a means, not an end—is just as important for the hunter as for the show jumper. Starting with two obstacles, the colt is schooled, as time goes on, over triple, quadruple, and quintuple in-and-outs. At the walk, the spacing between jumps for the green colt may be any distance from five yards up. At this gait, the obstacles are never over two and one-half feet in height and the colt easily alters his length of step so as to take off correctly. At the trot, the usual spacing is six yards; at the gallop, *with low obstacles not over three feet in height,* seven yards; and for obstacles four feet or higher at the gallop, eight yards. When, at five or six years of age, the horse becomes skillful, these distances may be changed, as for instance, by having only seven yards between two high obstacles; or four yards between two fairly low ones, which will require the horse to "pop" in and out without an intervening stride at the gallop. *As always, it is much practice over LOW in-and-outs which gives calmness and agility and ultimately makes a great jumper over any type of jump. Patience brings calmness, and calmness permits cleverness.* The distracted horse which fears and hates jumping can never be a consistent performer. Sad to relate, not over one out of ten hunters or jumpers receives thorough and gradual elementary education in jumping.

As an example of a training in-and-out for a four-year-old after five months' mounted work, a single bar two feet high may be followed at six yards by a small double fence two and one-half feet high, with the two fences two feet apart; this, succeeded at eight yards distance by a two and one-half foot wall. Later, five or six small obstacles may be arranged at varying intervals within a chute formed by wings or fences. When mounted, the objections found to jumping in a straight chute while at liberty are not present. The triple in-and-out described above may be taken at the walk, trot or gallop. The colt frequently should be halted between two of the obstacles, patted, turned about and jumped out over the one over which he entered. Or, he may be turned ninety degrees and taken out over a small barrier on one side of the chute. Obviously the arrangements may be varied infinitely and, as conditions allow, a slight change in direction after each jump is introduced. By the end of five months' training, gymnastic exercises will have made the colt supple and responsive to the legs and reins so that the halts and changes of direction during practice at jumping can be executed smoothly and calmly.

A colt, as he gains experience, may be longed over simple, and triple in-and-outs. The side of the obstacles away from the trainer must be walled, or fenced in by wings. The uprights toward him must have poles—with one end resting on the ground, the other on the top of the upright—so that the longe will slip over and not catch on the uprights. Here again, instruction begins at the walk. Punishment on the nose with the longe will prevent rushing, and since in-and-outs by their nature discourage it, the colt can be taught to go calmly. The trainer will find it necessary to "double time" parallel to the horse's croup as he longes him through an in-and-out, both because the longe is usually not long enough to permit his standing still, and because he must prevent the colt's stopping.

TRAINING THE HORSE TO JUMP

In addition to the in-and-outs, single jumps should be taken, preferably after work over the former, and when the horse is relaxed and calm. The single jumps are a little higher and broader than those comprising the in-and-outs. By jumping these, the colt gains confidence in his ability over larger obstacles, while his form is perfected over the small ones in the in-and-outs.

Exercise before Jumping

As a fixed rule, no jumping ever is done *during training* until the horse has been worked sufficiently at hacking, shoulder-in, changes of rate and gait, circles, serpentines, broken lines and other exercises—*according to his particular needs*—to wear off his first playfulness. He then will be calm, relaxed, obedient and softly on the hand.

In this connection, when work over obstacles *at the gallop* is initiated, the rider begins to maintain soft contact with the mouth and ceases to hold the pommel, as is done in the elementary lessons at the walk and trot. No matter what occurs, the fingers always ought to be semirelaxed at an obstacle, so that in case of a "bad jump" the reins may slip through them and the horse's mouth not be hurt.

With a finished jumper, the "higher" he feels before a jumping competition, the better are his prospects of winning. He has no need of all the calming exercises that a green horse must have prior to *training in jumping,* and the absurd habit of "working the horse down" before he enters the show ring simply takes a few potential inches off each leap. Of course, if he is old and stiff he must be "limbered up," but if not, a bit of cantering and a couple of jumps to warm his blood are all he needs. For a week before a competition the finished jumper requires only the lightest sort of work with almost no jumping. This permits him to store up an abnormal amount of energy for the crucial moments when big, strange obstacles confront him. Likewise a well trained hunter needs little schooling over obstacles, for he receives all the jumping necessary to keep him in form while hunting. On the contrary, if a horse is *not a trained jumper,* he is not ready to show or hunt, for the show ring and hunting field are not suitable places for him to learn the mechanics of jumping. He and his rider are nuisances to others, and the nerve-wracking conditions prevailing generally do the horse's disposition and jumping form more harm than good.

How To Ride over an Obstacle

The main and most difficult task of the trainer when riding over an obstacle is to "let the horse alone." Simple though this sounds, in practice it requires cool nerves and great coördination. Riding a jumper is a specialized form of athletics. It may be very well done by riders having little general ability in equitation or horse training, provided they have good natural balance and muscular control. Obviously the trainers of hunters and jumpers need perfect form in jumping to accomplish properly this phase of training.

Too often riders believe that they are assisting their horses over obstacles by using their hands and legs in various ways other than those to be described. The idea that one can "place" his horse for each jump over a course of big and imposing obstacles is erroneous. Many really brilliant riders have tried it, but without complete success. The horse must do the jumping and the less he is bothered, except to encourage and rate him, the better he will do. If "placed" for each jump, either his or the rider's nerve or judgment inevitably cracks at some point while traversing a difficult course. Under strain few horses will subordinate *completely* their will and actions to the men on their backs. *With the best-trained horses the tactful horseman sagaciously compromises when blood is hot and excitement rife.*

The following rules cover almost all there is to know about riding over obstacles:

The Approach

Approach the center of the obstacle perpendicularly. Sit in balance with loin hollowed out and body inclined well forward from the hip joints. Do not stand in the stirrups during the immediate approach, but allow your weight to settle on your thighs by relaxing the knee joints. Keep head and chest lifted.

If, as good jumpers often do, your horse starts with a rush at the first obstacle, lean, in preparation, a trifle farther forward from the hips than usual in order not to be "caught behind." The momentum of the quick start will throw your body upward and backward into the correct angle. If this is not done, you may be caught out of balance and forced to hang on the reins.

Do not lean forward or backward in anticipation or apprehension, just prior to the take-off. SIT STILL.

Keep the reins *very slightly stretched* and be certain that the hands, with relaxed fingers, *accentuate* the following of every oscillation of the horse's head and neck, beginning with his first stride in the direction of the obstacle. Pulling during the first few strides, as he gains impetus, will make a horse nervous, and eventually develop a frantic rusher. His "balancer" must have the absolute freedom that results from complete relaxation of finger, elbow and shoulder joints.

If the reins are barely taut, the slightest resistance by the fingers will collect and rate the horse during the approach (if that is necessary), *for the horse on a light rein is relaxed in poll and neck.* If, on the other

Excellent show jumping seat; rider's weight in heels; balance perfect; hands light; horse contented and free.

Correct form during descent. Note rider's weight in heels and on knees; seat out of saddle; hands feathery-light.

Correct form in landing. Weight received principally in heels; seat kept out of saddle by stiffening knee joints and setting muscles of back; hands low and soft; croup free of rider's weight which allows painless engagement of hind legs under the belly as they come to ground.

hand, you are resisting or pulling with the reins, he stiffens and resists so that your efforts have little effect in rating or changing direction.

While approaching, your legs are continuously active, with the intensity of action varying according to the sensibility of the horse, but always sufficient to sustain the speed required by the height and breadth of the obstacle. The best jumper in the world some day will refuse if the rider's legs are passive or weak. The legs' action may be intermittent and in rhythm with the strides, being performed by squeezing with the calves or tapping, when necessary, with the heels or spurs. During the last few strides before the obstacle, determined squeezing is usually sufficient encouragement. With legs tight to the horse the seat is secure and the spurs may be turned against his sides at the last instant if you sense a refusal. With experience, your hands and seat learn to anticipate any attempt at disobedience.

Combine the indications of heart, balance and legs to encourage the horse to gallop in his stride boldly over the obstacle. Indecision on the part of your mind, legs or position—which is usually abetted by apprehensive clutching of the reins—quickly transmits the same indecision to the horse and causes a run-out, refusal or "pecking," timid jump.

Pinch more tightly than usual with the knees during

the approach, in order to prevent slipping forward in the saddle, while the lower legs are engaged in driving the horse onward.

Be tactful in convincing your horse that he *must* jump, *for too much activity of legs and failure to sit quietly* before the take-off communicate similar excitement and nervousness to the horse with consequent loss of calmness and cleverness. He must know that you intend he shall jump, but he must not believe from your actions that you are excited about the matter.

Clearing the Obstacle

As the horse jumps, hold your forward inclination (with back straight, loin hollowed out, head and chest lifted) so that the whole body, from the knees up, is projected out of the saddle as a result of its inertia when the horse's forehand checks and rises. At this moment stiffen the knee joints as they perforce open part way, and allow your entire weight to sink into your depressed heels. Your knees remain pinched against the saddle. Thereafter, while clearing the obstacle, you remain in balance out of the saddle, supported by your knees and stirrups. The ankles, knees and hips are the springs and joints which open and close as necessary to maintain balance and to soften the shocks of the take-off and landing. Force your heels well down before starting for the obstacle so that

TRAINING THE HORSE TO JUMP

your feet are braced against the stirrups. This position of the heels automatically gives a strong grip with the calves, and helps balance immeasurably, both over the obstacle and upon landing.

Contact with the mouth, which by degrees should become feathery light during the approach, vanishes at the instant the horses rises over the obstacle to the mere weight of the reins. With any save a very expert horseman, it is far better to permit a floating rein during the period of suspension, for the slightest resistance, pull, or jerk against a delicate mouth prevents full use of the balancer and maximum folding of the knees and fetlocks. Consequently a fault by the fore legs is almost certain. In addition, a few blows to the mouth will dissipate calmness and boldness.

Over the jump, the horse pivots between your fixed knees, and although you feel your lower legs fairly snug against his sides, the stirrup straps necessarily move a trifle in rear of the perpendicular while he is ascending. As momentum dies out over the top of the jump, the stirrup straps become approximately perpendicular. In other words, your lower legs feel to be, but in reality are not, fixed to the horse's sides. The knees however remain fixed in position.

The habit, so irritating to the horse, of allowing the lower legs to slide far to the rear along his sides, is unsightly, upsetting to the horse, and destructive to security of seat. On the other hand, lower legs in the correct position, allow you to straighten up your body from the brace of your feet against the stirrups, in case of a bad landing, and so prevent your being pitched forward on the horse's neck or over his head, as is often the case where the legs slide to the rear and the toes point downward. The same conditions are applicable to refusals.

Landing

Upon landing, do not commit the vicious mistake of roughly snatching the reins, thereby terrifying the horse and hurting his mouth. He, if intelligent, can only interpret such treatment as punishment for jumping and soon will begin to refuse. Reëstablish normal contact with his mouth very gently during the first strides after landing.

As the horse descends, let your lower legs slip a trifle forward so that the stirrup straps are the least bit in front of the vertical. This position is favorable to receiving your weight in your heels and so maintaining balance while remaining out of the saddle upon landing. Your ankle, knee and hip joints absorb the shock, but remain elastically stiff so as to keep the seat entirely off the saddle.

Provided there is another obstacle close at hand to be jumped, relax your knees gradually two or three strides after landing, and sink into the saddle, your weight supported on the thighs and crotch.

If a turn in direction immediately after jumping the obstacle is obligatory, it is initiated by very softly using the opening rein while your horse is in the air over the obstacle. The lightest effect suffices and the opposite rein is allowed to be passive. Abrupt changes of direction should not be required until the horse has become a well trained and confident performer.

To prevent the colt's running out, and also when it is necessary to change direction just before or after a jump, the opening, or direct, rein is normally used. Neither the direct, nor the indirect reins of opposition should be used when the opening or bearing reins will accomplish the desired result. The latter are conducive to calmness, while the former distract the horse, when he is jumping.

Seat When Galloping across Country

When hunting, galloping across country, or between obstacles of a long jumping course, the weight is habitually supported on the knees and stirrups. You sit down in the saddle, by relaxing the knee joints, only when approaching a fence. This form of riding greatly facilitates the horse's work, and so tends to keep him calm and contented. After becoming accustomed to this seat, it is also much less tiring to the rider when covering long distances at the gallop. The essential points to bear in mind when riding in the stirrups are: to have the loin hollowed out, the buttocks well to the rear but off the saddle, the knees and heels thrust down as far as possible and the stirrup straps vertical or a bit to the rear thereof. In this position your center of gravity is approximately over the horse's elbows and you are balanced over your knees.

As you sit down in the saddle, about twenty yards before taking an obstacle, the upper body should maintain the same forward inclination as when riding in the stirrups.

Riding Courses of Jumps

When the colt becomes calm and proficient in jumping at the walk, trot and gallop, he should thereafter receive his principal jumping practice by galloping over progressively longer courses of obstacles. The courses are varied at each lesson as to succession, type, number, spacing and arrangement of obstacles. The sharpness of changes in direction and the length of the courses are increased very gradually. When executed at the gallop, the trainer endeavors to maintain a free, long-striding, uniform gait and encourages the horse to jump in his stride. If the colt shortens his stride excessively, or puts in extra strides before each jump, it generally indicates that jumping is painful to some part of his anatomy. Often his feet or muscles may be a little sore although no lameness is present. Rest is essential or bad habits and poor form will result.

The exercises in extending and slowing the gait which are being concurrently carried on, by this time should have made it possible to rate the horse readily. In approaching broad jumps where more speed is necessary, a somewhat stronger feel of the mouth should be maintained during the approach, and the legs act more vigorously to sustain impulsion in order to insure the horse's jumping in his stride. Often to put in a short stride before a broad jump means catastrophe. However, on straight up and down fences, a very light feel of the mouth as the obstacle is approached, permits the horse to place himself. There are times when a short stride before a vertical fence is the wisest course. Although before a broad jump a stronger feel is maintained, the hands, through the elasticity of the elbows, must continue to follow the backward and forward movement of the mouth. That is, the hands are never "fixed" so as to resist, nor are the fingers tightly closed. Tightly closed fingers tend to immobilize all joints of the arms and thus prevent following the mouth. In jumping, this resistance of stiff arms is fatal and no horse so abused can possibly become a confident or certain jumper.

The most pleasant characteristic of an excellent hunter or jumper is his willingness to be "rated." If trained for a year or more according to preceding chapters before he is called upon to hunt a difficult country, or to jump a full-sized course of imposing obstacles, rating will be possible. After all is said and done, the rider's main task when hunting and jumping is to establish the proper rate of speed according to the type and size of obstacles facing him; from then on, the horse handles the task. The numerous frenzied and uncontrollable horses seen in the hunting field and show ring are a sad commentary on their trainers. Riders of varying degrees of competence often attempt to conduct over obstacles horses which, in their untrained state, could not be ridden at a uniform gait around a circle in a riding hall by a most skillful horseman. In most cases these demonstrations are directly attributable to improper preparation.

Refusals

To refuse, the horse must drop back of bit and legs, and duck his head. An old rogue's favorite manner of accomplishing the trick is by approaching the obstacle with an enthusiastic rush. A few yards in front of the fence, with even greater enthusiasm, he suddenly checks, ducks his head, turns slightly to the right or left, and comes to a disconcerting stop. This abruptness causes the rider to lose simultaneously his seat, contact with the mouth and use of his spurs. The element of surprise abolishes all thoughts save that of staying on the horse.

To prevent a repetition, hold such a horse during the approach firmly in hand—at the same time following his mouth—so as to restrain his gait until within a few strides of the obstacle. If, from about fifteen yards in front of the fence, the reins are not suddenly thrown away, and if the legs continue to drive the horse up to his bit, it becomes almost impossible for him to refuse. Since almost every refuser invariably turns toward a particular side as he ducks his head the rein on the opposite side should be predominatingly tightened during the last few strides in order to block the route to his favorite escape. The other rein's tension is mildly diminished. As a refuser, until he has abandoned the vice, must be held quite strongly in hand with consequent limited freedom of head and neck, it follows that he cannot as accurately place himself for his take-off. Nevertheless, in all training, one thing must be corrected at a time, and although he undoubtedly will make mistakes at the obstacle, he first must be convinced that refusing is impossible. For the rider's safety, it is best to work such a horse over obstacles that are not too rigid.

The moment after a refusal occurs, the offender

should be faced squarely up against the center of the obstacle and punished sharply, just in rear of the cinch, with the spurs. Punishment is of no value whatever if administered as much as five seconds after the offense is committed. He then should be *turned in the opposite direction from that toward which he ducked* and taken back for another trial. For instance, in leaving the obstacle he should never be allowed to turn to the left if that is the direction in which he turned when refusing.

With refusers, as in all cases where defenses arise, it is best to revert to more elementary work and go over all early training in jumping. Nevertheless the horse must be forced to jump, *at the present time,* the identical obstacle refused, even if it is necessary to lower its height. Also, a thorough diagnosis should be made to discover if pain is the cause of the refusals.

Run-Outs

Running out is accomplished by a sudden check or lunging increase in speed, combined with dropping back of the bit in the first case, or throwing the weight on the rider's hand in the second. In either case, the horse needs more suppling with the direct rein and leg on the side away from the run-out. The opening rein, or *direct rein of opposition,* is used to prevent run-outs, for if a horse is forced into his jump with the *indirect rein of opposition,* his head is turned away from the obstacle and even though he is unsuccessful in running out, he very probably, because he cannot see well, will commit a serious mistake in jumping. If the rider, with a horse inclined to pop his shoulder out and to run out, either by increasing or by decreasing his speed, vibrates the bit well away from the obstacle, the defense can be broken up before initiated. In increasing the speed as he runs out (to the right, for example) a horse normally takes a strong feel of his bit and throws his weight violently onto his right shoulder. Consequently, if the rider, anticipating this trick, uses vibrations, the horse is unable to set his jaw against the bit and hence is unable to throw his weight on his right shoulder.

In run-outs accomplished by dropping back of the legs, and a decrease in speed, the seat is often displaced as in a refusal. Driving the horse up to his bit with the legs and using vibrations quickly will break up this form of disobedience. The horse needs lessons with the spur to inculcate frank, forward movement.

If a horse succeeds in running out to the left, for example, he should be instantly turned around to the right several times by the right direct rein while being punished simultaneously with the right spur (lateral aids). As he becomes docile and obedient to the aids, their action ceases and calmness is restored. Under no circumstances should he be permitted to turn about to the left, after running out in that direction, as the rider conducts him back for another trial at the obstacle. After preliminary vibrations, the right rein predominates during the next approach and both legs are very active.

With experienced jumpers, which for some unknown reason suddenly start running out, a more brutal but very efficacious cure may be instituted. The trainer arms himself with a small, stiff stick about three-quarters of an inch in diameter and eighteen inches long. It should have no flexibility. If the horse habitually runs out to the right, the trainer carries the stick in his right hand. He then encourages a run-out by partly abandoning the reins some distance in front of the obstacle. As the horse swerves in the run-out, he is struck smartly on the side of the face midway between the eye and nostril. Evidently this form of punishment should be administered by an expert and intelligent rider, not by an ill-tempered or clumsy groom. The blows need not be forceful, for the moral effect, not the physical, recalls obedience.

As in the case of refusers, the most effective and permanent corrective measures lie in first resuming elementary suppling and control exercises with no jumping involved, followed by a rehearsal of all preliminary exercises over obstacles.

A whip, carried in the hand on the side toward which the horse runs out or turns in refusing, used on the shoulder a few strides in front of the obstacle usually will eliminate those vices.

Rushers

Almost without exception, rushers are produced by heavy hands. The average colt, properly trained and gradually prepared for high obstacles, never acquires this disagreeable trait. It usually is inspired through the trainer's tightening the reins the moment an obstacle is faced, whereupon the horse, realizing that he needs a certain amount of momentum to jump, takes control of matters and bolts forward despite the rider's pulling. Not only does the horse realize he needs some speed, but when the heavy hands fail to allow him liberty of head and neck, he becomes frantic. Always a frantic or frightened horse seeks escape by running away. As mentioned previously, many excellent jumpers, particularly at the first obstacle of a course, gather impulsion quickly. If the rider is unperturbed, stays in balance, and follows the mouth from the first stride with light hands, his horse invariably steadies his gait so as to accurately gauge his take-off. This does not mean he should slow down and "peck" before each jump, but if he has been "let alone at his jumps" during training, experience will have taught him to measure carefully his last three or four strides, in order to take off at the most advantageous spot, just as the human high jumper does.

With all vices, a cure is much more difficult and laborious than is prevention. Work on the longe for horses that refuse, rush, or run out, will accomplish wonders. The rule, heretofore given, concerning exercises to calm and relax the horse prior to any jumping must necessarily be followed. With the rusher, to teach proper acceptance of the bit with the lowered and extended head and neck is the prime essential. It will be noted that most offenders of this type are horses which have been over-flexed, and fold their heads and necks into balls the moment their riders attempt to restrain them before an obstacle. To jump a rushing star-gazer is a dangerous ordeal. If he is rated, he cannot see the jump, and if turned loose too late, a calamity is always imminent. Until his head carriage is corrected, he should not be jumped.

Quietly galloping on a small circle just opposite one end of a small obstacle until a rusher is calmly on his bit with extended head and neck, and then occasionally swinging wide so as to let him hop over it, helps to cure rushing. Needless to say, the rider should allow an absolutely loose rein and hold to the pommel of the saddle, if necessary, until the horse discovers that his mouth will not be bothered while jumping. It

Photo: J. A. McClasky

Mrs. W. B. McIlvanie, Jr., illustrating form and calmness on "Brockway."

AMERICAN OFFICER
Illustration of light hands and relaxation of horse and rider.

also aids if, beyond the obstacle, the horse is faced at a few yards by a wall or other insurmountable barrier, so that after jumping he has "no place to go." After each jump the rusher should be gently halted and allowed to rest at a walk. Of course when out-of-doors he should not be jumped over obstacles while going toward his stable.

Jumping without Wings

As the horse becomes perfectly amenable to the various rein effects, during some jumping lessons wings should be eliminated. Again common sense dictates that work without wings first be done over the elementary obstacles with which the colt has long been familiar. Using a very soft vibration in anticipation of a run-out is a wise preventive measure. This is also applicable to an old horse when he faces a strange fence. It is a foolish risk, when avoidable, to attempt to put any horse over a large and strange obstacle for the first time if it is not framed by wings. Intelligent care may prevent a good horse's refusing or running out throughout his entire career. The trainer must recognize each colt's potential ability and never ask more than he can comfortably accomplish. Certain it is that many horses never can be outstanding jumpers. Great ability and boldness must be innate in truly famous performers. However, much can be done with little, where patience and intelligence serve proper methods. Ultimately, with proper training, a horse will have no need of wings because he knows that "crime doesn't pay."

Device for Making the Horse Stand Back
(See Sketch)

Instead of placing take-off bars on, or close to the ground, the device to be described provides a much more satisfactory and lasting effect in teaching a horse to stand back from straight up-and-down obstacles. Two small pieces of board about one by two by twelve inches are nailed, parallel to the ground, one or two inches below the ends of the top element of the obstacle to be jumped. They should project about eight inches outward from the obstacle in the direction from which the horse approaches, and be nailed to the standards, or sides of the imitation stone wall, or other obstacle. A hollow iron bar about one inch and a half in diameter is laid across these projecting pieces of wood and allowed to rest from two to eight inches away from, and parallel to, the top element of the obstacle. This places the bar a certain number of inches nearer the horse than the top of the obstacle. It is advisable to paint the bar the same color as the obstacle, but this is not essential.

In all training over stiff obstacles four feet or

TRAINING THE HORSE TO JUMP

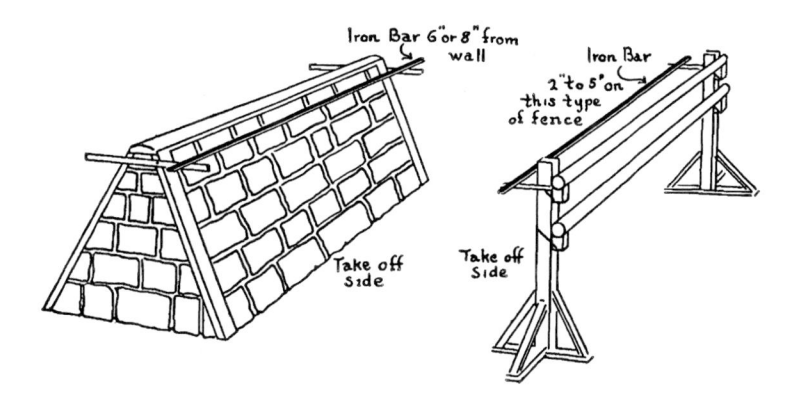

higher, the horse should be equipped with knee guards, and this is particularly necessary when jumping over obstacles armed with the device just described. The bar's effect is obvious; unless the horse stands back and folds well his knees and fetlocks, he will rap his feet or cannons against the bar, which then will roll on the supports against the obstacle. If frequently longed and ridden over obstacles where the bar is utilized, the normal horse of good breeding soon acquires the habit of standing well back and putting in several inches of height to spare when clearing a fence. When struck, the bar not only hurts the cannons, but also slightly overbalances the horse. This latter result seems to be more effective in teaching respect than the pain suffered. Such a device must be used with discretion and intelligence.

When the bar is used, the uprights, or the top blocks

of an artificial wall, should not be rigid or too heavy, for it is preferable that the whole obstacle fall, rather than violently throw the horse, in case he makes a bad mistake in jumping. Most of the practice when using this device should be given on the longe.

Rapping

If correctly used with careless or sluggish horses, rapping bars are beneficial. They should be "rapped" over low jumps, about two and one-half feet high, with a rapping bar handled by two men. When poorly manipulated—as is unavoidably the case with a single assistant—the bar can be seen by the horse, and his fear soon causes him to peck or refuse. Each of the two men holds one end of the bar which, from its concealed position back of the top element of the obstacle, is raised several inches just as the horse is actually clearing with his fore legs. In order not to frighten him the bar is raised quietly and not very high so that several jumps may be made before it is hit by the horse's front cannons. If, on the following jump, the horse adds several inches to the height of his leap, the rapping has accomplished its purpose; if not, the procedure is repeated. A broomstick may be used to tap the hind legs when necessary. Usually faults caused by dragging the hind feet result from heavy hands or a backward seat, which prevents the horse using his head and neck. A bar of hollow iron which is not exceedingly heavy but which will not bend, is most satisfactory.

If severely punished once or twice by rapping, a careless colt, for a long time afterward, usually will be much more attentive. Likewise an experienced but sluggish hunter may be made a safer conveyance by a little judicious rapping. This method of punishment has no place in the early training of a colt, and in general the use of rigid schooling jumps or the device described for making the horse stand back at his take-off are the most satisfactory means of instilling respect for all obstacles. For a horse so trained, rapping will be unnecessary.

To those who object to rapping, on the grounds of cruelty to animals, the answer is: it is better to make the horse's shins smart now and then than to let him break his own or his rider's bones.

Conclusion

IN writing a book of this nature, the author is constantly puzzled concerning the details which ought, or ought not, to be included. This, to some extent, is decided by the level of equestrian education of the readers for whom the book is written. Obviously a book for the man in his first year of riding is not suitable for one of several years' hunting experience. Too many details may smother the principles, while too few leave all, except the expert horseman, without a definite picture of methods. This work, as was stated in the preface, is for horse folk who have graduated from the primer class in equitation. For them, all the basic training necessary to proceed to the loftiest heights of horsemanship is embodied herein. Having mastered practically the principles and methods enunciated, the skill attained by any horseman will be limited only by his natural physical and mental endowments and the amount of sincere study and application he devotes to equitation.

TRAINING HUNTERS, JUMPERS AND HACKS

Training a horse, as he acquires brilliance, is a sport requiring intense mental and physical concentration. One's mind must be constantly active and alert during schooling, but this same concentration also completely relieves one from the many worries of life. Meanwhile the body receives most healthful exercise. The behavior of many horses, alas, presents irrefutable evidence of how little their masters have deemed it necessary to think while on horseback.

With the fear of wearying the reader, countless repetitions of the fundamental principles have been purposely made. For with these, the trainer must regulate the curriculum and decide the work necessary for each colt, since no two horses are more alike than are two human beings.

For the above reasons the basic framework of training is again recalled.

Seek an extended head and neck, with the horse on the bit, by keeping the hands soft and elastic. Calmness and confidence result.

Develop free, long strides and frank forward movement from the first lesson by use of vigorous legs and soft hands. Result—boldness.

Constantly improve suppleness, relaxation, balance and agility while securing relaxation of jaw, poll and loin, control of the forehand and prompt obedience of the hindquarters, through use of the exercises

CONCLUSION

detailed in Chapters IV and V on Breaking and Training.

Jumping is dealt with alone, but as has been reiterated, it is taught concurrently with other training. In warning, let it be said that jumping should lag well behind other work. This, sadly enough, is the reverse of what is generally seen; many colts are forced to jump before they are rudimentarily trained, which accounts for many a ruined horse.

As a final bit of advice, be sure that, prior to each day's training, a carefully laid-out program of work has been prepared, according to the needs of the individual colt, and that it is meticulously followed. Only by such systematic preparation can rapid progress be assured.

Comments on High-Schooling

High-schooling, since not essential to outdoor horses, is not covered. Briefly, it calls for greatly refining the aids and ever more closely associating their actions. Pirouettes at the gallop, gallop in place, changes of lead at every fourth, third, second, and at each stride are, with study and practice, within the ability of any horseman who succeeds in securing a nicely-balanced canter and a smoothly-executed single change of lead on a straight line.

Two-tracking is similar to shoulder-in on an oblique

line (*appuyer*) except that the horse's head and neck, rather than being turned away from, turn toward the direction of movement. His spine is not bent in two-tracking, and diagonal aids (right rein and left leg, if two-tracking to the right front) predominate. It is rarely well done by the average high-school rider because complete relaxation of poll, jaw and loin is not obtained. Perfectly executed, it demonstrates that the rider possesses great skill in use of the aids and that the horse is one step nearer complete domination. For the horse, shoulder-in is infinitely more valuable as a gymnastic.

The *passage* (a very lofty and cadenced trot) and the *piaffe* (the trot in place) are merely extremes of collection. Any horse can be taught to do them if the rider has the necessary technique and coördination. Naturally some horses are far more brilliant than others. These movements have no value for the horse except to teach him to work on a very short base of support, and to perfect obedience at slow gaits.

The Spanish Walk, Spanish Trot (requiring horizontal extension of the fore legs) and the gallop on three legs are closely associated. They are not difficult to obtain, once the trainer has learned how to teach them. The elevation and extension of the fore leg is usually taught while dismounted with a riding whip. Classically, it should be done mounted and without a

CONCLUSION

whip. Always the instantaneous reward and rest after the first perceptible *inclination* toward obedience is, as in all training, the secret of rapid progress in high-schooling.

All the airs of *haute école* have great value in developing in the horseman tact and artistic finesse. For the outdoor horse they are of little, if any, value. The high-school horse habitually works with an abnormal amount of weight on his hindquarters, and this is neither possible nor desirable at fast gaits. Also, as explained earlier, this form of collection in checking and halting is artificial and not what the outdoor horse or polo pony should be taught. A high-school horse has usually forgotten how to throw his weight forward, extend head and neck, and gallop with long, low strides on the hand.

If one has a good cross-country horse, the author deems it inadvisable to teach extreme collection or the delicately-balanced airs of the high-school. Putting the horse on the bit with a normal head carriage, improving his natural balance through the simple exercises detailed heretofore, and thereafter allowing him, as a rule, to go in the manner most comfortable to himself, is the safest and surest road to success and pleasure for the outdoor horseman.